Teach Yourself
VISUALLY™

Web Design

Visual

Rob Huddleston

KT-177-113

30131 05020900 3

LONDON BOROUGH OF BARNET

Teach Yourself VISUALLY™ Web Design

Published by
Wiley Publishing, Inc.
10475 Crosspoint Boulevard
Indianapolis, IN 46256

www.wiley.com

Published simultaneously in Canada

Copyright © 2011 by Wiley Publishing, Inc., Indianapolis, Indiana

No part of this publication may be reproduced, stored in a retrieval system or transmitted in any form or by any means, electronic, mechanical, photocopying, recording, scanning or otherwise, except as permitted under Sections 107 or 108 of the 1976 United States Copyright Act, without either the prior written permission of the Publisher, or authorization through payment of the appropriate per-copy fee to the Copyright Clearance Center, 222 Rosewood Drive, Danvers, MA 01923, 978-750-8400, fax 978-646-8600. Requests to the Publisher for permission should be addressed to the Permissions Department, John Wiley & Sons, Inc., 111 River Street, Hoboken, NJ 07030, 201-748-6011, fax 201-748-6008, or online at www.wiley.com/go/permissions.

Library of Congress Control Number: 2010935578

ISBN: 978-0-470-88101-9

Manufactured in the United States of America

10 9 8 7 6 5 4 3 2 1

Trademark Acknowledgments

Wiley, the Wiley Publishing logo, Visual, the Visual logo, Teach Yourself VISUALLY, Read Less - Learn More and related trade dress are trademarks or registered trademarks of John Wiley & Sons, Inc. and/or its affiliates. All other trademarks are the property of their respective owners. Wiley Publishing, Inc. is not associated with any product or vendor mentioned in this book.

LIMIT OF LIABILITY/DISCLAIMER OF WARRANTY: THE PUBLISHER AND THE AUTHOR MAKE NO REPRESENTATIONS OR WARRANTIES WITH RESPECT TO THE ACCURACY OR COMPLETENESS OF THE CONTENTS OF THIS WORK AND SPECIFICALLY DISCLAIM ALL WARRANTIES, INCLUDING WITHOUT LIMITATION WARRANTIES OF FITNESS FOR A PARTICULAR PURPOSE. NO WARRANTY MAY BE CREATED OR EXTENDED BY SALES OR PROMOTIONAL MATERIALS. THE ADVICE AND STRATEGIES CONTAINED HEREIN MAY NOT BE SUITABLE FOR EVERY SITUATION. THIS WORK IS SOLD WITH THE UNDERSTANDING THAT THE PUBLISHER IS NOT ENGAGED IN RENDERING LEGAL, ACCOUNTING, OR OTHER PROFESSIONAL SERVICES. IF PROFESSIONAL ASSISTANCE IS REQUIRED, THE SERVICES OF A COMPETENT PROFESSIONAL PERSON SHOULD BE SOUGHT. NEITHER THE PUBLISHER NOR THE AUTHOR SHALL BE LIABLE FOR DAMAGES ARISING HEREFROM. THE FACT THAT AN ORGANIZATION OR WEBSITE IS REFERRED TO IN THIS WORK AS A CITATION AND/OR A POTENTIAL SOURCE OF FURTHER INFORMATION DOES NOT MEAN THAT THE AUTHOR OR THE PUBLISHER ENDORSES THE INFORMATION THE ORGANIZATION OR WEBSITE MAY PROVIDE OR RECOMMENDATIONS IT MAY MAKE. FURTHER, READERS SHOULD BE AWARE THAT INTERNET WEBSITES LISTED IN THIS WORK MAY HAVE CHANGED OR DISAPPEARED BETWEEN WHEN THIS WORK WAS WRITTEN AND WHEN IT IS READ.

FOR PURPOSES OF ILLUSTRATING THE CONCEPTS AND TECHNIQUES DESCRIBED IN THIS BOOK, THE AUTHOR HAS CREATED VARIOUS NAMES, COMPANY NAMES, MAILING, E-MAIL AND INTERNET ADDRESSES, PHONE AND FAX NUMBERS AND SIMILAR INFORMATION, ALL OF WHICH ARE FICTITIOUS. ANY RESEMBLANCE OF THESE FICTITIOUS NAMES, ADDRESSES, PHONE AND FAX NUMBERS AND SIMILAR INFORMATION TO ANY ACTUAL PERSON, COMPANY AND/OR ORGANIZATION IS UNINTENTIONAL AND PURELY COINCIDENTAL.

Contact Us

For general information on our other products and services please contact our Customer Care Department within the U.S. at 877-762-2974, outside the U.S. at 317-572-3993 or fax 317-572-4002.

For technical support please visit www.wiley.com/techsupport.

WILEY   Sales | Contact Wiley at (877) 762-2974 or fax (317) 572-4002.

Credits

Acquisitions Editor
Aaron Black

Sr. Project Editor
Sarah Hellert

Technical Editor
Dennis R. Cohen

Copy Editor
Scott Tullis

Editorial Director
Robyn Siesky

Editorial Manager
Rosemarie Graham

Business Manager
Amy Knies

Sr. Marketing Manager
Sandy Smith

Vice President and Executive Group Publisher
Richard Swadley

Vice President and Executive Publisher
Barry Pruett

Project Coordinator
Patrick Redmond

Graphics and Production Specialists
Carrie Cesavice
Andrea Hornberger
Jennifer Mayberry

Quality Control Technician
Rebecca Denoncour

Proofreader
Jacqueline Brownstein

Indexer
Valerie Haynes Perry

Media Development Project Manager
Laura Moss

Media Development Assistant Project Manager
Jenny Swisher

Media Development Associate Producer
Shawn Patrick

Artists
Ana Carrillo
Ronda David-Burroughs
Cheryl Grubbs
Mark Pinto
Jill A. Proll

About the Author

Rob Huddleston has been developing Web pages and applications since 1994, and has been an instructor since 1999, teaching Web and graphic design to thousands of students. His clients have included the United States Bureau of Land Management, the United States Patent and Trademark Office, the States of California and Nevada and many other federal, city, and county agencies; the United States Army and Air Force; Fortune 500 companies such as AT&T, Bank of America, Wells Fargo, Safeway, and Coca-Cola; software companies including Adobe, Oracle, Intuit, and Autodesk; the University of California, San Francisco State University, and the University of Southern California; and hundreds of small businesses and nonprofit agencies, both in the United States and abroad. Rob is an Adjunct Professor in the Interactive Media program at the Art Institute of California, Sacramento. He is an Adobe Certified Instructor, Certified Expert, and Certified Developer, serves as an Adobe User Group Manager, and has been named as an Adobe Community Professional for his volunteer work answering user questions in online forums. He also helps users as an expert moderator on Adobe's Community Help system. Rob lives in Northern California with his wife and two children.

Rob is the author of *XML: Your visual blueprint for building expert Web sites with XML, CSS, XHTML, and XSLT; HTML, XHTML, and CSS: Your visual blueprint for designing effective Web pages; Master VISUALLY: Dreamweaver CS4 and Flash CS4 Professional; ActionScript: Your visual blueprint for creating interactive projects in Flash CS4 Professional;* and the *Flash Catalyst CS5 Bible.* You can visit Rob's blog at www.robhuddleston.com, or follow him on Twitter at twitter.com/robhuddles.

Author's Acknowledgments

Writing is mostly a solitary pursuit, but I wouldn't be able to continue doing it without the unwavering love and support from my wife and best friend, Kelley, and our two beautiful children, Jessica and Xander. I hope you kids enjoy seeing your pictures in the book.

The people at Wiley continue to be a wonderful group with whom to work. Acquisitions editor Aaron Black, who first approached me about this project, provided invaluable insight in getting started and then through some of the project's more trying moments. I was pleased and thankful to work again with project editor Sarah Hellert. Many thanks to tech editor Dennis Cohen and copy editor Scott Tullis for adding their expertise.

Bill Mead introduced me to an exciting new opportunity teaching at the Art Institute, and helped with this book by pointing me to the example used in the section on jQuery. Ted Fitzpatrick and Nolan Erck both helped explain some of the intricacies of the Mac to me. Thank you to each of you for your help and your friendship.

How to Use This Book

Who This Book Is For

This book is for the reader who has never used this particular technology or software application. It is also for readers who want to expand their knowledge.

The Conventions in This Book

❶ Steps

This book uses a step-by-step format to guide you easily through each task. **Numbered steps** are actions you must do; **bulleted steps** clarify a point, step, or optional feature; and **indented steps** give you the result.

❷ Notes

Notes give additional information — special conditions that may occur during an operation, a situation that you want to avoid, or a cross reference to a related area of the book.

❸ Icons and Buttons

Icons and buttons show you exactly what you need to click to perform a step.

❹ Tips

Tips offer additional information, including warnings and shortcuts.

❺ Bold

Bold type shows command names, options, and text or numbers you must type.

❻ Italics

Italic type introduces and defines a new term.

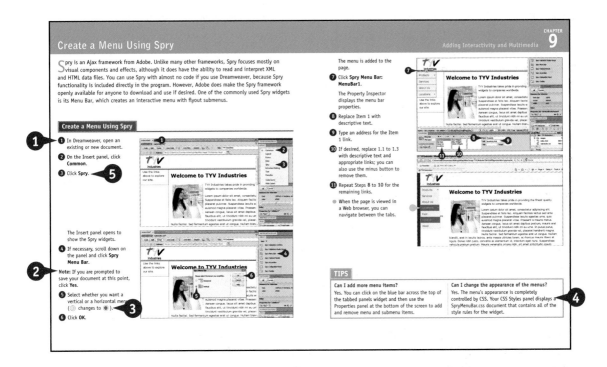

Table of Contents

Chapter 3 | Creating Images

Table of Contents

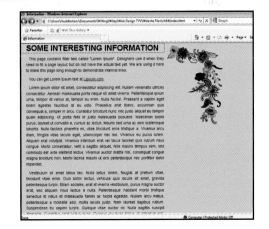

| Chapter 6 | Laying Out Pages |

| Chapter 7 | Adding Tables and Lists |

Table of Contents

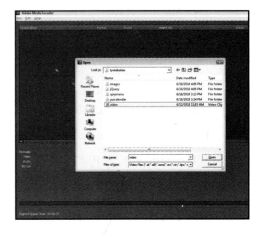

Chapter 10 Making Sites Accessible

Chapter 11 Adding Forms to Your Site

Table of Contents

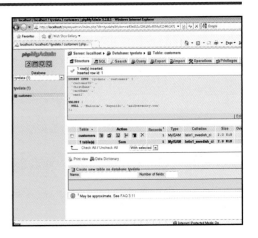

Chapter 14 Publishing Your Site and Getting Noticed

CHAPTER 1

The Tools of Web Design and Planning Your Site

Before you can dive into creating Web sites, you need to understand the tools that you need. This chapter shows you the software you need to create Web pages, add images to them, and preview the finished products. However, software alone cannot make a good Web site. You need to carefully plan your site's content, design and overall structure in order to create a site. Therefore, this chapter also details those steps you should undertake to plan your site before you begin building it.

Only twenty years after its invention, the World Wide Web has become commonplace and has fundamentally changed the way we work, live, and interact with others. However, the medium is in many ways still in its infancy, and as you progress in learning about designing Web pages, you will encounter many significant limitations primarily because the Web was not created as a place to sell books or keep in touch with friends from high school. Understanding why the Web was invented and what its original goals were will help you better understand these issues.

The Invention of the Web

The Web was invented in 1990 by Tim Berners-Lee. Berners-Lee was a physicist at CERN, the European laboratory for particle physics, located in Geneva, Switzerland. Berners-Lee noted that visiting scientists, while working on experiments that could have come straight from *Star Trek*, had to exchange most of their information with one another on paper because their computer systems were incompatible. He therefore created the Web as a way to allow these scientists to share their findings, regardless of what kind of computer system they used.

The Invention of the Internet

Jokes about politicians aside, no one person invented the Internet. Rather, it evolved over decades from a variety of other sources. Much of the early work on what became the Internet was done in the 1960s. Although the United States Department of Defense funded the early research, the Internet was not, contrary to popular belief, designed by or for the military directly.

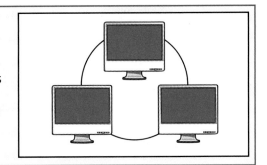

The Web versus the Internet

Many people confuse the Web with the Internet, but it is important to understand that they are not the same thing. The Web is best thought of as an application that runs on the Internet. E-mail is another application running on the Internet, entirely separate from the Web.

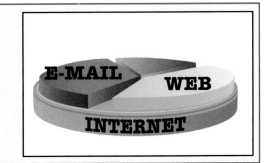

Protocols

Computer networking relies on *protocols*, which are essentially standards by which two computers can talk to one another using a common language. The Internet relies on a suite of two protocols: TCP, or Transmission Control Protocol, and IP, or Internet Protocol. TCP/IP was developed in the 1970s by Robert Kahn and Vinton Cerf. The Web primarily uses the Hypertext Transfer Protocol, or HTTP, developed in 1990 by Tim Berners-Lee.

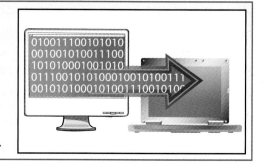

The Expansion of the Web

CERN did not show much interest in Berners-Lee's invention, and so allowed him to make it publicly available with no licensing restrictions. Soon, scientists at Stanford University and the National Center for Supercomputing Applications took his ideas and began building servers and browsers to work with. Companies soon followed, and by the mid-1990s, the Web had taken off.

The World Wide Web Consortium

In October 1994, Berners-Lee left CERN and founded the World Wide Web Consortium (W3C) as a sort of governing body for the development of the Web. Today, the W3C is still responsible for maintaining and adopting standards for languages such as HTML, or Hypertext Markup Language. They also promote standards for other aspects of the Web, such as graphics formats and cascading style sheets, or CSS.

The Web Today

Exact numbers are hard to find, but most estimates show that many billions of Web pages are in existence. Search engine Google announced in 2008 that it had indexed one trillion unique Web addresses. Hundreds of millions of Web sites are likely currently in operation. Considering that 2010 marks only the 20th anniversary of the Web, its expansion is truly amazing.

The primary means by which most people access the Web is via a browser. Browsers are simply software applications that read and interpret HTML pages. In a way, you can look at browsers as the canvas for which you design your page. Unfortunately, browsers are inconsistent in the ways in which they display pages, and remain the primary source of Web designers' headaches. Although you can minimize these differences on your pages, understanding browsers is an important first step to learning how to create sites that avoid these issues.

WWW: The First Browser

Tim Berners-Lee developed the first browser when he invented the Web. Although he considered many names for it, he finally settled on WorldWideWeb. His idea was to have browsers/editors, whereby users would rely on a single tool to both view and create pages.

NCSA Mosaic and Other Early Browsers

One of the first graphical browsers, capable of displaying images alongside text, was developed by the National Center for Supercomputing Applications. The lead designer of the Mosaic browser, Marc Andreessen, left soon after to found Netscape Communications and create Navigator, the first commercial, widely adopted browser.

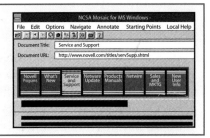

Internet Explorer

As the Web began to gain in popularity, Microsoft developed their own browser, which they called Internet Explorer, but which is most often referred to today simply as IE. Of the early browsers, IE is the only one still in existence in a recognizable form.

Mozilla Firefox

When AOL purchased Netscape, they decided that rather than compete with Microsoft, they would release the code upon which the Netscape browser was based as open source. The nonprofit Mozilla corporation used it as the basis for Firefox, which is today the second-most-popular desktop browser after IE.

Safari and Chrome

After years of relying on Netscape and Microsoft, Apple decided to build their own browser. Using the open-source WebKit browser code base, they released the Safari browser. Google, entering the browser market later, also used WebKit as the underpinning of their Chrome browser. Today, Safari is the main browser on Macintosh systems, although it is also available on Windows and Apple's mobile devices such as the iPhone and iPad. Chrome is increasingly popular on both Windows and Mac, along with mobile devices running the Android operating system such as the Nexus One and Droid phones.

Opera

Although Netscape briefly flirted with the idea of charging for their browser, Norway's Opera browser was available in paid and free versions for many years, finally becoming completely free-only in 2000. It offers many features that make it popular to technically inclined users, but the general public remains mostly unaware of it.

Browser Differences

Though the original idea of the Web was to be able to create pages that would look the same on all computers everywhere, browsers have long rendered pages differently. Today, most browsers are to some extent standards-based, meaning that they display most pages the same most of the time. However, differences still exist, requiring that you test your pages in multiple browsers.

The Mobile Web

More and more people today are using cell phones and the newest generation of so-called smart phones to surf the Web, posing a new set of challenges for Web designers. Fortunately, most smart phones today rely on standard browsers: the popular iPhone, for example, uses Apple's Safari browser.

Upgrading Browsers

New versions of browsers are being constantly released. Unfortunately for you as a designer, each browser company releases their software on different schedules, making keeping up with the latest browsers challenging. Even though the browsers are free, many users do not upgrade their browsers, forcing designers to worry not only about new versions, but several iterations of old ones as well.

All Web pages are, in the end, simple text files that contain the code the browser needs in order to display the page. Although HTML and CSS are not complicated programming languages, many designers would prefer to write as little code as possible. Many visual design tools over the years have attempted to come up with a way to allow designers to create pages using no code at all. Unfortunately, none have succeeded, so you need to gain an understanding of the code. That said, visual design tools allow you to minimize the amount of code you need to write.

Adobe Dreamweaver

Dreamweaver has been the industry-standard design tool for many years. Originally created by Macromedia, Dreamweaver has existed as an integral part of Adobe's Creative Suite toolset since 2005. Dreamweaver provides both a Design view that approximates a browser window with a Live view feature that relies on an actual browser-rendering engine. Dreamweaver CS5 was released in April 2010.

Microsoft Expression Web

Microsoft's primary Web design tool, a direct competitor to Dreamweaver, shares many of the same features. It contains a design interface that allows you to create pages without writing code, along with tools to help manage your site's files. Expression Web 3 was released in 2008, and a new version is expected sometime in mid- to late-2010.

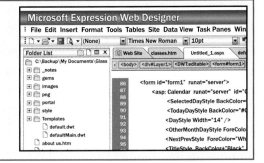

Legacy Programs

For many years, the go-to product for individuals and small businesses who wanted to create Web sites was Microsoft's FrontPage. FrontPage was discontinued in 2003, but some designers continue to use it today.

Before their acquisition of Macromedia, Adobe manufactured a competitor, GoLive. GoLive focused more heavily on design features than most other tools. It was discontinued in 2008.

Because learning how to write HTML and CSS remains important for successful Web designers, many have decided that if they must write code anyway, they would prefer to use a pure code editor rather than rely on visual tools to do it for them. Perhaps the biggest advantage to code editors over visual design tools is that many hundreds of code editors exist as free downloads, whereas all of the best visual editors are commercial products that must be purchased. Using a coding tool also gives you complete control over your code.

TextEdit and Notepad

Because HTML can be created in any text tool, some designers who do not want to purchase or download other tools use the free text editors that ship with operating systems, including TextEdit on Macintosh and Notepad on Windows.

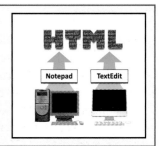

Dreamweaver and Expression Web

Although primarily visual tools, both Dreamweaver and Expression contain powerful code-editing capabilities. In fact, many day-to-day users of each program never use the visual tools at all, preferring to rely on them as code editors.

Eclipse

Eclipse is an open-source development toolset. Although it has no specific HTML-editing capabilities by itself, free plug-ins are available for it that add that functionality. Eclipse is available for free from www.eclipse.org; HTML and other plug-ins can be downloaded at www.eclipse.org/downloads.

HomeSite

For many years, HomeSite was packaged with Dreamweaver. No new version of HomeSite has been released since 2003, and Adobe officially discontinued its development in 2009. However, many developers enjoyed its powerful code-editing features and have continued to use their old copies of it.

The Web is a visual medium. As such, images and graphics play an important role in your site's development. Today, powerful graphics tools are available that enable you to create professional-quality images. The photographs you plan to use on your site may need colors corrected, they may need to be cropped or resized, or you may want to apply special visual effects. You may also need to create images from scratch, such as a site logo, buttons, or other icons. You therefore need to understand the tools available to you.

Adobe Photoshop

Photoshop has been the industry-standard tool for manipulating images for so long that its name is almost synonymous with editing. Today, Photoshop combines the same powerful tools for editing images with an ever-growing array of features targeted specifically at Web designers. The latest version, CS5, was released in April 2010.

Adobe Illustrator

Illustrator is to vector-based drawing programs what Photoshop is to photo editing. Artists and graphic designers have relied on it for decades to create everything from logos to full print campaigns. Like Photoshop, many of its newer features are targeted at Web designers. Illustrator CS5 was released in April 2010.

Adobe Fireworks

Originally created by Macromedia as a competitor to both Photoshop and Illustrator, Fireworks today is the graphics tool of choice for many Web designers due to its ease of use, wide set of tools, and extremely efficient graphics optimization features. Fireworks CS5 was released in April 2010.

Corel Draw

Corel Draw is, like Adobe Illustrator, a vector-based drawing tool. Today, it contains many features similar to Illustrator, making it an ideal tool for working on Web graphics. A new version, known as X5, was released in February 2010. Its only main disadvantage to designers today is that it is available only for Windows-based systems.

GIMP

An open-source graphics toolset designed to mimic many of the features of Photoshop and other commercial products, GIMP, whose name is short for **GNU Image Manipulation Program**, is a viable option for budget-minded designers. It can be downloaded for free from www.gimp.org.

Adobe Photoshop Elements

The full version of Photoshop is designed with professionals in mind. Adobe created Photoshop Elements for hobbyists and home users. However, even though its price is roughly 1/5 of that of Photoshop, Photoshop Elements actually contains a very large number of Photoshop's features.

Aperture

Aperture is manufactured by Apple and is the preferred image-editing tool for many Macintosh users. It has many features in common with Photoshop, including a set of tools designed specifically for use on the Web. Its main disadvantage is that it is available only for Macintosh computers.

Although you may be tempted to sit down at your computer and simply start coding your site, good Web sites do not come together by chance. Rather, careful planning is needed to ensure that your site's content is organized logically, that your site fits your user's needs, and that your navigation works and is intuitive. Planning a site may not be the most exciting task in the overall process, but it is perhaps the most important. In general, well-planned sites come together much more quickly and are more likely to end up being something you can be proud of.

Brainstorm Design Concepts

Most successful finished designs are the result of taking parts from several ideas and combining them into a whole. In your brainstorming session, whether you are working alone or in a team, always remember that no idea should be rejected out-of-hand.

Wireframe the Design

A wireframe is simply a representation of the site's structure and layout. It does not need to be fancy — many wireframes are simply boxes with labels — but you should try to get proportions correct to make sure the design works. You can draw the wireframes by hand or use a graphics program such as Adobe Fireworks.

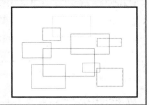

Storyboard Pages

Storyboards provide more detailed representations of your design. You can use storyboards to see how the color scheme from your project will work and begin to get an idea of what graphics you might use. You can create a storyboard for each page in your site, although sites with animated elements may require multiple storyboards.

Develop a Timeline for Completion

If you are working for a client or developing a Web site for your company, you need to discuss with your client or boss a realistic timeline that includes deadlines along the way in which you can complete the project. If you are creating a personal site, a timeline can be just as important to keep you on track.

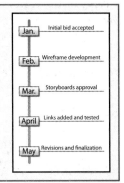

The Web is a user-centric environment. Almost all of your users will approach your site with a "what's in it for me" attitude. Traditional businesses can, to a point, rely on the fact that by the time a customer walks in their door, the customer has already invested something in the trip, such as time and gas. Thus, they may be more likely to endure a certain level of inconvenience. On the Web, your customers have invested next to nothing in getting to your site. Understanding your audience is the key to being able to meet their needs and keep them on your site.

Market Studies

Companies have long understood the importance of studying the market in which they plan to do business in order to target advertising and products to their important customers. Many Web sites, however, forego this step, to their peril. Web market studies are every bit as important as those for traditional offline businesses.

Demographics

Demographics is the study of populations. You need to get an idea of the demographics of your potential audience in order to ensure that your site meets their needs. General questions to research include your audience's age, educational level, socioeconomic background, and more.

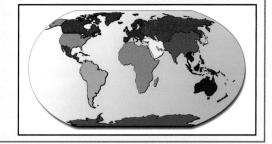

Local Businesses with Global Customers

The global scope of the Web is one of its more exciting aspects. Even the smallest of businesses can now reach companies on the other side of the world, but that same global scope presents many challenges as well. How will you handle foreign orders? Will you present your site in multiple languages?

uilding a Web site requires that you manage a host of assets, from the pages themselves to the style sheets that control their appearance to the images, ads, and videos you use. Keeping yourself organized makes the whole process much simpler. Whether you are working with a large site with many hundreds, or possibly thousands of files, or a smaller site with only a few dozen files, disorganization can quickly eat up large amounts of your time and thus the site's budget. There is not one correct way to organize your site; use whatever method works best for you.

Root Folder

All of your Web site's files and assets eventually need to reside within a single folder on your hard drive. Thus, you should begin by creating this folder and moving any existing assets into it. The folder can be anywhere on your computer, and can be named however you want, but in Web terms the folder is known as the *root*.

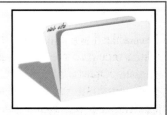

Images

Most sites require a lot of images. At this opening stage, you should be thinking about the images you need and begin collecting them, whether from your own collection, your company's media department, or online stock-image resources.

Multimedia Assets

If you plan to use audio and video files, you should begin to prepare for them early on because production of that media can require a lot of additional time and effort. If you have existing multimedia that you plan to use, copy it to your root now. Otherwise, begin the preproduction process as soon as you can to ensure that it does not delay the project.

Source Documents

Many companies have marketing and other materials already prepared in various electronic formats. You should try to collect those documents that contain information you need and place them in your root folder for easy access later.

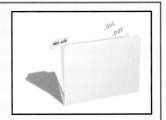

Carefully laid-out navigation makes your site easy and intuitive to use, which in turn ensures that users have a more successful experience in your site. You should plan your navigation early in the design process, to make sure that all important pages are navigable and to ensure that the navigation works with your design. Sites with poorly designed navigational structures quickly confuse and frustrate your users, which is likely to cause them to give up and find another site. Good navigation should be so intuitive that the user never has to consciously think about it.

Main Navigation

Your site's main navigation is the area that contains links to the primary sections of your site, such as your home page and departmental pages. The main navigation will likely appear on every page in the site, and is traditionally displayed either horizontally near the top of the site or vertically along the left side.

Section Subnavigation

Each section of your site will likely require its own navigation to the pages within the section. Section navigation can be presented directly below or next to the main navigation, or as an independent unit. It should be visually obvious to users that these areas represent links within the section.

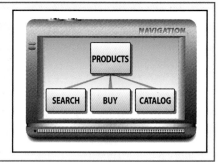

Think Like Users

Do not organize your site's navigation based on the internal organization of your company. Rather, approach the site from an outsider's view, and organize your navigation based on the needs of your prospective users.

Your site's file structure is mostly for your benefit. You want to be sure that your site is organized in such a way as to allow you to easily find files as you need them. As with organizing the site's files, there is not any one "correct" way to lay out your site structure; you simply need to make sure that it makes sense to you. Most designers rely on nested folders to keep files organized. As important as the folder structure is the naming of folders: be sure that you use logical names.

Organizing Below the Root

Some designers prefer to place only the home page directly in the root folder, and then place all other pages in the site in subfolders of the root. Others prefer to have all top-level pages directly in the root, with subfolders for each section. Use whatever plan makes sense to you, but be consistent.

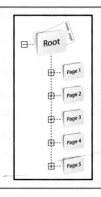

Naming Folders

The names of the folders in your site are visible to your site's users on their browser's navigation bar, so be sure to give your folders names that make sense to you but also assist your users in navigating the site. Folder names must begin with a letter and cannot contain spaces.

Images Directory

Most designers place an *images* folder in the root, and put all of the site's graphics in it. Bigger sites might require that the image folder contain subfolders, or you might prefer each section of the site have its own images directory. As long as the organization is logical, you can use whichever method works best for you.

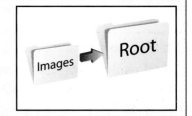

Other Assets

Multimedia should most likely be placed in a single directory, although media-heavy sites may need further organization. Every site will contain one or more style sheets, which can either be placed directly in the root, in their own directory, or in each section's directory. See Chapter 5 for more details on style sheets.

CHAPTER 2

Getting Started with HTML

HTML is the language of the Web, and in this chapter, you learn the fundamentals of the language and get started building your first pages.

Introduction to HTML

Hypertext Markup Language (HTML) is the fundamental language for Web pages and an essential starting point for anyone wanting to learn Web design. Thankfully, HTML is not a programming language. You do not need to learn complicated logic processes or worry about performing mathematical computations. Instead, HTML is best seen as a set of relatively simple instructions to the Web browser, telling the browser how it should interpret the text. HTML is completely free, so you never have to worry about paying to use it.

Tags

HTML documents are made up of text surrounded by *tags*. A tag is an instruction to the software that displays the page — usually a Web browser — on how the text contained within the tag should be interpreted and displayed. A tag is made up of angle brackets and an element name, and sometimes includes attributes.

Elements

Elements are the basic pieces that make up HTML. The language contains roughly 100 elements, and when placed in a tag and inserted into your page, they tell the browser how to render the text. Examples of elements include `html`, `body`, `p`, and `table`.

Attributes

Often, the element alone does not provide enough information to tell the browser exactly how to handle text. In these cases, you also need to add attributes, which provide the additional details on how that element should display. Attributes go inside tags, after the element.

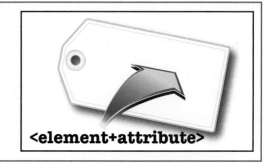

Container Tags

Most HTML tags are *container* tags that wrap around blocks of text in your document to tell the browser both when to begin applying formatting and when to end. Container tags are used in sets, with an opening and a closing tag. The closing tag contains the angle brackets and the element, and also includes a backslash.

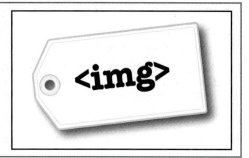

Empty Tags

A few HTML tags are essentially instructions to the browser. For example, the <img> tag tells the browser where to insert an image. Empty tags do not have or require closing tags, but are instead placed in the document alone.

Whitespace and Capitalization

HTML is both whitespace- and case-insensitive. You should include whitespace in your code to make it more readable, but it does not impact the display of the page. Element names and attributes can be written in any case, also without affecting the page display.

```
<html>
<head>
<TITLE>My Web Site</title>
                ← white space
</head>
</HTML>
```

HTML versus XHTML

XHTML is merely a version of HTML that requires a stricter syntax. In XHTML, all element and attribute names must be lowercase, and attribute values must be enclosed in quotation marks. XHTML has no empty tags — all tags, including instructional tags such as <img>, must always be closed.

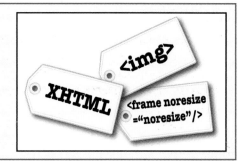

Create Your First Web Page

You can begin building simple Web pages in your editor of choice. Web pages use sets of HTML tags to define their content. Although the content of each page will vary greatly, all pages contain the same basic set of starting tags. These tags begin by telling the browser that the document does in fact contain HTML tags, and then divide the page into two sections: a head, with information for the browser, and a body, which contains everything the user actually sees on the page. The head section also contains the title, which appears on the browser's title and tab bars.

Create Your First Web Page

1 Open your editor to a new blank page.

Note: The examples in this chapter use Windows Notepad, but you can use any editor to complete these sections. See Chapter 1 for more information on editors.

2 Type <html>.

3 Press Enter.

4 Type <head>.

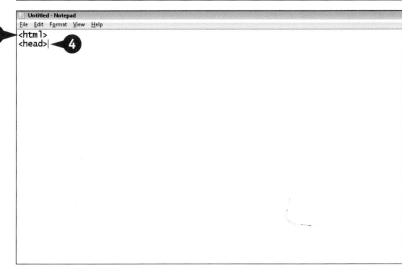

5 Press Enter.

6 Type `<title>My First Page</title>`.

7 Press Enter.

8 Type `</head>`.

9 Press Enter.

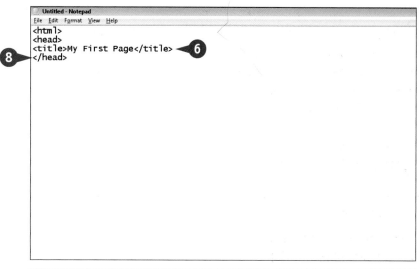

10 Type `<body>`.

11 Press Enter.

12 Type `</body>`.

13 Press Enter.

14 Type `</html>`.

The document now contains the basic tags needed for a Web page.

TIPS

Do capitalization and spacing matter?
XHTML requires that all tags and attributes be written in lowercase letters. Whitespace, however, does not matter; the examples above and throughout the book separate code onto distinct lines to make it more readable, but a page where all of the code is written on a single line is also valid.

Do I need all of these tags in every document?
Browsers will display your page if you do not have these basic tags, but they may not do so correctly, so you should always include them. Most dedicated HTML editors add them automatically when you create a new document.

Save Your Web Page

efore you can preview your page or allow others to see it, you need to save your document. Saving a Web page does not involve any special steps — simply use your editing program's Save feature. You need to be sure that you save the file into your Web site's root folder, or a subfolder of the root. Your file's name must start with a letter, and can contain only letters, numbers, and underscore characters. Your pages can end with either .html or .htm. Your homepage will likely need to be saved as either index.htm or index.html.

Save Your Web Page

1 Click **File**.

2 Click **Save As**.

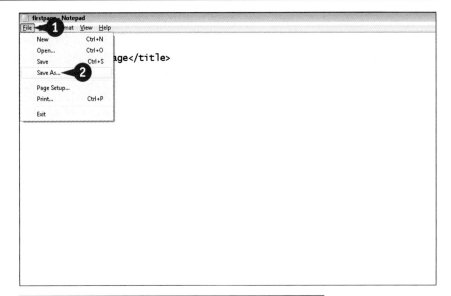

The Save As dialog box appears.

3 Type a name for your Web page.

④ Type **.html** as the file extension.

⑤ Click **Save**.

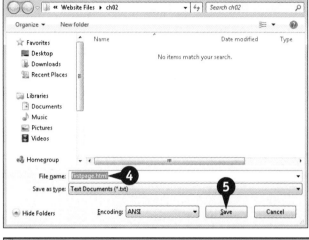

The dialog box closes, and the file is saved.

TIPS

Can I name my file anything I want?
The Web is much more restrictive on filenames than your operating system. The most important thing to remember is that your filename absolutely cannot contain spaces. It should also begin with a letter, and should not contain any characters other than letters, numbers, dashes, and underscores.

Is there a difference between the .html and .htm extensions?
No. Either will work in all browsers on all computers. The only important thing is that you make sure that you are consistent within a site, because you do not want some files to have an .html extension while others have .htm.

Preview a Page in a Browser

Throughout the design process, you will want to regularly check your page in a Web browser to ensure that it looks the way you expect it to. Ideally, you should check your page in more than one browser because browsers may not display the page in the same way. Many visual design tools have a way to automatically send the page to a browser for previewing, but the steps below demonstrate how to open the page manually in case you are not using a tool that opens it for you.

Preview a Page in a Browser

1 Open a Web browser.

2 Click **File**.

3 Click **Open**.

Note: Depending on the browser, the name of the menu item might vary slightly.

Note: If you are using Internet Explorer on Windows, you may need to press **Alt** on your keyboard to make the menus appear.

The Open dialog appears.

4 Click **Browse**.

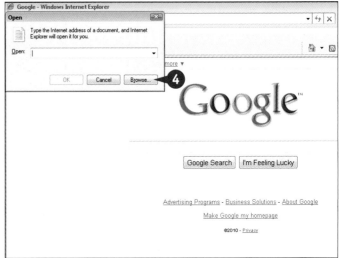

The browse file dialog box appears.

5 Navigate to the folder into which you saved your Web page.

6 Click the page.

7 Click **Open**.

The dialog box closes.

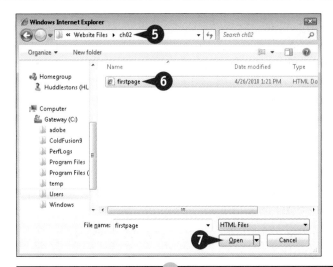

● The page opens in the browser.

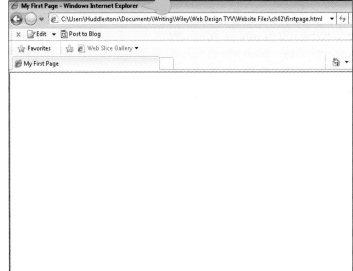

TIPS

Can I use any browser to test my pages?
Although browsers have become consistently better over the last few years about displaying pages the same, differences still exist. Technically the answer is yes, you can use any browser, but you should ideally use several browsers instead of any one. At a minimum, Windows users should test their pages in Internet Explorer, Firefox, and Safari, and Macintosh users should test on Safari and Firefox.

Can I leave my page open in my editor when I test it in the browser?
Yes. Most designers keep their editor and their browser open together, and simply switch back and forth between them as needed to test their pages. Be sure to save the page in the editor before switching to the browser, and be sure to refresh the browser's view each time you go back to it to ensure that you are seeing the latest version of the page.

Declare Your Document Type

Before a browser can correctly render your HTML, it needs to know what version of the language you are using. Both HTML and XHTML support three subsets or flavors: Strict, Transitional, and Frameset. You can set this version in your document by adding a document type declaration, or DOCTYPE. This special code, which is not an HTML tag, goes at the very top of your document; in fact, some browsers may render your page incorrectly if any code, including even a blank line, appears before the DOCTYPE. Most modern sites use the Transitional version of XHTML.

Declare Your Document Type

1 Open an HTML document.

2 Click at the top of your document.

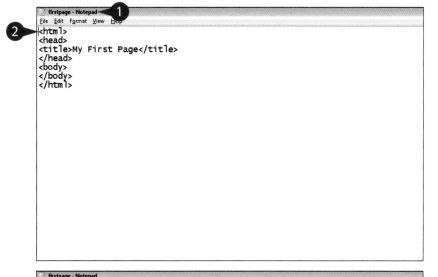

```
firstpage - Notepad
File Edit Format View Help
<html>
<head>
<title>My First Page</title>
</head>
<body>
</body>
</html>
```

3 If necessary, press **Enter** to create a new line above the `<html>` tag.

4 Type the appropriate document type declaration.

● For XHTML Transitional, type
`<!DOCTYPE html`
`PUBLIC "-//W3C//DTD`
`XHTML 1.0`
`Transitional//EN"`
`"http://www.w3.org/`
`TR/xhtml1/DTD/`
`xhtml1-transitional.`
`dtd">`.

```
firstpage - Notepad
File Edit Format View Help
<!DOCTYPE html PUBLIC "-//W3C//DTD XHTML 1.0 Transitional//EN"
"http://www.w3.org/TR/xhtml1/DTD/xhtml1-transitional.dtd">
<html>
<head>
<title>My First Page</title>
</head>
<body>
</body>
</html>
```

● For XHTML Strict, type
`<!DOCTYPE html PUBLIC "-//W3C//DTD XHTML 1.0 Strict//EN" "http://www.w3.org/TR/xhtml1/DTD/xhtml1-strict.dtd">`.

```
strictdoctype - Notepad
File  Edit  Format  View  Help
<!DOCTYPE html PUBLIC "-//W3C//DTD XHTML 1.0 Strict//EN"
"http://www.w3.org/TR/xhtml1/DTD/xhtml1-strict.dtd">
<html>
<head>
<title>My First Page</title>
</head>
<body>
</body>
</html>
```

● For HTML 4.01 Transitional, type `<!DOCTYPE HTML PUBLIC "-//W3C//DTD HTML 4.01 Transitional//EN" "http://www.w3.org/TR/html4/loose.dtd">`.

The document type declaration is added to the page.

```
firstpage - Notepad
File  Edit  Format  View  Help
<!DOCTYPE HTML PUBLIC "-//W3C//DTD HTML 4.01 Transitional//EN"
"http://www.w3.org/TR/html4/loose.dtd">
<html>
<head>
<title>My First Page</title>
</head>
<body>

</body>
</html>
```

TIPS

Am I required to add the declaration to the page?
Browsers will display your page without it, but some browsers are more likely to make mistakes in the rendering if you do not have a proper document type, so adding the declaration is strongly recommended. Most dedicated HTML editors add the declaration for you, so you may not have to actually type it.

What is the difference between the types?
HTML and XHTML Transitional are the least restrictive types and the most appropriate for most documents. Strict forces you to exactly follow the syntax of the languages and Web standards, so it is more difficult to code. Frameset provides additional tags for use in frames, but few Web sites use frames anymore.

Add Headings

M any studies have been conducted that show that most people scan Web pages rather than read them closely. Thus, headings are important to let your user know what topics are on the page that they might want to stop and read. The headings on your Web page serve the same purpose as headings in printed materials. For example, this book contains a main heading above this paragraph that allows you as a reader to quickly determine that these pages cover the topic of adding headings to your page. Just as that heading helps you find information in this book, headings on your Web page help your user.

Add Headings

1 Open a Web page in your editor.

2 Place the cursor between the opening and closing `<body>` tags.

3 Type `<h1>`.

4 Type text for the heading.

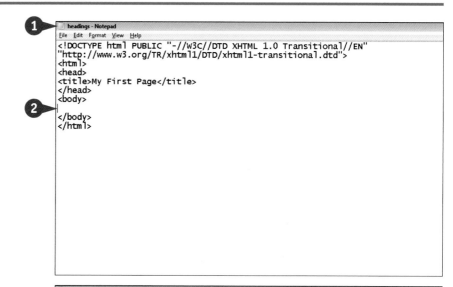

5 Type `</h1>`.

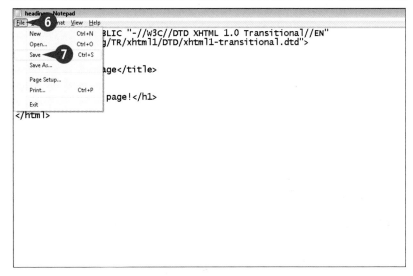

6 Click **File**.

7 Click **Save**.

The page is saved. The heading is added to the page.

Note: If you want to see how the heading will appear, follow the steps outlined above to preview the page in a browser.

TIPS

Does HTML provide for more than one level of heading?
Yes. HTML actually contains six heading levels. The elements are essentially the same: Each is the letter *h* followed by a number, 1–6. Your main topics should be designated with H1. Subtopics under the main should be H2, with subtopics under that H3, and so on.

Can I change the size and font of the heading?
Yes. Web designers have access to a powerful formatting language known as Cascading Style Sheets (CSS) that allows you to change the appearance of most anything on the screen, including the size and font of headings. CSS is covered in detail later in Chapters 4 and 5.

Add Paragraphs

Any logical block of text not already defined as a heading is likely going to be a paragraph. XHTML designates paragraphs using the `<p>` tag. You should wrap each logical block of text within this tag. When displayed within the browser, paragraphs appear with a blank line both above and below, rather than indenting the first line. Keep in mind that XHTML ignores whitespace in your code, so simply adding line breaks between blocks of text does not create that space in the browser; you need to use the `<p>` tag.

Add Paragraphs

① Open the page to which you want to add text.

② Type `<p>`.

③ Type text.

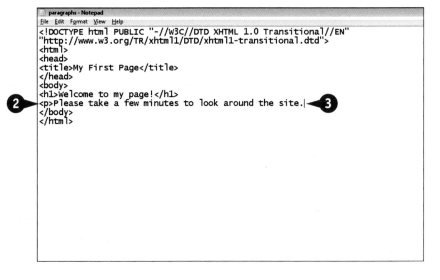

④ Type `</p>`.

⑤ Repeat Steps 2 to 4 to add additional paragraphs.

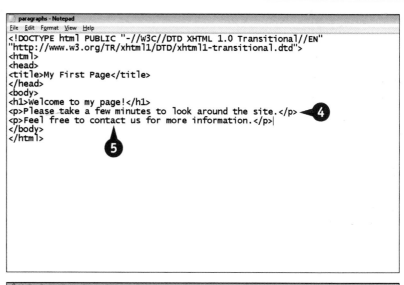

● When viewed in a Web browser, the text appears separated into distinct paragraphs.

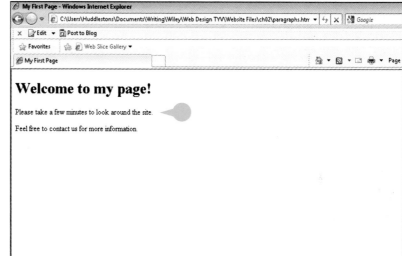

TIPS

Can I control how much space appears between paragraphs?

Yes. Cascading Style Sheets (CSS) allows you to precisely control the spacing between paragraphs, along with the font and color of the text and almost everything else with the paragraph's appearance. CSS is covered in detail in later chapters.

Why can I not just press the Enter key in my code to create paragraphs? Why do I need the <p> tag?

HTML is whitespace-insensitive, so pressing `Enter` in your code does not create paragraph breaks on the page in the browser. You can separate the text only by using the HTML tags.

Apply Logical Formatting

The formatting of your page can be done through either HTML tags or CSS. You should use the HTML tags only when the formatting affects the underlying meaning of the page and is not being used purely for visual effect. For example, if you want to make the name of your company visually stand out by making it bold, you are formatting for visual effect, and should use CSS. On the other hand, if you are using bold to emphasize the text, you should use HTML.

Apply Logical Formatting

1 Open the page to which you want to add formatting.

```
logicalformatting - Notepad
File  Edit  Format  View  Help
<!DOCTYPE html PUBLIC "-//W3C//DTD XHTML 1.0 Transitional//EN"
"http://www.w3.org/TR/xhtml1/DTD/xhtml1-transitional.dtd">
<html>
<head>
<title>My First Page</title>
</head>
<body>
<h1>Welcome to my page!</h1>
<p>Please take a few minutes to look around the site.</p>
<p>Feel free to contact us for more information.</p>
</body>
</html>
```

2 Before a word you want to make bold, type `<strong>`.

3 Type `</strong>` after the word.

```
logicalformatting - Notepad
File  Edit  Format  View  Help
<!DOCTYPE html PUBLIC "-//W3C//DTD XHTML 1.0 Transitional//EN"
"http://www.w3.org/TR/xhtml1/DTD/xhtml1-transitional.dtd">
<html>
<head>
<title>My First Page</title>
</head>
<body>
<h1>Welcome to my page!</h1>
<p><strong>Please</strong> take a few minutes to look around the site.</p>
<p>Feel free to contact us for more information.</p>
</body>
</html>
```

4 Before a word you want to italicize, type <em>.

5 After the word, type </em>.

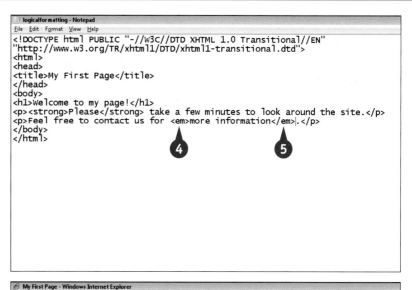

● When viewed in a browser, the formatted text is bold or italic.

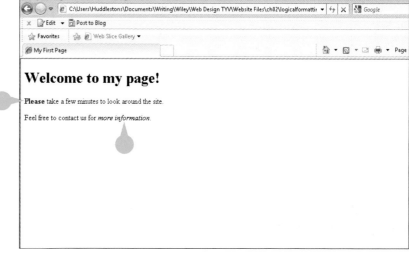

TIPS

I have seen pages that use <b> for bold. What is the difference?

The <strong> tag is used to add strong emphasis to a word, whereas the <b> tag means "bold." Visually they are identical, but <strong> provides more semantic meaning — you are saying that the word is bold because you are emphasizing it, rather than merely providing a formatting instruction. The same is true with <em>, for emphasis, and <i>, for italic.

Are there other tags besides <i> to italicize text?

Yes. In fact, there are quite a few, but all have specific semantic meanings. For example, <cite> renders its text in italic, but logically marks the text as a citation. The <address> tag, used for denoting an address on a page, also renders in italic.

Understanding URLs and File Paths

Your Web site is a collection of linked pages. You can have links on your pages that take your user to other pages in your site, other sites on the Web, other places within the same document, or e-mail addresses. The details of creating each of these links are covered in the following sections, but before you can start understanding the HTML syntax for links, you need to understand how to reference other pages in your document and other sites on the Web.

Relative Paths

Pages within your site can be referenced from one another via a *relative path*, where you tell the browser where the page to which you are linking is in relation to the current page. Think of this like giving directions to someone on the street, where you tell them how to go based on your current location.

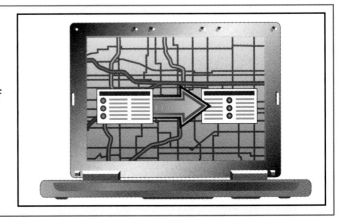

Pages in Folders

When providing a relative path, you may have files to which you are linking that are in folders other than the one that contains the file with the link. If the page to which you are linking is in a folder, and that folder is in the same folder as the page with the link, you simply provide the folder name, a slash, and the filename, as in `products/widget.html`.

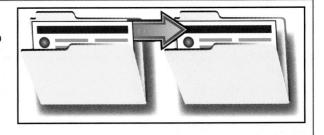

Absolute Paths

Hyperlinks to other sites on the Web need to use *absolute paths* for reference. Absolute paths contain the complete address to the site, including http://. Using an absolute path is similar to how you address a letter in the mail: You provide the complete address, regardless of where the letter originates.

http://www.example.com

HTTP Prefix

Absolute paths require that you use the complete address to the page in question. For most sites, this begins with http://, which is a way of telling the browser that you are using the HTTP protocol for this connection. Another common prefix is https://, the secure version of HTTP. You need to use whatever prefix is required by the site to which you are connecting.

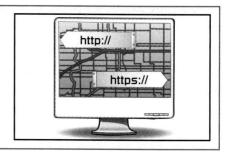

Host, Domain, and Top-Level Domain Name

The part of the address that follows the prefix is made up of the host, the domain name, and the top-level domain (TLD). In the example www.wiley.com, the host is www, the domain name is wiley, and the TLD is .com. Some sites, such as twitter.com, do not use a host. Other familiar TLDs include .net and .org.

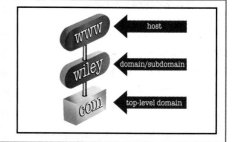

Folder Path

When you link to any page other than the home page in a site, the host, domain, and TLD are followed by the folder path to the page being requested. For example, a link to the address www.robhuddleston.com/books/tyvwebdesign.html is asking for a document, tyvwebdesign.html, in a folder called books at that site.

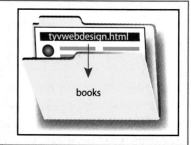

Requesting the Default Document

Anytime you link to a site without requesting a specific page, as when you provide only the prefix, host, domain, and TLD, or anytime you link to a folder within a site, you are requesting that site's or folder's default document, more commonly called the home page. For example, a link to http://www.yoursite.com/products actually returns the home page within the `products` folder.

Link to Other Pages in Your Site

Hyperlinking is a core concept behind the Web, which was originally conceived as a set of hyperlinked documents. Your Web site's navigation will consist of a set of hyperlinks to other pages in your site. Hyperlinks in HTML are created by using the anchor tag, which the language abbreviates to simply <a>. The tag has a required attribute, href, the value of which is set to the path to the page to which you are linking. Most of the time, you should do this by using relative paths for links to pages within your site.

Link to Other Pages in Your Site

1 Open a page on which you want to add a hyperlink.

```
links - Notepad
File  Edit  Format  View  Help
<!DOCTYPE html PUBLIC "-//W3C//DTD XHTML 1.0 Transitional//EN"
"http://www.w3.org/TR/xhtml1/DTD/xhtml1-transitional.dtd">
<html>
<head>
<title>My First Page</title>
</head>
<body>
<h1>Welcome to my page!</h1>
<p><strong>Please</strong> take a few minutes to look around the site.</p>
<p>Feel free to contact us for <em>more information</em>.</p>
<p>Second page</p>
</body>
</html>
```

2 Before the text that will be linked, type `<a href="?">`, replacing *?* with the path to the page to which you are linking.

```
links - Notepad
File  Edit  Format  View  Help
<!DOCTYPE html PUBLIC "-//W3C//DTD XHTML 1.0 Transitional//EN"
"http://www.w3.org/TR/xhtml1/DTD/xhtml1-transitional.dtd">
<html>
<head>
<title>My First Page</title>
</head>
<body>
<h1>Welcome to my page!</h1>
<p><strong>Please</strong> take a few minutes to look around the site.</p>
<p>Feel free to contact us for <em>more information</em>.</p>
<p><a href="secondpage.html">Second page</p>
</body>
</html>
```

3 After the link text, type </a>.

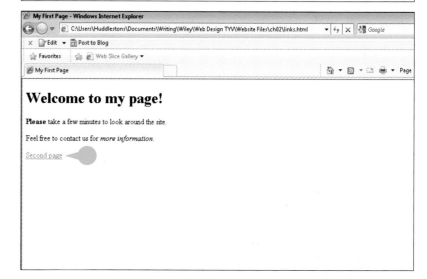

● When viewed in a browser,
the text appears blue and
underlined. Click it to
navigate to the other page.

TIPS

Can I change the appearance of the link?
Yes. CSS can be used to alter the color of the link
text, remove the underline, or otherwise format the
link. CSS is covered in later chapters.

**When I view the page in the browser and click
the link, I get an error. Why?**
The most common reason for errors when you click
links is an incorrect file path in the href attribute.
Double-check that you spelled the page name
correctly, and that it is in the location specified. If
you are viewing a site that has been uploaded to
the Web, make sure that the page to which you are
linking has also been uploaded.

Link to Pages on the Web

You can link to other sites on the Web by using the exact HTML code used in linking to pages in your site: an anchor tag with an `href` attribute. However, these links require that you use an absolute path. Depending on the operating system on which the site is hosted, the path may or may not be case-sensitive, so you need to pay attention to capitals. A simple way of ensuring that your link will work is to use your Web browser to navigate to the page, copy the address, and paste it into your code.

Link to Pages on the Web

1 Open the page onto which you want to add the link.

```
weblinks - Notepad
File  Edit  Format  View  Help
<!DOCTYPE html PUBLIC "-//W3C//DTD XHTML 1.0 Transitional//EN"
"http://www.w3.org/TR/xhtml1/DTD/xhtml1-transitional.dtd">
<html>
<head>
<title>My First Page</title>
</head>
<body>
<h1>Welcome to my page!</h1>
<p><strong>Please</strong> take a few minutes to look around the site.</p>
<p>Feel free to contact us for <em>more information</em>.</p>
<p><a href="secondpage.html">Second page</a></p>
<p>Search Google</p>
</body>
</html>
```

2 Before the text that you want to have linked, type `<a href="?">`, replacing *?* with the absolute path to the site to which you want to link.

Note: Be sure to include the prefix, such as `http://`, or the link will not work.

```
weblinks - Notepad
File  Edit  Format  View  Help
<!DOCTYPE html PUBLIC "-//W3C//DTD XHTML 1.0 Transitional//EN"
"http://www.w3.org/TR/xhtml1/DTD/xhtml1-transitional.dtd">
<html>
<head>
<title>My First Page</title>
</head>
<body>
<h1>Welcome to my page!</h1>
<p><strong>Please</strong> take a few minutes to look around the site.</p>
<p>Feel free to contact us for <em>more information</em>.</p>
<p><a href="secondpage.html">Second page</a></p>
<p><a href="http://www.google.com">Search Google</p>
</body>
</html>
```

3 After the text, type `</a>`.

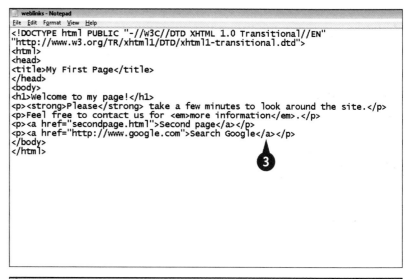

● When viewed in a Web browser, the text is blue and underlined. Click the text to navigate to the other site.

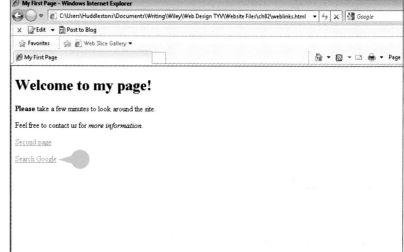

TIPS

Can I really link to any other page on the Web?
For the most part, yes. The Web was built for exactly this purpose. The only time you will be unable to link to a page is if that page requires that the user log in, in which case you will likely only be able to link to the login page.

Is there an easy way to get the address to a page I want to link to?
Yes. Simply use your Web browser to navigate to the page as you normally would. Then, you can copy the address from the browser's address bar and paste it into your code.

Link within a Page

If you have a particularly long document, you may want to provide links internally; that is, links from the top of the document to headings within the document, or a link at the bottom back up to the top. When creating these links, you will need to once again add an anchor tag, but you must also add some HTML code at the point to which you want to link. This becomes the target of the link. The easiest way to do this is to add an ID attribute to an existing tag. Your anchor tag's `href` attribute then begins with a pound sign, followed by the ID.

Link within a Page

1 Open the page on which you want to add internal links.

2 Before the text you want to use as the link, type `<a href="#?">`, replacing *?* with an identifier for the point on the page to which you want to link.

Note: The identifier must be a single word without spaces.

3 After the text, type `</a>`.

④ Scroll in the document to the point to which you want the link to go when clicked.

⑤ In the existing tag at that point, type id="?", replacing ? with the same identifier you used in Step 2.

Note: The identifier is case-sensitive, so be sure it matches exactly.

Note: If no tag exists at the point to which you want to link, you can use <span id="?">, again replacing ? with the identifier from Step 2. Be sure to add a closing </span> tag.

● When viewed in a browser, the link is blue and underlined. Click it to have the browser scroll to the other point in the document.

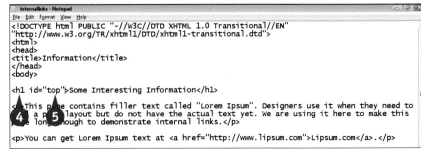

TIPS

What is the ID attribute?
The ID attribute can be used to identify a particular element. In addition to becoming the target of links, IDs can also be used in CSS and JavaScript. You can add an ID attribute to almost any tag in your HTML document.

Are there restrictions on what I can use for an ID?
The value of the ID attribute cannot contain spaces, but almost more important is that it must be unique on a page. You cannot have two elements share the same ID on the same page; if you do, you get unpredictable results in various browsers. The ID value is also case-sensitive, so be sure to stay consistent in how you capitalize it.

Link to an E-mail Address

You will likely want your users to be able to contact you from your site, whether to order products, get more information, or simply communicate. The easiest way to facilitate this contact is by providing a link to your e-mail address. Once again, you use the anchor tag with an `href` attribute, but this time, the attribute's value begins with `mailto:`, followed by the address to which you want the e-mail to be sent. When your user clicks the link, a new e-mail message is created in your user's e-mail program, with the address you specified filled into the To: field.

Link to an E-mail Address

1 Open the page onto which you want to add the link.

```
emaillinks - Notepad
File  Edit  Format  View  Help
<!DOCTYPE html PUBLIC "-//W3C//DTD XHTML 1.0 Transitional//EN"
"http://www.w3.org/TR/xhtml1/DTD/xhtml1-transitional.dtd">
<html>
<head>
<title>My First Page</title>
</head>
<body>
<h1>Welcome to my page!</h1>
<p><strong>Please</strong> take a few minutes to look around the site.</p>
<p>Feel free to contact us for <em>more information</em>.</p>
<p><a href="secondpage.html">Second page</a></p>
<p><a href="http://www.google.com">Search Google</a></p>
</body>
</html>
```

2 Before the text that you want to have linked, type `<a href="mailto:?">`, replacing *?* with your e-mail address.

```
emaillinks - Notepad
File  Edit  Format  View  Help
<!DOCTYPE html PUBLIC "-//W3C//DTD XHTML 1.0 Transitional//EN"
"http://www.w3.org/TR/xhtml1/DTD/xhtml1-transitional.dtd">
<html>
<head>
<title>My First Page</title>
</head>
<body>
<h1>Welcome to my page!</h1>
<p><strong>Please</strong> take a few minutes to look around the site.</p>
<p>Feel free to <a href="mailto:contact@somesite.com">contact us for <em>more
information</em>.</p>
<p><a href="secondpage.html">Second page</a></p>
<p><a href="http://www.google.com">Search Google</a></p>
</body>
</html>
```

③ After the text, type `</a>`.

```
emaillinks - Notepad
File  Edit  Format  View  Help
<!DOCTYPE html PUBLIC "-//W3C//DTD XHTML 1.0 Transitional//EN"
"http://www.w3.org/TR/xhtml1/DTD/xhtml1-transitional.dtd">
<html>
<head>
<title>My First Page</title>
</head>
<body>
<h1>Welcome to my page!</h1>
<p><strong>Please</strong> take a few minutes to look around the site.</p>
<p>Feel free to <a href="mailto:contact@somesite.com">contact us</a> for <em>
information</em>.</p>
<p><a href="secondpage.html">Second page</a></p>
<p><a href="http://www.google.com">Search Google</a></p>
</body>
</html>
```

● When viewed in a Web browser, the text is blue and underlined. Click the text. A new e-mail message should open from your computer's e-mail program.

```
My First Page - Windows Internet Explorer
    C:\Users\Huddlestons\Documents\Writing\Wiley\Web Design TYV\Website Files\ch02\emaillinks.html   Google
  Edit    Post to Blog
  Favorites      Web Slice Gallery
  My First Page                                                                    Page
```

Welcome to my page!

Please take a few minutes to look around the site.

Feel free to contact us for *more information*.

Second page

Search Google

TIPS

Linking to an e-mail address seems very easy, but I do not see this very much on the Web. Why?

Even though linking to an e-mail address is in fact easy, it has significant downsides. First, your users must be using their own computer and must have a properly set-up e-mail program such as Microsoft Outlook in order for the link to work. Second, it is unfortunately very easy for spammers to find your address when you use this technique, so you will likely see a dramatic increase in the junk mail in your inbox.

What other methods exist for allowing users to contact me?

You can use an HTML form and server-side scripting, both of which are covered in later chapters (Chapters 11 and 12, respectively), to overcome the downsides mentioned above and yet still allow users to contact you. This is a far more common method on the Web today.

Link to Other Document Types

In addition to linking to other Web pages, you can link to other types of documents as well. For example, you might have a user manual saved in the Adobe PDF format that you want users to access. Fortunately, the process for linking to these documents is the same as that for linking to Web pages: You add an anchor tag, and then provide either an absolute or relative path to the document. Depending on the type of document to which you are linking, it either opens within a plug-in in the user's browser, or the browser asks the user to download and save it.

Link to Other Document Types

1 Open the page onto which you want to add the link.

```
documentlinks - Notepad
File  Edit  Format  View  Help
<!DOCTYPE html PUBLIC "-//W3C//DTD XHTML 1.0 Transitional//EN"
"http://www.w3.org/TR/xhtml1/DTD/xhtml1-transitional.dtd">
<html>
<head>
<title>My First Page</title>
</head>
<body>
<h1>Welcome to my page!</h1>
<p><strong>Please</strong> take a few minutes to look around the site.</p>
<p>Feel free to <a href="mailto:contact@somesite.com">contact us</a> for <em>
information</em>.</p>
<p>You can also learn more about us by downloading our PDF.</p>
<p><a href="secondpage.html">Second page</a></p>
<p><a href="http://www.google.com">Search Google</a></p>
</body>
</html>
```

2 Before the text that you want to have linked, type `<a href=" ?">`, replacing *?* with the absolute path to the document to which you want to link.

Note: Be sure to include the appropriate file extension, such as .pdf.

```
documentlinks - Notepad
File  Edit  Format  View  Help
<!DOCTYPE html PUBLIC "-//W3C//DTD XHTML 1.0 Transitional//EN"
"http://www.w3.org/TR/xhtml1/DTD/xhtml1-transitional.dtd">
<html>
<head>
<title>My First Page</title>
</head>
<body>
<h1>Welcome to my page!</h1>
<p><strong>Please</strong> take a few minutes to look around the site.</p>
<p>Feel free to <a href="mailto:contact@somesite.com">contact us</a> for <em>
information</em>.</p>
<p>You can also learn more about us by <a href="info.pdf">downloading our PDF
<p><a href="secondpage.html">Second page</a></p>
<p><a href="http://www.google.com">Search Google</a></p>
</body>
</html>
```

③ After the text, type `</a>`.

● When viewed in a Web browser, the text is blue and underlined. Click the text to open or save the document.

TIPS

Can I control whether the browser asks my user to save the document instead of just opening it?

No. If the user has the correct plug-in for the document type, such as Adobe Reader for PDF files, the document simply opens. If the user does not have the correct plug-in, the browser asks the user to download the file. If you want to ensure that the file is downloaded, save it as a Zip file because all browsers download Zips instead of opening them.

What happens if I link to a Microsoft Office document?

Office documents are treated the same as any other. If the user is on Windows and using Internet Explorer and has Office installed, the document opens in a special plug-in within the browser. If the user is not on Windows, or is using a different browser, the user is prompted to download and save the document.

Show Tool Tips for Links

You can display a tool tip, or small pop-up message, when your user moves her mouse over a link to provide some details about the target page when she clicks the link. This can help assure your user that the link is safe to follow. You use the optional `title` attribute of the anchor tag to add this tool tip. Be sure that the tool tip text accurately describes the page to which the user will be taken when she clicks the link.

Show Tool Tips for Links

1 Open a page that contains a hyperlink.

```
tooltips - Notepad          1
File  Edit  Format  View  Help
<!DOCTYPE html PUBLIC "-//W3C//DTD XHTML 1.0 Transitional//EN"
"http://www.w3.org/TR/xhtml1/DTD/xhtml1-transitional.dtd">
<html>
<head>
<title>My First Page</title>
</head>
<body>
<h1>Welcome to my page!</h1>
<p><strong>Please</strong> take a few minutes to look around the site.</p>
<p>Feel free to <a href="mailto:contact@somesite.com">contact us</a> for <em>
information</em>.</p>
<p>You can also learn more about us by <a href="info.pdf">downloading our PDF
<p><a href="secondpage.html">Second page</a></p>
<p><a href="http://www.google.com">Search Google</a></p>
</body>
</html>
```

2 Click within an existing anchor tag, after the `href="?"` but before the `>`.

```
tooltips - Notepad
File  Edit  Format  View  Help
<!DOCTYPE html PUBLIC "-//W3C//DTD XHTML 1.0 Transitional//EN"
"http://www.w3.org/TR/xhtml1/DTD/xhtml1-transitional.dtd">
<html>
<head>
<title>My First Page</title>
</head>
<body>
<h1>Welcome to my page!</h1>
<p><strong>Please</strong> take a few minutes to look around the site.</p>
<p>Feel free to <a href="mailto:contact@somesite.com">contact us</a> for <em>
information</em>.</p>
<p>You can also learn more about us by <a href="info.pdf" >downloading our PD
<p><a href="secondpage.html">Second page</a></p>
<p><a href="http://www.google.com">Search Google</a></p>    2
</body>
</html>
```

3 Type `title=" ?"`, replacing *?* with appropriate text describing the link's target page.

● When viewed in a browser, the link appears as it did before. When you position your mouse pointer over the link without clicking, the title text appears as a tool tip.

TIPS

How long can the title text be?

In theory, you can have as much text as you want in the title, but you should try to keep it short and to-the-point. Your users want to be able to glance at it and see where they will go when they click, rather than needing to read a lot.

Can I add the tool tip to any other elements?

Yes. Technically, HTML allows for the `title` attribute to appear in any element, and browsers display the tool tip for any title. Tool tips are rarely used for elements other than links because the user is not likely to mouse over other items on the page, but using them is still allowed.

CHAPTER 3

Creating Images

The Web is a visual medium, and effectively using images will greatly enhance your page designs. This chapter will introduce you to some of the industry-leading image-editing tools and show how to put those images onto your pages.

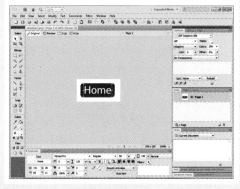

Understanding Image Formats

Depending on how the image was created, images you want to use on your Web site can potentially come in any one of hundreds of formats, but the Web supports only three: GIF, JPEG, and PNG. Before you can begin working with images on your pages, you need to understand these formats so that you can choose the one that works best. Each format has specific advantages and disadvantages, and you will need to evaluate each image to determine the format that works best for it.

The Formats for the Web

Browsers can natively display images saved in the JPEG, GIF, and PNG formats. Any other format requires that the browser use a plug-in, so these three are commonly thought of as the formats the Web supports. If you have an image in any other format, you will need to convert it to one of these.

JPEG

JPEG is short for Joint Photographic Expert's Group, the organization that originally developed the format. The JPEG format supports millions of colors and is thus best for photographic images. Most of today's digital cameras save images as JPEGs by default.

GIF

Originally developed in the 1980s by CompuServe, the Graphics Interchange Format has long been a standard on the Internet, even before the Web. GIFs support a maximum of 256 colors, and today are primarily used for logos, line art, and buttons. Unlike JPEG, GIFs support transparency and animation.

PNG

Developed as an alternative to GIF, the Portable Network Graphics format combines the best features of the JPEG and GIF formats. Like JPEG, a PNG can have millions of colors, and like GIF, PNGs can support transparency.

Legally Acquiring Stock Images

Any creative work is protected by copyright. This applies to written works such as this book as well as artistic works such as photographs. You are of course free to use any image that you create yourself. If you work for a large company, they will likely have sets of images that they have already acquired that are again safe to use on the company's Web sites. Before you can use an image that you or your company did not create, you need to be sure that you have the legal right to use it.

Royalty-Free Images

If you want to use someone else's work, you must pay them for that work through royalties every time you use it. However, you may be able to pay for an image once and then freely use that image from then on. Such images are known as *royalty-free* images. Note that you may have to pay a fee upfront, so royalty-free does not necessarily mean free.

Stock Images

Stock images are generally royalty-free images made available for use by companies and organizations. Stock images tend to be somewhat general in their subject matter: groups of people, animals, and scenery are common subjects for stock images.

When in Doubt, Do Not Use It

The penalties for using someone else's copyrighted material can be severe. The simplest way to protect yourself from getting sued for illegally using images is to never use something unless you are absolutely certain doing so is okay. Do not use an image off a site unless you can find text on the page from which you are getting the image that clearly states that it is okay.

Understanding Image Optimization

Every image you add to a page increases the time the page takes to load in a browser. Optimizing your image is the process of reducing its file size while minimizing the impact of that reduction on the quality of the image. Every major graphics program offers tools to optimize images, but these generally provide an array of options that can be highly confusing, so you should gain a basic understanding of the various ways in which graphics can be optimized in order to better understand the process.

JPEG Optimization

JPEGs are optimized by compressing the image. Unfortunately, this uses a technique known as *lossy compression*, where data is removed from the image. Therefore, the more you optimize an image, the worse it will look. The compression is often expressed as a percentage, with 100% indicating that all of the original data has been retained and thus no compression.

GIF Optimization

You can optimize a GIF by removing unnecessary colors from it. GIFs can contain up to 256 colors, but they do not need to use all of those. A simple logo may be made up of only one or two colors, so saving additional color information is nothing more than a waste of space. However, more complex images may start to lose quality if you remove needed colors.

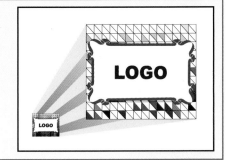

PNG Optimization

PNG files can be compressed via lossy compression, just like JPEGs, or via removing colors, like GIFs. PNGs can also contain additional embedded data that describes the image to editing software but is unnecessary when used on Web pages, so removing this data can be seen as a form of optimizing for the format.

GIF and PNG Features

GIF supports optional features such as animation and transparency. PNG supports transparency. Adding these can make your image look better, but also adds to the file size. Therefore, choosing to not use these features reduces the size of the images.

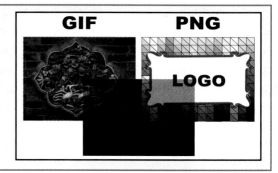

Choosing the Right Format

Because the JPEG and GIF formats were specifically designed for a particular image type, each is inherently more efficient when used on the correct type of image. Therefore, an image that should be saved as a JPEG will be larger if you attempt to save it as a GIF, and vice versa.

Scale and Crop Images

Images with needlessly large pixel dimensions will also be needlessly large files. Using a good image-editing tool to reduce the dimensions of the image dramatically reduces its file size. You can also crop unneeded portions out of the image to reduce its size.

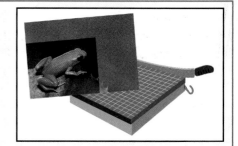

Resolution

Image resolution describes the number of pixels per inch in an image. Whereas images for print need to have a high resolution, images for the Web should never be more the 72 dots or pixels per inch. Many computer screens are simply incapable of displaying higher-resolution images, so keeping the image at a higher resolution simply wastes file size.

Download a Stock Image from the Web

The Web site at www.istockphoto.com is an excellent resource for finding royalty-free images. Although you need to pay for most of the images, they do provide a single image each week that can be freely downloaded and used. You begin the process of getting images at the site by creating a free account. You can use this account to search the site and download the free image of the week. As with other sites that you have accounts with, you should pick a strong password that is easy for you to remember but hard for others to guess.

Download a Stock Image from the Web

Sign Up for a Free Account

1. Open a Web browser and go to www.istockphoto.com.

2. Click **Sign up**.

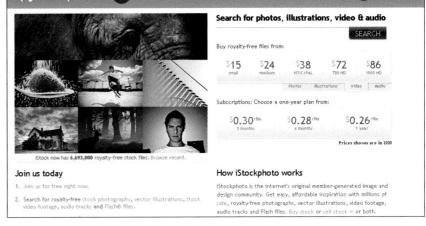

A signup form appears.

3. Fill in the requested information on the form.

4. Click **I agree to the Membership Agreement** (☐ changes to ☑).

5. Click **Sign me up!**

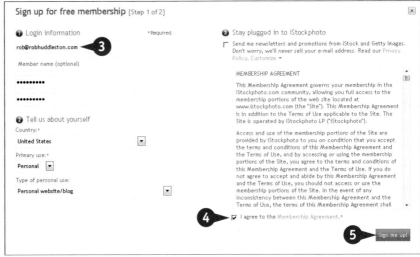

A confirmation screen appears.

6 Double-check that the information is correct.

7 Click **Confirm**.

The You're Done screen appears.

8 Click **Continue**.

The signup process is complete, and you are returned to the home page.

TIPS

What other stock image sites exist online?
There are too many to count, but SpiderPic, at www. spiderpic.com, is a good place to start. Unlike other sites, SpiderPic does not sell their own images; instead, they allow you to comparison-shop across many other stock sites, often allowing you to find the same image for less.

Are there places to get completely free, royalty-free images?
Yes. Stock.xchng, at www.sxc.hu, has many royalty-free images that you do not have to pay for. Be sure to read the license carefully for each image, however, because the permissions vary from one picture to the next.

continued ▶

Once you have signed up for a free account at iStockphoto, you can either purchase credits to buy images or visit the site every week to download their free image of the week. Credits are about $1 each, but as with many other sites, the price per credit drops if you purchase more at one time. However, plan carefully, because credits expire one year after you purchase them. You should therefore try to plan ahead so that you can purchase enough credits for the year to take advantage of discounts while not buying so many that you end up losing some.

Download a Stock Image from the Web (continued)

Download the Free Image of the Week

1 On the iStockPhoto home page, click the image above the heading Free Photo of the Week.

The free photo page loads.

2 Select the image size you want to download.

3 Click **Buy**.

The Download Free File of the Week page appears.

4 Click **Accept Agreement & Start Download**.

Note: If a page appears asking you to complete your membership profile, fill out the form and click **Update Profile**.

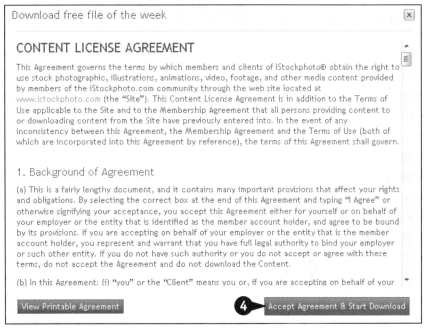

The File Download dialog box appears.

5 Click **Save**.

The image is downloaded to your computer.

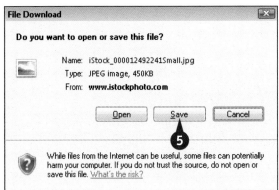

TIPS

Where will the image be saved?
Depending on which browser you use, you are either asked for a location to save the file or it just downloads. In the latter case, the file will likely be placed either in your Downloads folder or on your desktop.

What size image should I choose?
For the free image of the week, you should just download the largest size available, because this gives you the most flexibility in working with the image later. Images can be easily scaled down, but not up, so for images you are purchasing, you should get the largest size you think you might need.

Get to Know the Photoshop Interface

 or over 20 years, graphic designers and photographers have relied on Photoshop for image manipulation and correction. Today, Photoshop is also a staple for Web designers who need to make their images ready for their sites. Unlike software created by many other companies, Adobe's Creative Suite products, including Photoshop, place the tools and most features in panels, which are docked along the left and right sides of the screen. This gives you much faster access to these features than what you find in other programs, but can make the interface appear overwhelmingly complex at first.

Menu Bar

Menus for working with files, changing views, and accessing other commands.

View Buttons

These buttons allow you to change your view, zoom in and out, and access Bridge.

Workspace Menus

You can change the layout of the program by selecting one of these workspaces.

Toolbox

All of the basic tools for working in Photoshop are accessible here.

Document Tabs

Switch between open documents by clicking these tabs. If you use a Mac, you may not see these tabs.

Panels

Most of Photoshop's controls are available via these panels.

Document Information

The size and current magnification of the document are shown here.

Photoshop Elements was created for amateur and home users who want to be able to clean up and manipulate photos but who do not need the full feature set of Photoshop. Photoshop Elements is considerably less expensive than Photoshop.

Menu Bar

Most of the commands in the program are available in the menus.

Common Tasks

Reset the interface, undo changes, and launch the Organizer from here.

Command Bar

The buttons on the command bar change according to the currently selected tool.

Toolbox

The tools for working in and manipulating your images can be accessed from here.

Project Bin

The photos you are currently working in can be accessed in the bin.

Panels

Apply effects or work with layers using these panels.

Mode Switcher

Switch between Edit, Create, and Share modes in the program.

Use Photoshop to Fix Colors

Most digital cameras today are fairly good at adjusting settings to capture good images, but almost all will get colors wrong. When you move from one lighting situation to another, the camera must reinterpret what it sees as white. For example, fluorescent lights cast a distinctly yellowish hue on everything. Therefore, a picture taken outside generally looks right, whereas pictures taken in offices are yellowish. Photoshop makes it easy to correct for this with color adjustment tools. You can simply drag sliders back and forth and see the corrections directly on your image.

Use Photoshop to Fix Colors

① Click **File**.

② Click **Open**.

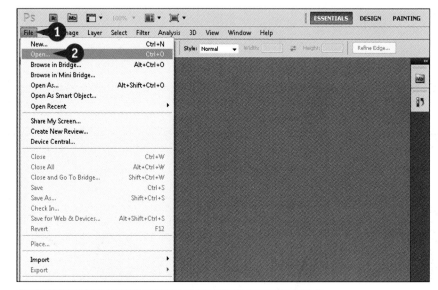

The Open dialog box appears.

③ Navigate to the folder containing your image.

④ Double-click the image.

The image opens in Photoshop.

5 Click **Window**.

6 Click **Adjustments** to open the Adjustments panel.

7 Click the **Color Balance** button (⬚).

The Color Balance adjustment sliders appear.

8 Drag the color sliders to achieve the desired color balance.

● The image's colors are corrected.

TIPS

What are the other adjustments?
Almost all images from your digital camera will require color adjustment. The other adjustment types allow you to change the color balance through various other techniques. You can also apply a few effects in the panel, such as converting the image to black and white.

Why did adjusting the color add a new layer?
Photoshop relies on nondestructive editing to apply changes. By adding the color balance as a new layer, Photoshop applies the effect without changing the original image, so if you want to remove the change, you can at any point simply delete the color balance layer.

Crop and Resize an Image in Photoshop

Once you have corrected the colors on the image, you must resize the image to something more appropriate to what your Web site needs. Most modern digital cameras take very large images, but for most Web sites, you will want much smaller pictures, if for no other reason than that you need your image to fit within the page. You can reduce the entire image by resizing it, or you can cut unwanted portions of the image out through a process known as *cropping*. Photoshop makes both very easy.

Crop and Resize an Image in Photoshop

Crop the Image

1 On the Toolbox, click the **Crop** tool.

2 Click and drag on the image to define an area to keep.

Note: You can adjust the crop box after you draw it by dragging the handles.

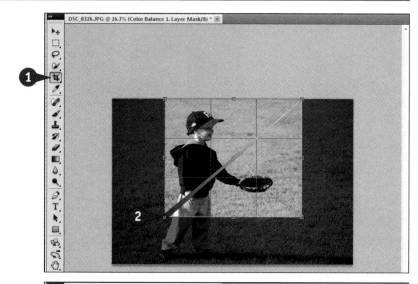

3 Double-click within the crop box.

● The image is cropped.

Resize the Image

1 Click **Image**.

2 Click **Image Size**.

The Image Size dialog box appears.

3 Enter a desired width.

Note: The height adjusts automatically as you enter a value for width.

4 Click **OK**.

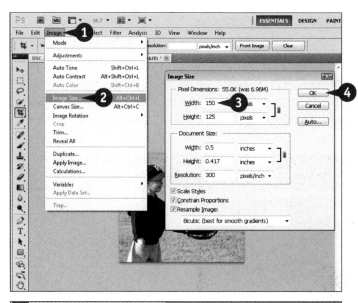

● The image is resized.

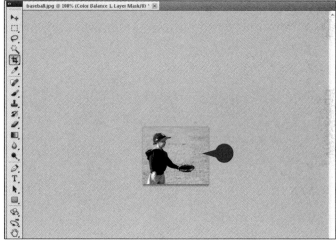

TIPS

How do I know how big to make the image?
The image needs to fit in your design. Hopefully, you had carefully planned out your design before going into Photoshop and know how big to make the image. As long as you preserve the original image, saving the cropped and resized image as a copy, you could always return to it and resize if needed.

What is the grid that appears when I crop my image?
Photographers have long followed a "rule of thirds" in composing images. Basically, the idea is that if you divide the image into nine equal parts and put the focal point of the image at the intersection of two of the grid lines, you will have a more visually interesting image. Photoshop's Crop tool provides the grid to help you achieve this.

Save an Image for the Web in Photoshop

Photoshop uses a native format, PSD, to save its images. Most of the adjustments and edits you make to images in the program cause it to save the image to this format, regardless of the format in which the image began. You therefore need to save it for the Web as a GIF, JPEG, or PNG once you have completed editing. Photoshop's Save for Web & Devices dialog box provides an easy way to optimize the image and then save it to the appropriate format. Most images that you create or modify in Photoshop work best as JPEGs.

Save an Image for the Web in Photoshop

1 Click **File**.

2 Click **Save for Web & Devices**.

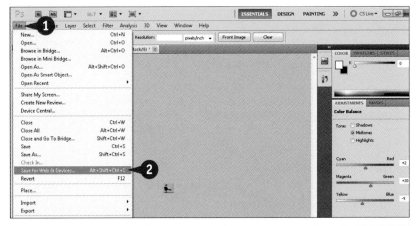

The Save for Web & Devices dialog box appears.

3 Select a format from the pop-up menu.

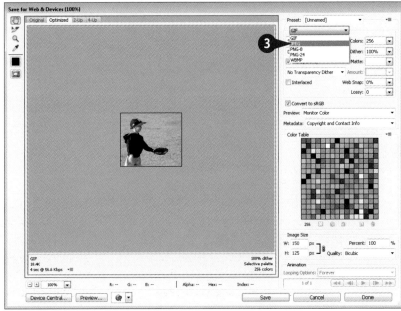

- If you select JPEG, select a quality preset.

- You can also manually set the quality percentage.

④ Click **Save**.

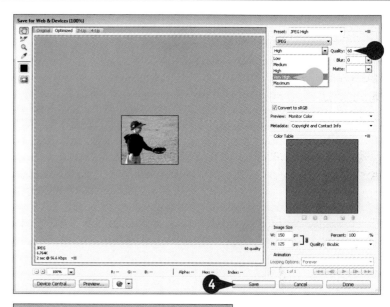

The Save Optimized As dialog box appears.

⑤ Navigate to the folder that contains your Web site's images.

⑥ Type a name for the image.

⑦ Click **Save**.

The image is saved.

TIPS

Can I compare different quality settings to see which one I like best?
Yes. Click the **2-Up** or **4-Up** buttons in the top corner of the dialog box. Then, click one of the previews and change the settings. Click another preview to modify the settings. Finally, click the preview with the best results and click **Save**.

I can see only a portion of my image. How do I view the rest of it?
You can move around on the image by simply clicking and dragging on the preview. You can also zoom out by selecting a different magnification level in the bottom right corner, but choosing optimization settings while viewing at 100% is best.

Open an Image for Editing in Photoshop Elements

Photoshop Elements is designed to make not only editing images easy, but also organizing images and sharing them. When you first launch the program, you do not see the main interface, but instead are presented with a Welcome screen that offers buttons to the editing and organizing sections of the program, along with links to help files. In order to make adjustments or edits to your picture, you need to go into the Editor by clicking the appropriate button on the Welcome screen. From there, you can open your image and begin making changes to it.

Open an Image for Editing in Photoshop Elements

1 On the Photoshop Elements Welcome screen, click **Edit**.

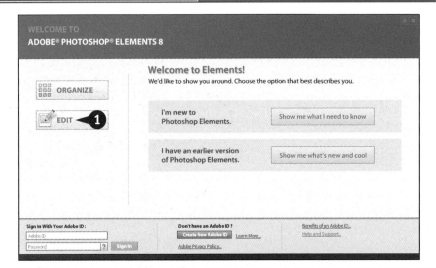

The Editor launches.

2 Click **File**.

3 Click **Open**.

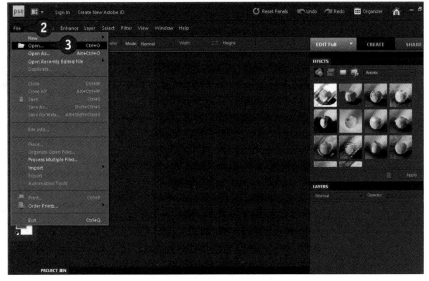

The Open dialog box appears.

4 Select the image you want to open.

5 Click **Open**.

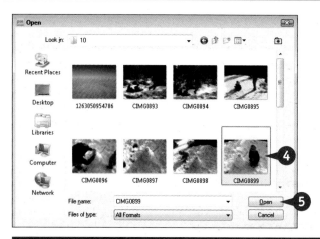

● The image opens in Photoshop Elements and can now be edited.

TIPS

How can I use Photoshop Elements to organize images?

One of the nicest things about digital photography is that, unlike in the days of film, you can take an unlimited number of images. Unfortunately, returning home from vacation with 2,000 pictures can be overwhelming. The Organizer, accessible from the Welcome screen or from the top right corner of the Editor window, provides tools to help manage your photographic collection.

What options are available to share images from Photoshop Elements?

Photoshop Elements provides easy-to-use tools to create online photo albums, e-mail pictures, burn images to CDs or DVDs, or create PDF-based slide shows. Click the **Share** button in the top right corner of the Editor to explore the available options.

Use Photoshop Elements to Fix Colors

Photoshop Elements has most of the power of Photoshop in a vastly simplified interface. In both Photoshop Elements and Photoshop, you can make the manual adjustments to fix problems with images such as incorrect colors, but both programs also feature a set of automatic adjustments that work well in most cases. These automatic adjustments provide a very fast way to fix colors, which can be particularly important if you need to fix a lot of images in a short time.

Use Photoshop Elements to Fix Colors

① Click **Enhance**.

② Click **Auto Color Correction**.

- The color correction is applied to the image.

Rotate an Image in Photoshop Elements

You may have pictures that you took by rotating your camera. You need to rotate these images so that they are oriented the correct way when you insert them into your page. Fortunately, Photoshop Elements automates this process. All you need to do to rotate an image is open the image in Photoshop Elements and then save it. When you open the image, Photoshop Elements analyzes it to see if it needs to be rotated. Once you save the image, the rotation is saved with it.

Rotate an Image in Photoshop Elements

1 Click **File**.

2 Click **Open**.

The Open dialog box appears.

3 Select an image that is rotated incorrectly.

4 Click **Open**.

● Photoshop Elements automatically rotates the image to the correct orientation.

Crop an Image in Photoshop Elements

Many images contain unwanted details along the edges. You can ensure that users focus on the portions of the image that you want them to by cropping it.

Crop an Image in Photoshop Elements

1 Click the **Crop** tool (⛶) in the Toolbox.

2 Adjust the crop box's handles.

Note: Press and hold **Shift** to maintain the image proportions as you crop.

3 Click the **Commit** button (✔) just below the crop area.

● The image is cropped.

Resize an Image in Photoshop Elements

The primary feature digital camera marketers focus on is megapixels. Contrary to popular belief, this has nothing to do with the quality of the image; rather, it is merely a measurement of the size of the image that the camera can take. A 6-megapixel camera likely takes images that are far too big for a Web site: about 3,000 pixels wide by 2,000 pixels tall. Most Web sites can more effectively use images between 100 and 600 pixels wide. You can use Photoshop Elements to scale them down to a size that better fits your site's design requirements.

Resize an Image in Photoshop Elements

1 Click **Image**.

2 Click **Resize**.

3 Click **Image Size**.

The Image Size dialog box appears.

4 Click **Resample Image** (☐ changes to ☑).

5 Enter a new width for the image in the Pixel Dimensions section.

6 Click **OK**.

● The image is resized.

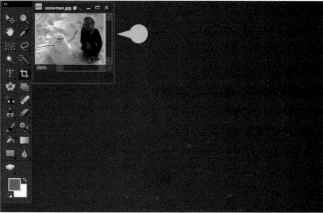

Save an Image for the Web in Photoshop Elements

Like Photoshop, images in Photoshop Elements are saved by default in the PSD format. To put the image on the Web, you need it saved as a JPEG, PNG, or GIF, although most photographs need to be JPEGs. You also need to optimize the image to maximize its quality while simultaneously minimizing its file size. The Save for Web feature in Photoshop Elements allows you to accomplish all of these goals.

Save an Image for the Web in Photoshop Elements

1 Click **File**.

2 Click **Save for Web**.

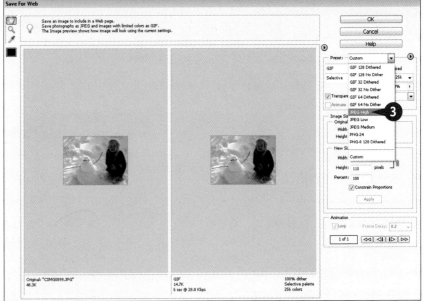

The Save For Web dialog box appears.

3 Choose one of the presets from the pop-up menu.

- If you want, you can modify the preset's settings by manually adjusting the quality percentage.

4 Click **OK**.

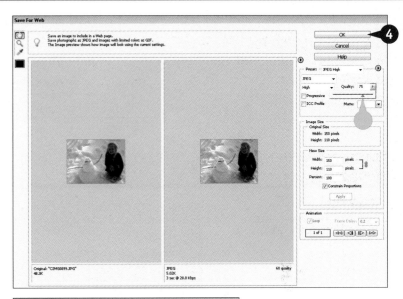

The Save Optimized As dialog box appears.

5 Navigate to your Web site's images folder.

6 Type a name for your image.

7 Click **Save**.

The optimized image is saved.

TIPS

What format should I use?

Most of the time, images you work with in Photoshop Elements are photographs, so either JPEG or PNG-24 gives you the smallest files with the best quality. GIFs and PNG-8s, because they are designed for images with only a few colors, tend to look poor and result in bigger files.

How can I tell how big my file is going to be?

Photoshop Elements displays the file size of the image after optimization in the lower right corner of the preview pane. You can adjust the settings and see how the file size will be impacted by looking here.

Get to Know the Fireworks Interface

Fireworks was created by a company called Macromedia. Unlike Photoshop, which at the time was its main competitor, Fireworks was specifically engineered to create Web graphics. Although now a part of the Adobe lineup, Fireworks continues to be a favorite among many Web designers because of its Web-centric focus. Its interface is designed to look and feel like the other Creative Suite products, and like those products its features are organized into panels, grouped primarily along the right side of the screen. Fireworks also contains a set of tools that allow you to perform various manipulations on the image.

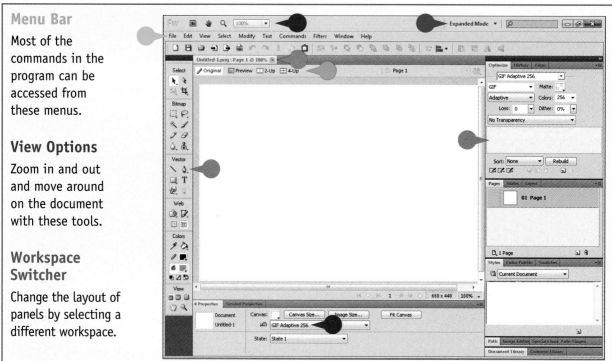

Menu Bar

Most of the commands in the program can be accessed from these menus.

View Options

Zoom in and out and move around on the document with these tools.

Workspace Switcher

Change the layout of panels by selecting a different workspace.

Panels

Most of your work in Fireworks will be done through panels.

Properties

This panel is dynamic, and presents different options depending on the tool or object currently selected.

Toolbox

The drawing tools in Fireworks can be found here.

Document Tabs

You can switch between open documents by selecting the document's tab.

Preview Options

Choose to view your document in original, preview, 2-up, or 4-up mode.

Get to Know the Illustrator Interface

Almost all computer graphics are either bitmaps, meaning that they are composed of small, square pixels, or vectors, which are constructed by defining points and using mathematical algorithms to draw lines between the points. Illustrator is an extremely powerful vector-based design tool. Many of the logos that represent major corporations were designed in Illustrator. Like its Creative Suite counterparts, Illustrator's interface contains a series of panels, from which most of the program's features can be accessed, and a set of drawing tools.

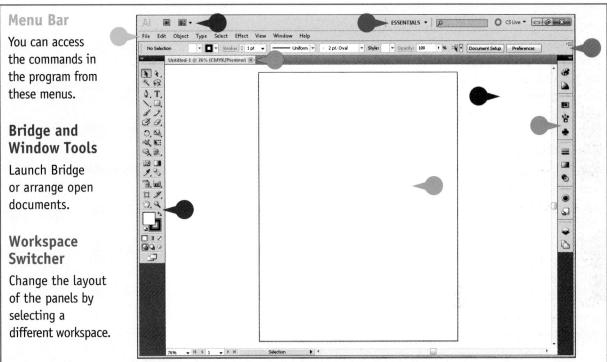

Menu Bar

You can access the commands in the program from these menus.

Bridge and Window Tools

Launch Bridge or arrange open documents.

Workspace Switcher

Change the layout of the panels by selecting a different workspace.

Panels

Most of your work in Illustrator will be done with these panels. Click a panel's icon to expand it.

Toolbox

The drawing and other tools in the program can be accessed from the Toolbox.

Control Bar

The items available on the Control bar differ depending on the currently selected tool.

Document Tabs

You can switch between open documents by selecting its tab.

Canvas

The drawing area for your document.

Artboard

The area surrounding the canvas can be used as a virtual desktop to place items you plan to use later.

Create a Button in Fireworks

You can make your Web site more visually interesting by using graphical buttons for your navigation. You can use the drawing tools in Fireworks to quickly create these graphics. Before you begin, you need to create a new document. You should size the document based on how big you need the button to be. You can use the color tools in Fireworks to set the background of the button to match the visual design you have in mind.

Create a Button in Fireworks

1 From the Fireworks Welcome screen, click **Fireworks Document**.

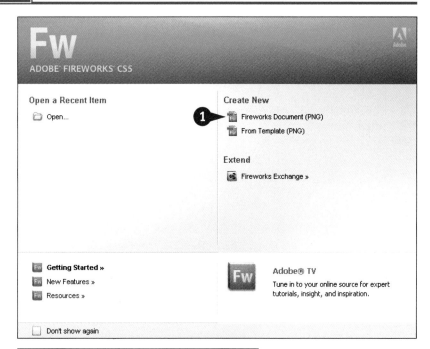

The New Document dialog box appears.

2 Enter the dimensions you want for your button.

3 Click **OK**.

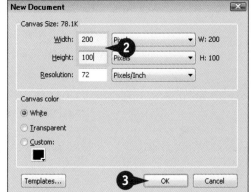

● The new document is created.

④ Click the **Rectangle** tool (▭).

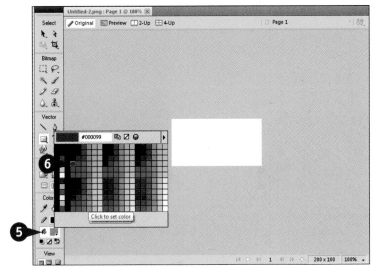

⑤ Click the **Fill Color** tool (▨).

⑥ Select a color to use for the fill.

The tool is ready to use.

TIPS

Can I modify existing images as well as create new ones in Fireworks?

Yes. Fireworks provides tools not only for creating new images, but also for manipulating existing images. In fact, most of the things you can do to images in Photoshop can be done in Fireworks.

When I click the Color Picker, I do not see many colors to choose from. Are more available?

Yes. Fireworks displays a limited color palette at first, but you can click the small color wheel in the top right corner of the Color Picker to open a dialog box from which you can select almost any color.

continued ▶

Drawing in Fireworks is similar to drawing in most other graphics programs: You select the tool that creates the shape you want, then click and drag on the canvas. The program allows you to add rounded corners to your rectangle while you draw by using the arrow keys on your keyboard. Fireworks includes a Text tool that allows you to add text to artwork. Because the text will be an integrated part of your button, you can use any font installed on your computer, although you should make sure that the font fits in your page design.

Create a Button in Fireworks (continued)

⑦ Press and hold the mouse button and drag on the canvas to draw the rectangle.

Note: Do not release the mouse button yet.

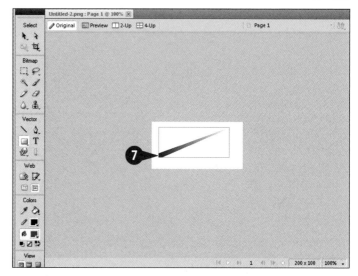

⑧ While still holding down the mouse button, press 🔼 several times to add rounded corners.

⑨ Release the mouse button.

The rectangle is drawn on the canvas.

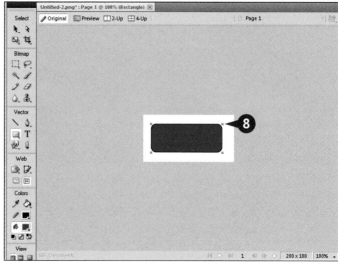

10 Click the **Text** tool (T).

11 Use the Properties panel to select a font.

12 Use the Properties panel to select a text color.

13 Use the Properties panel to set a font size.

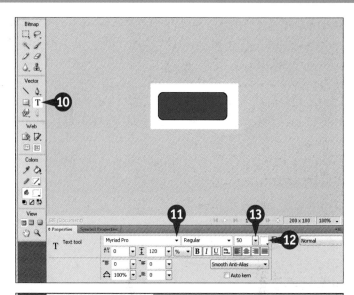

14 Click the canvas.

15 Type the label for the button.

16 If necessary, click the **Pointer** tool ( ) and move the text to position it correctly.

The button is completed.

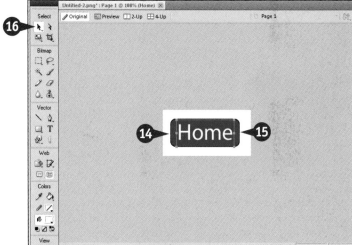

TIPS

Should I worry about extra room on my canvas?
The final size of your image will be the size of the canvas, so for something like a button, you want to ensure that the canvas matches the size of the artwork. You can click **Modify**, **Canvas**, and **Trim Canvas** to have Fireworks remove the extra space.

How big should I make my button?
The exact size of your button depends on the design of your site. Most buttons are around 150 pixels wide by around 50 pixels tall, but you should not feel bound by these numbers.

Save an Image for the Web in Fireworks

Fireworks' native file format is PNG. However, the Fireworks version of the format contains additional data to store information about features of the program such as layers. Fireworks also contains a set of tools for optimizing images for the Web so that you end up with files much smaller than those saved from other graphics programs while still maintaining the visual quality. Optimization is done directly in the program with a panel devoted to the task, and saving the image to JPEG, GIF, or PNG is done by exporting it.

Save an Image for the Web in Fireworks

1 Click **Window**.

2 Click **Optimize**.

● The Optimize panel opens.

3 Select the file format you want to save the image as.

④ Click **File**.

⑤ Click **Export**.

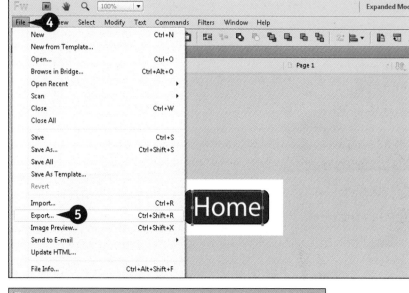

The Export dialog box appears.

⑥ Navigate to your Web site's images folder.

⑦ Type a name for the image.

⑧ Ensure that the Export setting is **Images Only**.

⑨ Click **Save**.

The image is exported in the correct format.

TIPS

How can I compare different optimization settings?

You can click the **2-Up** and **4-Up** buttons to view several versions of your image at once. Then, you can click each version and choose different optimization settings so that you can compare the results and select the one that looks the best while resulting in the smallest file.

What are the other export options in the Export dialog box?

Fireworks can export its images in a wide variety of formats. Most of the time, you will likely select Images Only, but you can export more complex designs as HTML and Images, or to other programs such as Dreamweaver or Lotus Domino Designer.

Create a Logo in Illustrator

Illustrator contains a set of powerful drawing tools that allow artists to draw images limited only by their creativity and imagination. As a vector-based program, its tools are designed around drawing new images, rather than editing existing ones. As with other tools, you begin by creating a new document, and setting Illustrator's artboard — its drawing area — to the size you need for your image. Illustrator's Text tool allows you to create images that use any font you have installed.

Create a Logo in Illustrator

1 From the Illustrator Welcome screen, click **Web Document**.

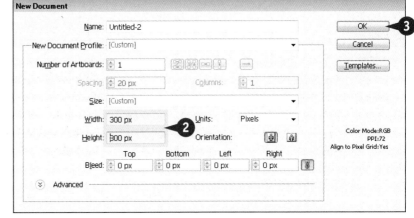

The New Document dialog box appears.

2 Set the width and height to your desired values.

3 Click **OK**.

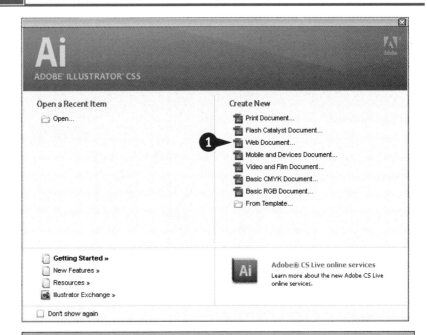

The new document is created.

4 Click the **Type** tool (T).

5 Click the canvas.

6 Type your company or organization's name.

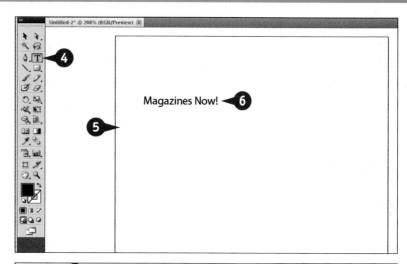

7 Click the **Selection** tool.

The text object is selected.

8 From the Control bar, click the Fill Color control and select a color for the text.

TIPS

How can I add more colors to the Fill Color drop-down menu?

Illustrator displays the current document's swatches in the Fill Color drop-down menu. You can add new colors by clicking **Window** and **Color** and dragging the sliders to create a color. Then, click the pull-down menu in the top right corner of the panel and select **Create New Swatch**.

Do I need to select the text with the Type tool to change font properties?

No. You can change the font, color, size, alignment, and other font properties from the Control bar if you have the text box selected with the Selection tool, or if you select the text directly with the Type tool.

continued ▶

Illustrator's Extrude & Bevel command allows you to easily add 3D effects to objects, including text. You can change the light source, angle, and other properties to create the look that you want. Although you will not at first be able to see the settings applied to your artwork, the command's dialog box includes a check box that enables you to preview its effects so that you can see exactly what your art will look like when you are done. Even though creating 3D effects can add to the visual effect of your pages, you should be careful to ensure that the text remains readable.

Create a Logo in Illustrator (continued)

9 Click **Effect**.

10 Click **3D**.

11 Click **Extrude & Bevel**.

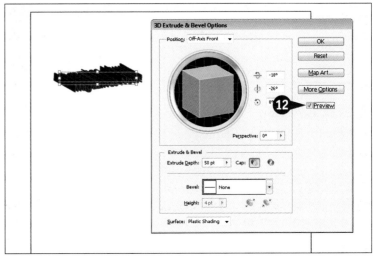

The 3D Extrude & Bevel Options dialog box appears.

12 Click **Preview** (☐ changes to ☑).

Note: You may need to move the dialog box to see your artwork.

The canvas updates to show the effect.

⓭ Experiment with the settings in the dialog box to achieve the look you want for your text.

⓮ Click **OK**.

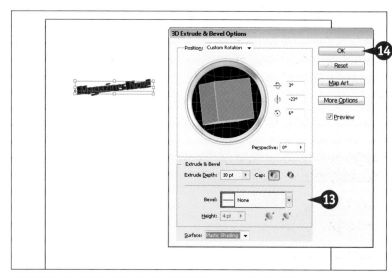

● The artwork is updated with the 3D effect.

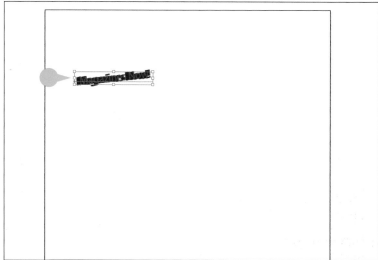

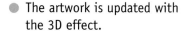

How can you change the color of the 3D portion?
In the 3D Extrude & Bevel Options dialog box, click **More Options** to reveal a drop-down menu to change the shading color. Select **Custom** from the box, and then pick a color. You can change the color of the front portion of the artwork after you close the dialog box by selecting a color from the Toolbox.

Save an Illustrator Image for the Web

All images you create in Illustrator are saved in Illustrator's native AI format. Similar to the Photoshop PSD format, images in the AI format cannot be placed directly on your Web site, but instead need to be saved using the Save for Web & Devices command. This command opens a dialog box almost identical to the one found in Photoshop that allows you to choose what Web-appropriate format you want to use and to select the optimization settings that work best for your image.

Save an Illustrator Image for the Web

1 Click **File**.

2 Click **Save for Web & Devices**.

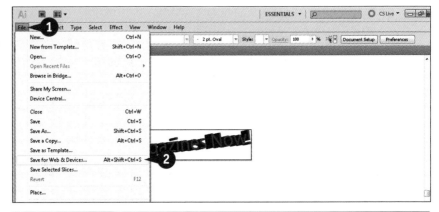

The Save for Web & Devices dialog box appears.

3 Select a preset.

● You can also modify the settings manually.

4 Click **Save**.

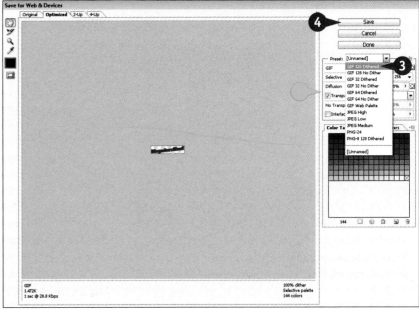

The Save Optimized As dialog box appears.

5 Navigate to your Web site's images folder.

6 Type a name for the image.

7 Click **Save**.

The image is saved in the correct format.

TIPS

Should I also save the original AI file?
Yes. If you need to make changes to the logo, you will find it very difficult to edit the optimized image. You should always save your original images so that you can return to them when needed.

What if my canvas is bigger than my logo?
You should make sure your canvas size matches your logo size, or you will have an image that is needlessly big. You can have Illustrator remove excess canvas by clicking **Object**, **Artboards**, and **Fit to Artwork Bounds**.

Add an Image to Your Web Page

You can use the HTML <img> tag to add images to your page. The tag has a required attribute, src, which takes a relative or absolute file path to the image you are adding. Unlike other tags you have worked with, <img> is an empty tag, meaning that it does not wrap around text, but instead stands alone as an instruction to the browser to place an image at that point. If you are using an XHTML document type, you must end the tag with a closing slash to designate it as empty.

Add an Image to Your Web Page

1 Open the page to which you want to add the image in your Web editor.

```
index - Notepad
File  Edit  Format  View  Help
<!DOCTYPE html PUBLIC "-//W3C//DTD XHTML 1.0 Transitional//EN"
"http://www.w3.org/TR/xhtml11/DTD/xhtml11-transitional.dtd">
<html>
<head>
<title>Magazines Now Home Page</title>
</head>
<body>

</body>
</html>
```

2 Within the body, type <img src=" ?", replacing ? with the path to your image.

```
index - Notepad
File  Edit  Format  View  Help
<!DOCTYPE html PUBLIC "-//W3C//DTD XHTML 1.0 Transitional//EN"
"http://www.w3.org/TR/xhtml11/DTD/xhtml11-transitional.dtd">
<html>
<head>
<title>Magazines Now Home Page</title>
</head>
<body>
<img src="images/logo.gif"
</body>
</html>
```

3 Type `/>` to finish the tag.

● When viewed in a browser, the image appears.

TIPS

Can I set the size of the image in my HTML?
The `<img>` tag does support optional width and height attributes. Although including these attributes is a good idea, you should always set them to the actual dimensions of the image. Resizing the image using HTML almost always degrades the quality of the image; if you need to resize it, return to your image editor and do it there.

How many images can I place on a page?
In theory, a single Web page can contain any number of images. However, each image you add does add additional loading time to the page, so without careful optimization, pages with a lot of images load very slowly.

Make Your Images Accessible

Ensuring that users with different physical needs can access your page is important so that you do not turn away potential customers or users. In order for blind users to make sense of your page, you should provide a text description of your image. You can add this description with the `alt` attribute to the `<img>` tag. Every image that you add to your page with HTML needs descriptive alternate text. The attribute is actually a requirement of HTML and XHTML; in many jurisdictions, it may be a legal requirement as well.

Make Your Images Accessible

1 Open a page that contains an `<img>` tag in your editor.

```
index - Notepad                                    1
File  Edit  Format  View  Help
<!DOCTYPE html PUBLIC "-//W3C//DTD XHTML 1.0 Transitional//EN"
"http://www.w3.org/TR/xhtml1/DTD/xhtml1-transitional.dtd">
<html>
<head>
<title>Magazines Now Home Page</title>
</head>
<body>
<img src="images/logo.gif" />|
</body>
</html>
```

2 Within the tag, before the closing `/>`, type `alt`.

```
index - Notepad
File  Edit  Format  View  Help
<!DOCTYPE html PUBLIC "-//W3C//DTD XHTML 1.0 Transitional//EN"
"http://www.w3.org/TR/xhtml1/DTD/xhtml1-transitional.dtd">
<html>
<head>
<title>Magazines Now Home Page</title>
</head>
<body>
<img src="images/logo.gif" alt|/>
</body>
</html>
                              2
```

3 Type =" *?* ", replacing *?* with a description of the image.

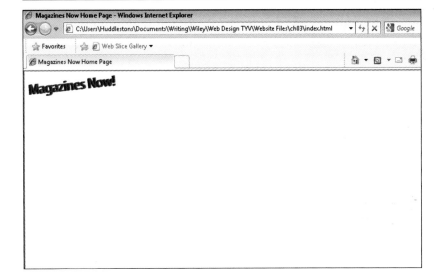

```
index - Notepad
File  Edit  Format  View  Help
<!DOCTYPE html PUBLIC "-//W3C//DTD XHTML 1.0 Transitional//EN"
"http://www.w3.org/TR/xhtml11/DTD/xhtml1-transitional.dtd">
<html>
<head>
<title>Magazines Now Home Page</title>
</head>
<body>
<img src="images/logo.gif" alt="Magazines Now"/>
</body>
</html>
```

When viewed in a browser, the page should not appear any differently than it did before. Alternate text is provided for people with disabilities, and does not affect the way the page displays.

TIPS

A client using Internet Explorer 6 says that he can see the alternate text when he mouses over the image. Why is this?

Older versions of Microsoft's Internet Explorer browser displayed image alternate text as a tool tip. This was never a part of the official specification for browsers, so no other browser did it. Microsoft discontinued the practice in the newer versions of IE.

How do blind users surf the Web?

Blind users rely on software called screen readers, which read aloud everything on the screen. Screen readers read the alternate text descriptions of images on your page as your blind user navigates around the document.

Use Images as Links

Images can stand in for text in hyperlinks. A common practice is to link the site's logo to its home page. Many sites also use graphical buttons for navigational elements. You can combine what you already know about creating links with what you know about adding images, because an image as a link is nothing more than an `<img>` tag wrapped in an `<a>` tag. The `<img>` src attribute, as normal, points to the image, and the href attribute of the anchor, as usual, points to the page to which you are linking.

Use Images as Links

1 In your editor, open the page on which you want to add a hyperlink around an image.

```
index - Notepad
File  Edit  Format  View  Help
<!DOCTYPE html PUBLIC "-//W3C//DTD XHTML 1.0 Transitional//EN"
"http://www.w3.org/TR/xhtml1/DTD/xhtml1-transitional.dtd">
<html>
<head>
<title>Magazines Now Home Page</title>
</head>
<body>
<img src="images/logo.gif" alt/>
</body>
</html>
```

2 Before the `<img>` tag, type `<a href=" ?">`, replacing ? with the path to the page to which you want to link.

```
index - Notepad
File  Edit  Format  View  Help
<!DOCTYPE html PUBLIC "-//W3C//DTD XHTML 1.0 Transitional//EN"
"http://www.w3.org/TR/xhtml1/DTD/xhtml1-transitional.dtd">
<html>
<head>
<title>Magazines Now Home Page</title>
</head>
<body>
<a href="index.html"><img src="images/logo.gif" alt/>
</body>
</html>
```

3 After the <img> tag,
type </a>.

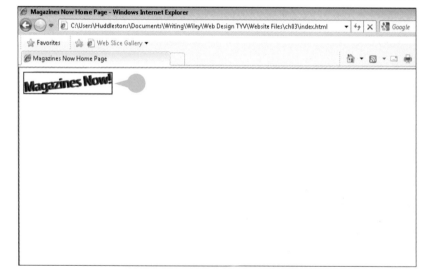

● When viewed in a browser, the
image is now a link. You can
click the image to navigate to
the specified page.

TIPS

My image now has a blue or purple border around it. How can I get rid of that?

The border is the browser's way of indicating that the image is a link, in the same way that turning text blue and adding the underline designates text as a link. You can remove the border using CSS, which is covered in Chapter 4.

How will my users know that they can click the image?

You should make sure that the image is obviously a navigational element via the design of the image. Placing descriptive text on it, or making it a recognizable icon such as a shopping cart, should provide the user with the necessary clue that the image is a hyperlink.

Formatting Your Pages

Web pages rely on another language, known as Cascading Style Sheets (CSS), to apply formatting. This chapter introduces you to the language and allows you to start making your pages more beautiful.

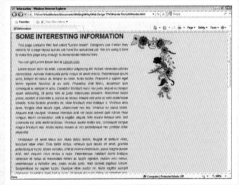

Introduction to CSS

HTML is a language designed to define the structure of a document. As it evolved, tags were added to HTML to handle formatting, but these were difficult to work with, difficult to edit, and added considerably to the page's file size. Cascading Style Sheets (CSS) was introduced both to solve all of these issues as well add additional formatting controls. With CSS, you can change your text properties, control the spacing between elements on your page, draw borders, add images, and much more. You can use CSS to format any Web page, regardless of the version of HTML or XHTML you are using.

Writing CSS

Like HTML, CSS documents are plain text and can be written in any text editor. Modern HTML editors include support for CSS as well, so the editor in which you are writing your HTML should also work for your CSS.

CSS Syntax

The syntax of CSS is quite a bit different from HTML. CSS documents are made up of a series of rules. Each rule includes a selector and a declaration. Selectors are case-sensitive, whereas the values and properties that make up declarations are not. Like HTML, CSS is whitespace-insensitive.

Selectors

Selectors define the parts of the HTML document to which the rules will apply. Selectors can be HTML elements, or they can correspond to the values of ID or class attributes within HTML. More complex selectors allow you to apply rules to elements based on their position relative to other elements.

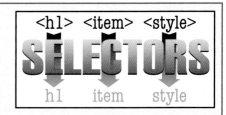

Declarations

CSS declarations are made up of properties and values. The properties define the category of formatting to be applied. The property is then set to a value. Properties and their values are separated by a colon, and each pair ends in a semicolon. All of the declarations to be applied to a particular selector are enclosed within curly braces. You can find a complete list of properties and values available in CSS in *HTML, XHTML, and CSS: Your visual blueprint for designing effective Web pages* (Wiley, 2008).

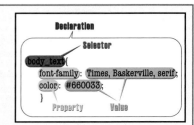

Embedded Style Sheets

Styles that you want to apply to one particular Web page can be embedded directly within the page by placing a `<style>` tag block in the head of the document and then putting your style rules within the tag block.

External Style Sheets

Groups of styles can be combined in a single document, with a .css extension, to create an external style sheet. External style sheets can be linked to any number of HTML documents, so you can create a single style sheet that defines and controls the formatting of your entire Web site.

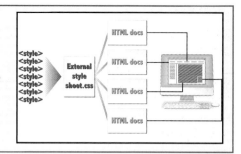

Inline Styles

Style properties and values can be placed directly within HTML tags using the `style` attribute. This is the least flexible method of applying CSS and should be avoided if at all possible because it makes it much more difficult to maintain a consistent look and feel for your site.

Browser Support

Today, most modern browsers support CSS in much the same way. You will still find issues with older browsers, such as Microsoft Internet Explorer 6, so you should carefully test your pages to be sure that they display the way you want them to.

Create an Embedded Style Sheet

mbedded style sheets place the style rules directly within an HTML page. They are a useful starting point in learning CSS because you only have to refer to one document. Embedded styles are placed in the head of the document within a `<style>` tag block. The tag has a required attribute, `type`, which is always set to a value of `text/css`. Be sure to remember to add the closing `</style>` tag, because without it the browser does not display anything on the page.

Create an Embedded Style Sheet

1 In your editor, open the page into which you want to add the styles.

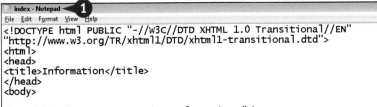

```
index - Notepad   1
File  Edit  Format  View  Help
<!DOCTYPE html PUBLIC "-//W3C//DTD XHTML 1.0 Transitional//EN"
"http://www.w3.org/TR/xhtml1/DTD/xhtml1-transitional.dtd">
<html>
<head>
<title>Information</title>
</head>
<body>

<h1 id="top">Some Interesting Information</h1>

<p>This page contains filler text called "Lorem Ipsum". Designers use it
fill a page layout but do not have the actual text yet. We are using it
page long enough to demonstrate internal links.</p>

<p>You can get Lorem Ipsum text at <a href="http://www.lipsum.com">Lipsu

<p>Lorem ipsum dolor sit amet, consectetur adipiscing elit. Nullam venen
consectetur. Aenean malesuada porta neque sit amet viverra. Pellentesque
tempor et varius at, tempor eu enim. Nulla facilisi. Praesent a sapien e
faucibus at eu odio. Phasellus erat libero, accumsan quis consequat a, s
Curabitur tincidunt nunc nec justo aliquet eu tempor quam adipiscing. Ut
justo malesuada posuere. Maecenas turpis purus, laoreet ut convallis a,
Mauris sed urna ac sem scelerisque lobortis. Nulla facilisis pharetra mi
```

2 Within the head section, type `<style`.

```
index - Notepad
File  Edit  Format  View  Help
<!DOCTYPE html PUBLIC "-//W3C//DTD XHTML 1.0 Transitional//EN"
"http://www.w3.org/TR/xhtml1/DTD/xhtml1-transitional.dtd">
<html>
<head>
<title>Information</title>

<style   2

</head>
<body>

<h1 id="top">Some Interesting Information</h1>

<p>This page contains filler text called "Lorem Ipsum". Designers use it
fill a page layout but do not have the actual text yet. We are using it
page long enough to demonstrate internal links.</p>

<p>You can get Lorem Ipsum text at <a href="http://www.lipsum.com">Lipsu

<p>Lorem ipsum dolor sit amet, consectetur adipiscing elit. Nullam venen
consectetur. Aenean malesuada porta neque sit amet viverra. Pellentesque
tempor et varius at, tempor eu enim. Nulla facilisi. Praesent a sapien e
faucibus at eu odio. Phasellus erat libero, accumsan quis consequat a, s
```

3 Type `type="text/css">`.

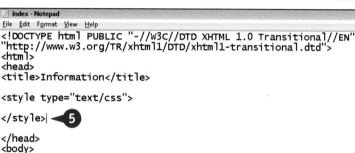

4 Press **Enter** twice.

5 Type `</style>`.

The embedded style sheet is created in the page.

TIPS

What does the type attribute do?
The `type` attribute instructs the browser that the style has been written in plain text and is using CSS. Currently, no other options exist, but adding the attribute now future-proofs your document: If another option is developed later, future browsers will not have to guess what your page uses.

Does the style sheet have to appear at the end of the head section?
No. The style can be placed anywhere within the head. It is traditionally placed toward the bottom of the section, but that is not a requirement.

Understanding Units of Measurement

M any CSS properties require that you specify a unit of measurement, such as spacing between elements, border widths, and font size. The language supports a wide variety of units of measurement. Understanding which one to use in what situations helps you become a better CSS designer and helps avoid common errors that occur when measurements do not work the way a designer expected. Units available range from those with which you are familiar to some you may have never heard of before. In most page designs, you will use a combination of several units of measurement.

English and Metric Units

CSS supports measuring values in inches, centimeters, and millimeters. However, the actual size of an inch, centimeter, or millimeter cannot be predicted from one computer monitor to the next, so using these units under any circumstance is not recommended.

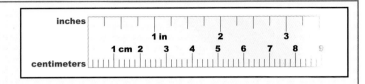

Pixels

Pixels are the building blocks of your computer monitor. Like the English and metric units, the exact size of a pixel cannot be predicted, but because it is a real unit of measurement in computer monitors, many CSS designers use pixels for setting widths of borders, padding, and margins around elements. Using pixels for font sizes is not recommended.

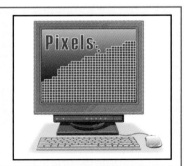

Points and Picas

Graphic designers for centuries have relied on points and picas. There are 72 points in one inch, and 6 picas in an inch, so logically there are 12 points in 1 pica. Even though you are probably familiar with sizing text via points, they are not recommended on the Web because they are based on inches, which is an unreliable unit.

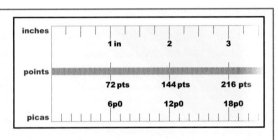

Ems and Exes

An *em* is a unit of measurement defined as the width of a capital letter *M* in the current font. In practice, browsers treat an em as an equivalent to the font size, so if your text is 16 pixels, 1 em would equal 16 pixels. If your text is 14 pixels, 1 em equals 14 pixels. Exes are defined as the width of a lowercase *x*, but most browsers treat it simply as 1/2 em.

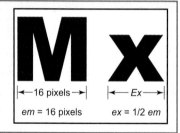

←16 pixels→ ← Ex →

em = 16 pixels ex = 1/2 em

Percents

You can also measure elements using percentages. CSS rules inherit from other rules, so a property with a percentage value will be that percent of whatever the element in question's parent element is, or failing that, the size defined in the body. For example, if you set the size of the body at 90%, and then a paragraph at 80%, the paragraph's size would be 80% of 90% of the default size.

Parent
100%

Header
75%

Body
50%

0%

Internet Explorer and Font Scaling

Browsers are supposed to allow users to resize the text on their screen. However, IE does not quite follow this rule; instead, it allows the user to resize text only if the designer set that text using a relative unit of measure. Therefore, this text scaling works in IE only if you set your font size in ems, exes, or percents. Note that this applies only to font size; other properties are not affected.

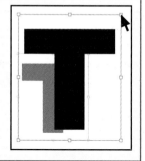

Specifying Units

CSS does not define a default unit of measure, so you must always provide it. Most units have associated abbreviations, so if you want to use pixels, you can write `px`. The only time this does not apply is when the value is 0, because a unit is obviously not needed.

CSS units of measure abbreviations	
Absolute measurement	
points	pt
picas	pc
centimeters	cm
inches	in
millimeters	mm
Relative measurement	
pixels	px
em space	em
x space	ex

Set the Font and Text Size on Your Page

Typography is very limited on the Web. Web pages do not contain embedded fonts; rather, they merely contain a set of instructions to the browser as to what font should be used. The CSS `font-face` property is used to provide these instructions on what fonts to use. The `font-size` property allows you to set the size of your text. These properties can be applied to any element that can contain text, such as a heading or paragraph, or to the page as whole, as in the example below.

Set the Font and Text Size on Your Page

1. In your editor, open a page that contains an embedded style sheet.

2. Within the style block, type `body`.

3. Press **Enter**.

4. Type `{`.

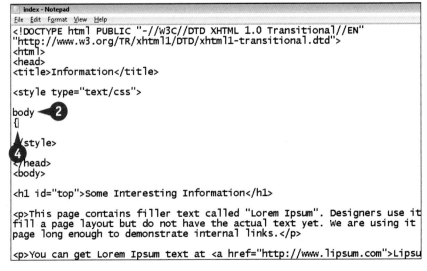

5 Type font-family: ?, replacing ? with a set of font names or categories such as Arial, Helvetica, sans-serif;.

6 Press Enter.

7 Type font-size: ?, replacing ? with a value and unit of measurement, such as 90%;.

8 Press Enter.

9 Type }.

● When viewed in a browser, the text on the page now appears in the font face and size you specified.

TIPS

Can I set my text in any font?

No. You are not embedding the font file in your document. Instead, you are merely asking the browser to use that font, which it can do only if your user has the same font installed. Most designers limit themselves to Arial, Times New Roman, Verdana, and Courier, although other fonts such as Georgia are becoming popular.

Why do I need to provide a list of fonts?

The list provides backup fonts in case your user does not have the same fonts that you do. If you set the font-face property to Arial, Helvetica, sans-serif, you are saying that you would prefer Arial, but if it is not available, use Helvetica. If that font is not on the system, fall back to a generic sans-serif font.

Understanding Color on the Web

Color is an important part of any design. Choosing the right color scheme for your site can have a huge impact on the mood, look, and feel of your site. Take a look at some of your favorite Web sites and think about the impact of color on your impression of the sites. Bright colors usually convey a lighter, happier sense than dark colors, but depending on the purpose of the site, either might be appropriate. In order to effectively use color, you need to have an understanding of how color works on the Web.

RGB

Computer monitors generate color by combining red, green, and blue light, and are thus known as RGB devices. Each color is expressed numerically, with values ranging from 0 to 255. Therefore, you can express purple as rgb(128,0,128) — 128 of red, no green, and 128 blue.

Hexadecimal

Hexadecimal is a counting system that uses 16 primary digits, rather than the 10 you are used to. The additional 6 digits are represented by the first 6 letters of the English alphabet, A through F. Hexadecimal allows you to count from 0 to 255 using only 2 digits rather than 3, and is thus useful for color values. Purple is expressed in hexadecimal as #800080.

#800080

Named Colors

The official specification identifies 16 named colors for the Web: aqua, black, blue, fuchsia, gray, green, lime, maroon, navy, olive, purple, red, silver, teal, white, and yellow. In practice, however, all modern browsers recognize 140 named colors. You can view a list of all of the colors in the appendix.

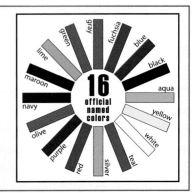

The Web-Safe Palette

In the early days of the Web, most monitors were capable of displaying only 256 colors, of which only 216 were shared between Windows and Macintosh systems. Thus, the Web-safe palette, representing those 216 colors, was developed. Today, there is no reason to limit yourself to this palette because all modern monitors can handle millions of colors.

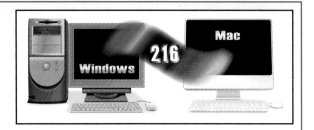

Accessibility and Colors

Current estimates are that about 5% of the population is to some degree color blind. Color blindness normally manifests itself as an inability to distinguish contrasts between similar colors. When you are picking your site's color palette, keep this issue in mind and be sure to select colors with sufficient contrast. This is particularly important when picking your text and background colors. Web sites such as www.vischeck.com/vischeck/vischeckURL.php can be helpful in checking your site's colors.

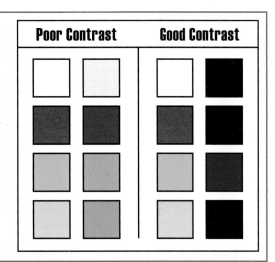

CSS 3 and Alpha

Version 3 of the CSS specification will add the ability to specify an alpha channel, or transparency, to colors. You can use the RGBA syntax: `rgba(128,0,128,.5)`, which creates a purple with 50 percent transparency. Browser support for CSS3 is still very sporadic, so you should carefully test this to ensure that it works in your target browser set.

RGB (128,0,128)

RGBA (128,0,128,.5)

Determine a Color Scheme Using Kuler

Adobe Kuler is a free online resource that allows designers to access and use color schemes created by others in the community. As an online service, it is available anytime you are connected to the Internet. You can use Kuler to select from one of thousands of color schemes. Once you have found a set of colors that you like, you can get the specific values of those colors so that you can use them in your site's design. You can also change individual colors within each set if you want.

Determine a Color Scheme Using Kuler

1 In your Web browser, go to http://kuler.adobe.com.

The Kuler home page opens.

2 Click the arrow buttons to browse through the color schemes.

● You can also search for schemes by name.

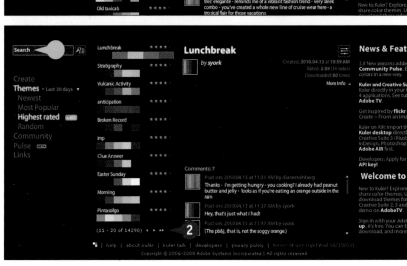

3 Click a scheme you want to use.

4 Click the **Make changes to this theme and view color values button** (▤).

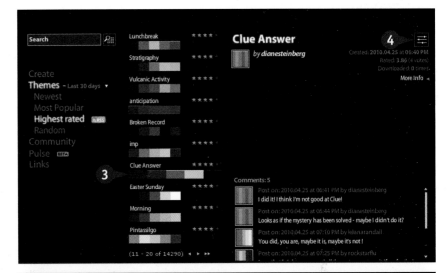

The color values page opens.

5 Note the hexadecimal or rgb values of each color in the scheme.

You can now use these colors on your page.

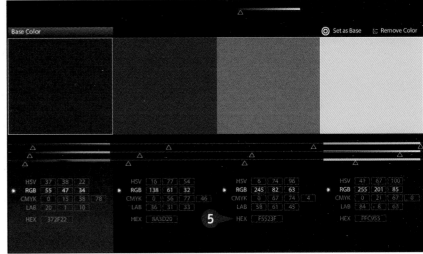

TIPS

Can I create and upload my own color schemes to the Kuler Web site?

Yes. You must create a free Adobe.com account if you do not already have one. Then, click the **Sign In** link in the top right corner of the page. From there, you can create and save your own schemes.

Can I use Kuler to determine the colors in an image?

Yes. From the navigation in the top right corner, click **From an Image**. The next page prompts you to upload an image. Kuler analyzes the image and displays a color scheme using the five most prominent colors from the image.

Set Text Color

The CSS `color` property technically applies a color to the foreground of any element. In practice, however, only text is in the foreground; thus, the property is used most often to change the color of text. Be sure that the color you choose fits within your site's design, but also provides sufficient contrast with the background of your page to ensure that the text remains readable. You can apply color to entire blocks of text, or, as is shown in later sections, to individual words or even characters.

Set Text Color

1 In your editor, open a page that contains an embedded style sheet with an existing `body` style declaration.

2 Within the declaration, type `color: #?;`, replacing *?* with a hexadecimal value for the color you want to use.

● When viewed in a browser, the text on the page is now in the specified color.

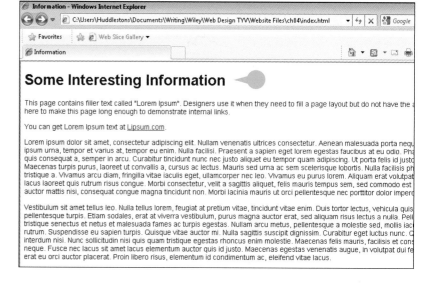

Set a Background Color

You can change the background color of your page or of elements within the page with the CSS `background-color` property. The background color needs to contrast with the text color to ensure readability. The default value of `background-color` is `none`, meaning that elements are transparent. Almost every browser sets the background of the body to white, although if you want to use a white background, you may want to expressly set the body's background to white to safeguard against browsers that might have a different default.

Set a Background Color

1 In your editor, open a document that contains an embedded style sheet and an existing `body` declaration.

2 Within the declaration, type `background-color: #?;`, replacing `?` with a hexadecimal value for the color you want to use.

● When viewed in a browser, the page now has the specified background color.

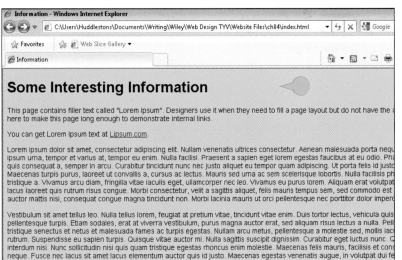

Add a Background Image

You can use an image as the background on your page with the CSS `background-image` property. A background image can be placed within any element on the page, although putting it in the body so that it comprises the background for the entire page is common. Although you can in theory use any JPEG, GIF, or PNG for your background, you should be careful to ensure that the image does not distract from the page, so you should pick an image that does not contain a lot of contrast and is overall fairly subtle.

Add a Background Image

1 In your editor, open a document that contains an embedded style sheet and an existing `body` declaration.

```
index - Notepad
File  Edit  Format  View  Help
<!DOCTYPE html PUBLIC "-//W3C//DTD XHTML 1.0 Transitional//EN"
"http://www.w3.org/TR/xhtml11/DTD/xhtml11-transitional.dtd">
<html>
<head>
<title>Information</title>

<style type="text/css">

body
{
font-family: Arial, Helvetica, sans-serif;
font-size: 90%;
color: #540907;
background-color: #FFC955;|
}

</style>

</head>
<body>

<h1 id="top">Some Interesting Information</h1>
```

2 Within the declaration, type `background-image:`.

```
index - Notepad
File  Edit  Format  View  Help
<!DOCTYPE html PUBLIC "-//W3C//DTD XHTML 1.0 Transitional//EN"
"http://www.w3.org/TR/xhtml11/DTD/xhtml11-transitional.dtd">
<html>
<head>
<title>Information</title>

<style type="text/css">

body
{
font-family: Arial, Helvetica, sans-serif;
font-size: 90%;
color: #540907;
background-color: #FFC955;
background-image:|
}

</style>

</head>
<body>

<h1 id="top">Some Interesting Information</h1>
```

③ Type url("?");, replacing ? with a relative or absolute path to the image you wish to use.

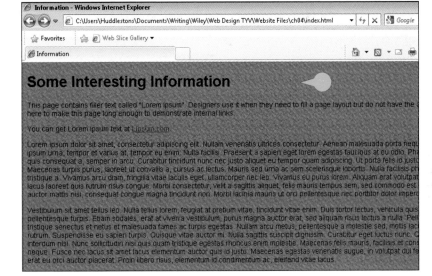

● When viewed in a browser, the image appears, tiling horizontally and vertically on the screen.

TIPS

Can I add more than one image as the background?
Unfortunately, CSS only allows you to place one image per element in the background. You can create the illusion of having multiple backgrounds, however, by placing other images in other elements on the page. For example, you can place a background image in a div, and then another in a paragraph within the div. See Chapter 5 for more about divs.

What makes a good background image?
Good background images are ones with very little contrast, because images with very dark and very light areas cause readability problems. Also, the background image should enhance the overall look of the page, instead of detracting or distracting from it, so subtle images work better.

Control Background Image Tiling

By default, background images tile both horizontally and vertically. The `background-repeat` property allows you to control this behavior. A value of `repeat-x` causes the image to only tile horizontally; `repeat-y` creates a vertical tile, and `no-repeat` prevents tiling altogether. If you can use an image with a transparent background, the background color of the page shows through the transparent areas of the image. You may want to set a background color on the page even if the image is not transparent as a fallback in case the image fails to load.

Control Background Image Tiling

1 In your editor, open a document that contains an embedded style sheet and an existing `body` declaration with a `background-image` rule.

2 Within the declaration, type `background-repeat: ?`, replacing `?` with either `repeat-x`, `repeat-y`, or `no-repeat`.

● When viewed in a browser, the image either repeats horizontally, vertically, or not at all.

112

Position Background Images

Background images are initially positioned in the top right corner of the element into which they are placed, but the `background-position` property allows you to control this. The property takes two values, separated by commas: the first the distance from the top edge, the second the distance from the left. These distances can be set using any valid unit of measurement. If you set the position using pixels, the image remains in place even if the browser is resized, but using percentages as the values allows the image to move as the browser scales.

Position Background Images

1 In your editor, open a document that contains an embedded style sheet and an existing body declaration and `background-image` rule.

2 Within the declaration, type `background-position: ? ?`, replacing the first *?* with the distance from the top of the page, and the second with the distance from the left.

Note: Be sure to include the unit of measurement you want to use.

● When viewed in a browser, the image is now positioned at the indicated spot. If the image is set to tile, it tiles from that location.

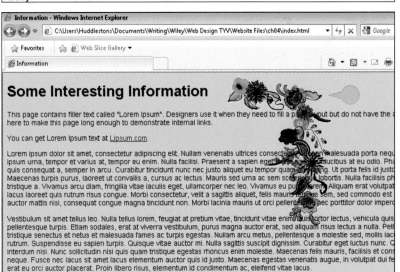

Apply Additional Text Formatting

In addition to setting the font and color, you can also control additional text properties including line height and capitalization. The CSS `line-height` property is the distance from the bottom or baseline of one line of text to the baseline of the next line. Adjusting the `line-height` can help improve readability by spacing out the text, but be careful to not add so much that you begin to have the opposite effect. The `transform` property, which accepts values of `uppercase`, `lowercase`, and `capitalize`, allows you to control the capitalization of text, which is particularly helpful with headings.

Apply Additional Text Formatting

1 In your editor, open a document that contains an embedded style sheet.

2 Within the style sheet, type h1.

3 Press **Enter**.

4 Type {.

```
index - Notepad                        1
File  Edit  Format  View  Help
<!DOCTYPE html PUBLIC "-//W3C//DTD XHTML 1.0 Transitional//EN"
"http://www.w3.org/TR/xhtml1/DTD/xhtml1-transitional.dtd">
<html>
<head>
<title>Information</title>

<style type="text/css">

body
{
font-family: Arial, Helvetica, sans-serif;
font-size: 90%;
color: #540907;
background-color: #FFC955;
background-image:url("images/flowers.gif");
background-repeat: no-repeat;
background-position:550px 0;      2

}

h1
{|      4
</style>
```

5 Type text-transform: ?;, replacing ? with uppercase, lowercase, or capitalize.

6 Press **Enter**.

7 Type }.

```
index - Notepad
File  Edit  Format  View  Help
<!DOCTYPE html PUBLIC "-//W3C//DTD XHTML 1.0 Transitional//EN"
"http://www.w3.org/TR/xhtml1/DTD/xhtml1-transitional.dtd">
<html>
<head>
<title>Information</title>

<style type="text/css">

body
{
font-family: Arial, Helvetica, sans-serif;
font-size: 90%;
color: #540907;
background-color: #FFC955;
background-image:url("images/flowers.gif");
background-repeat: no-repeat;
background-position:550px 0;
}

h1
{
text-transform: uppercase;      5
}|      7
```

8 Type p.

9 Press Enter.

10 Type {.

11 Type line-height: ?;, replacing ? with the height you want to apply.

12 Press Enter.

13 Type }.

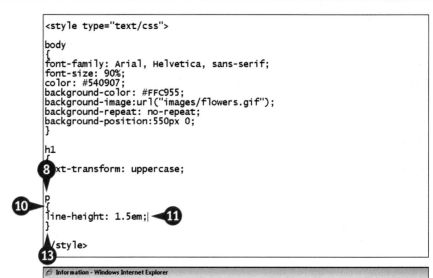

```
<style type="text/css">

body
{
font-family: Arial, Helvetica, sans-serif;
font-size: 90%;
color: #540907;
background-color: #FFC955;
background-image:url("images/flowers.gif");
background-repeat: no-repeat;
background-position:550px 0;
}

h1
{
text-transform: uppercase;
}

p
{
line-height: 1.5em;|
}

</style>
```

● When viewed in a browser, the main heading on the page has the text transformation applied, and the paragraphs have the line height.

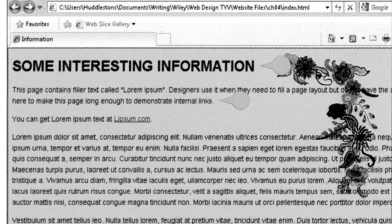

TIPS

What unit of measurement should I use for line-height?

Many designers rely on ems to set line height. Because the exact size of an em is dependent on the font size, using ems for line height ensures that the height scales with the font. You can use decimals to set fractional line height, so for example 1.5 ems sets the line height to one and a half times the text size.

What is the advantage of using text-transform for headings? Can I just not type the heading using the correct case?

Large sites may have many people adding content, and you cannot always control how they type the content. Using text-transform guarantees that headings use consistent casing.

Indent and Align Text

CSS can be used to control indentation of the first line of text and its alignment. The `text-indent` property indents the first line of a block of text such as a paragraph. Note that only the first line of text is indented. You can use any valid unit of measurement for this property, although pixels and ems are the most common, and should experiment to determine what value gives you the best look. The `text-align` property allows for values of `center`, `left`, `right`, and `justify`.

Indent and Align Text

1 In your editor, open a document that contains an embedded style sheet.

```
index - Notepad ◄──1
File  Edit  Format  View  Help
<!DOCTYPE html PUBLIC "-//W3C//DTD XHTML 1.0 Transitional//EN"
"http://www.w3.org/TR/xhtml1/DTD/xhtml1-transitional.dtd">
<html>
<head>
<title>Information</title>

<style type="text/css">

body
{
font-family: Arial, Helvetica, sans-serif;
font-size: 90%;
color: #540907;
background-color: #FFC955;
background-image:url("images/flowers.gif");
background-repeat: no-repeat;
background-position:550px 0;
}

h1
{
text-transform: uppercase;
}
```

2 Within an existing `p` declaration, type `text-indent: ?;`, replacing `?` with the amount of first-line indentation you want.

```
body
{
font-family: Arial, Helvetica, sans-serif;
font-size: 90%;
color: #540907;
background-color: #FFC955;
background-image:url("images/flowers.gif");
background-repeat: no-repeat;
background-position:550px 0;
}

h1
{
text-transform: uppercase;
}

p
{
line-height: 1.5em;
text-indent: .75em;|
}

</style>

</head>
<body>

<h1 id="top">Some Interesting Information</h1>

<p>This page contains filler text called "Lorem Ipsum". Designers use it
```

3 Within an existing p declaration, type `text-align: ?;`, replacing *?* with `right`, `left`, `center`, or `justify`.

```
body
{
font-family: Arial, Helvetica, sans-serif;
font-size: 90%;
color: #540907;
background-color: #FFC955;
background-image:url("images/flowers.gif");
background-repeat: no-repeat;
background-position:550px 0;
}

h1
{
text-transform: uppercase;
}

p
{
line-height: 1.5em;
text-indent: .75em;
text-align: justify;|
}

</style>

</head>
<body>

<h1 id="top">Some Interesting Information</h1>
```

● When viewed in a browser, the first line of each paragraph is indented and aligned according to the values you set.

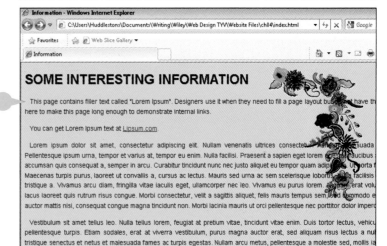

TIPS

Can I make my first line indentation increase or decrease automatically if I change my font size?
Yes. Set the `text-indent` in ems to have it scale with the font. For example, if you are using 14-pixel text, you could set `text-indent: 1.5 ems` to have a 21-pixel indentation. If you later changed the text to 10 pixels, the indentation would automatically adjust to 15 pixels — one and a half times the font.

Can I indent the whole paragraph, instead of just the first line?
Yes. The margin and padding properties in CSS allow you to control the spacing around elements on the page. Both of those properties are discussed later in this chapter.

117

Apply Spacing with Padding

The space around elements on your page is defined by something known as the *box model*. The innermost section of the model is the element's content. The content is surrounded on all four sides by padding, which in turn is surrounded by a border. Outside the border is a margin. The `padding` property allows you to control the space between the content and the border; in essence, it allows you to move the element within the box. You can easily remember this by thinking of a physical package: You add padding between the fragile contents and the edge of the package.

Apply Spacing with Padding

1 In your editor, open a document that contains an embedded style sheet.

```
index - Notepad
File  Edit  Format  View  Help
<!DOCTYPE html PUBLIC "-//W3C//DTD XHTML 1.0 Transitional//EN"
"http://www.w3.org/TR/xhtml1/DTD/xhtml1-transitional.dtd">
<html>
<head>
<title>Information</title>

<style type="text/css">

body
{
font-family: Arial, Helvetica, sans-serif;
font-size: 90%;
color: #540907;
background-color: #FFC955;
background-image:url("images/flowers.gif");
background-repeat: no-repeat;
background-position:550px 0;
}

h1
{
text-transform: uppercase;|
}
```

2 Within an existing `h1` declaration, type `padding-left: ?;`, replacing *?* with the amount of padding you want to apply.

3 Press Enter.

```
body
{
font-family: Arial, Helvetica, sans-serif;
font-size: 90%;
color: #540907;
background-color: #FFC955;
background-image:url("images/flowers.gif");
background-repeat: no-repeat;
background-position:550px 0;
}

h1
{
text-transform: uppercase;
padding-left: 20px;|
}

p
{
line-height: 1.5em;
text-indent: .75em;
text-align: justify;
}

</style>

</head>
<body>

<h1 id="top">Some Interesting Information</h1>
```

4 Within an existing `p`
declaration, type `padding-
left: ?;`, replacing *?* with
the amount of padding you
want to apply.

```
body
{
font-family: Arial, Helvetica, sans-serif;
font-size: 90%;
color: #540907;
background-color: #FFC955;
background-image:url("images/flowers.gif");
background-repeat: no-repeat;
background-position:550px 0;
}

h1
{
text-transform: uppercase;
padding-left: 20px;
}

p
{
line-height: 1.5em;
text-indent: .75em;
text-align: justify;
padding-left: 20px;
}

</style>

</head>
<body>
```

● When viewed in a browser,
the headings and paragraphs
have the specified padding.

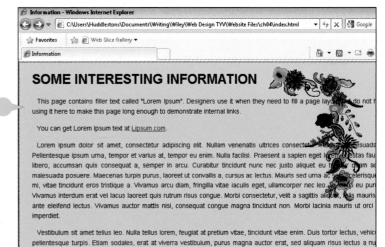

SOME INTERESTING INFORMATION

This page contains filler text called "Lorem Ipsum". Designers use it when they need to fill a page layout. I do not h
using it here to make this page long enough to demonstrate internal links.

You can get Lorem Ipsum text at Lipsum.com.

Lorem ipsum dolor sit amet, consectetur adipiscing elit. Nullam venenatis ultrices consectetur. Vivamus malesuada
Pellentesque ipsum urna, tempor et varius at, tempor eu enim. Nulla facilisi. Praesent a sapien eget lorem egestas fau
libero, accumsan quis consequat a, semper in arcu. Curabitur tincidunt nunc nec justo aliquet eu tincidur diam ac
malesuada posuere. Maecenas turpis purus, laoreet ut convallis a, cursus ac lectus. Mauris sed urna ac sem scelerisque
mi, vitae tincidunt eros tristique a. Vivamus arcu diam, fringilla vitae iaculis eget, ullamcorper nec leo. Vivamus eu pur
Vivamus interdum erat vel lacus laoreet quis rutrum risus congue. Morbi consectetur, velit a sagittis aliquet, felis mauris
ante eleifend lectus. Vivamus auctor mattis nisi, consequat congue magna tincidunt non. Morbi lacinia mauris ut orci
imperdiet.

Vestibulum sit amet tellus leo. Nulla tellus lorem, feugiat at pretium vitae, tincidunt vitae enim. Duis tortor lectus, vehic
pellentesque turpis. Etiam sodales, erat at viverra vestibulum, purus magna auctor erat, sed aliquam risus lectus a nu

TIP

Can I set padding on all four sides?
Yes. You can set each side individually with the four padding properties: `padding-left`, `padding-right`, `padding-top`, and `padding-bottom`. You can also use the shortcut padding property. As a shortcut, provide a single value to set the same padding on all four sides; two values where the first is the padding for the top and bottom, and the second is the value for the right and left; or four values, where the first is top, the second right, the third bottom, and the fourth left.

Control Whitespace with Margins

The outermost section of the box model is the margin, which represents the space between elements on the page. CSS contains five properties for setting margins: `margin-top`, `margin-right`, `margin-bottom`, and `margin-left` let you set each side individually, whereas the `margin` property is a shortcut for setting all four margins together. This shortcut property can take a single value to set all four margins. You can also provide two values, where the first applies to the top and bottom and the second to the left and right, or four values, where the first sets the top, the second the right, the third the bottom, and the fourth the left.

Control Whitespace with Margins

1 In your editor, open a document that contains an embedded style sheet and an existing `body` declaration.

```
index - Notepad        1
File  Edit  Format  View  Help
<!DOCTYPE html PUBLIC "-//W3C//DTD XHTML 1.0 Transitional//EN"
"http://www.w3.org/TR/xhtml1/DTD/xhtml1-transitional.dtd">
<html>
<head>
<title>Information</title>

<style type="text/css">

body
{
font-family: Arial, Helvetica, sans-serif;
font-size: 90%;
color: #540907;
background-color: #FFC955;
background-image:url("images/flowers.gif");
background-repeat: no-repeat;
background-position:550px 0;
}

h1
{
text-transform: uppercase;
padding-left: 20px;
```

2 Within the `body` declaration, type `margin:0;`.

3 Within the existing `h1` declaration, type `margin-top:0;`.

4 Press `Enter`.

5 Type `margin-bottom: ?;`, replacing `?` with the amount of bottom margin you want.

```
body
{
font-family: Arial, Helvetica, sans-serif;
font-size: 90%;
color: #540907;
background-color: #FFC955;
background-image:url("images/flowers.gif");
background-repeat: no-repeat;
background-position:550px 0;
margin:0;                          2
}

h1
{
text-transform: uppercase;
padding-left: 20px;
margin-top:0;                      3
margin-bottom:10px;|               5
}

p
{
line-height: 1.5em;
text-indent: .75em;
text-align: justify;
padding-left: 20px;
}

</style>
```

6 Within the existing p declaration, type `margin-top:0;`.

7 Press `Enter`.

8 Type `margin-bottom: ?;`, replacing *?* with the desired amount of bottom margin.

```
}
h1
{
text-transform: uppercase;
padding-left: 20px;
margin-top:0;
margin-bottom:10px;
}

p
{
line-height: 1.5em;
text-indent: .75em;
text-align: justify;
padding-left: 20px;
margin-top:0;        ← 6
margin-bottom: 10px;|   ← 8
}

</style>

</head>
<body>

<h1 id="top">Some Interesting Information</h1>
```

● When viewed in a browser, the page no longer has space around the edges. The space between the headings and the paragraphs has also changed.

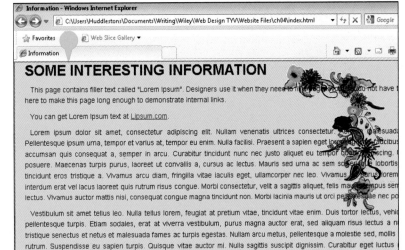

TIPS

I want to move paragraphs closer together. When I set the bottom margin, nothing happens. Why is this?

Adjacent vertical margins collapse into one another in CSS. Therefore, you must work with both the top and bottom margins in order to move elements closer to one another. In the examples above, the top margins are zeroed-out so that the bottom margin alone can control the spacing.

Can I eliminate the space around the edge of the page with margins?

Yes. Browsers apply a default margin to the body. Unfortunately, they are inconsistent as to the amount of margin they apply, so many designers set the margin of the body to 0 to eliminate this space between their content and the edge of the window. Note that because CSS has no default unit of measurement, you must always provide one, except when setting the value to 0.

Specify Widths

By default, elements are as wide as the element that contains them. Elements directly within the body of the document are as wide as the browser window. You can control this behavior using the CSS `width` property. The width is calculated as only the width of the element's content, so the total size of the element is actually its width, plus the left and right padding values, plus the left and right border widths. Keep this in mind when you are attempting to calculate the space needed to place elements next to each other on the page.

Specify Widths

1 In your editor, open a document that contains an embedded style sheet and an existing `body` declaration.

```
index - Notepad ◀── 1
File Edit Format View Help
<style type="text/css">

body
{
font-family: Arial, Helvetica, sans-serif;
font-size: 90%;
color: #540907;
background-color: #FFC955;
background-image:url("images/flowers.gif");
background-repeat: no-repeat;
background-position:550px 0;
margin:0;
}

h1
{
text-transform: uppercase;
padding-left: 20px;
margin-top:0;
margin-bottom:10px;
}

p
```

2 Within the existing `h1` declaration, type `width: ?;`, replacing ? with the desired width of the element.

```
h1
{
text-transform: uppercase;
padding-left: 20px;
margin-top:0;
margin-bottom:10px;
width: 520px;|  ◀── 2
}

p
{
line-height: 1.5em;
text-indent: .75em;
text-align: justify;
padding-left: 20px;
margin-top:0;
margin-bottom: 10px;
}

</style>

</head>
<body>
```

3 Within the existing p declaration, type width: ?;, replacing ? with the desired width of the element.

```
color: #540907;
background-color: #FFC955;
background-image:url("images/flowers.gif");
background-repeat: no-repeat;
background-position:550px 0;
margin:0;
}

h1
{
text-transform: uppercase;
padding-left: 20px;
margin-top:0;
margin-bottom:10px;
width: 520px;
}

p
{
line-height: 1.5em;
text-indent: .75em;
text-align: justify;
padding-left: 20px;
margin-top:0;
margin-bottom: 10px;
width: 520px;|
}

</style>

</head>
<body>
```

● When viewed in a browser, the elements have the specified widths. This is most apparent on the paragraphs.

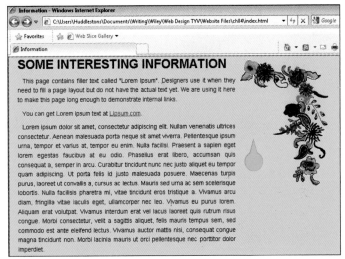

TIP

Can I also control the height of content?
Yes, but be aware that although an element's width is determined by its parent element, an element's height is determined by its own content. Thus, setting the width to 100% expands the element horizontally to fill its container, whereas setting its height to 100% does not expand it vertically. You also need to be careful about setting too small a height, because browsers vary greatly on how they treat elements with specified heights too small to fit the content.

Add Borders

You can draw visual lines around elements using the CSS border property. To add a border, you need to set its width, color, and style. These three properties can be set in any order. You can also use border-top, border-bottom, border-left, or border-right to set individual borders. Each of these takes the same three values as noted above: width, color, and style. The width of the border can be set in any unit of measurement, but pixels are used most often. The color can be any valid color name or a hexadecimal value. The style is set using one of ten keywords.

Add Borders

1 In your editor, open a document that contains an embedded style sheet.

```
index - Notepad    1
File  Edit  Format  View  Help
<style type="text/css">

body
{
font-family: Arial, Helvetica, sans-serif;
font-size: 90%;
color: #540907;
background-color: #FFC955;
background-image:url("images/flowers.gif");
background-repeat: no-repeat;
background-position:550px 0;
margin:0;
}

h1
{
text-transform: uppercase;
padding-left: 20px;
margin-top:0;
margin-bottom:10px;
width: 520px;
}
```

2 Within the existing h1 declaration, type border:.

```
margin:0;
}

h1
{
text-transform: uppercase;
padding-left: 20px;
margin-top:0;
margin-bottom:10px;
width: 520px;
border:|    2
}

p
{
line-height: 1.5em;
text-indent: .75em;
text-align: justify;
padding-left: 20px;
margin-top:0;
margin-bottom: 10px;
width: 520px;
}

</style>

</head>
```

3 Type *? ? ?;*, replacing the first *?* with the desired width,
the second with the desired color, and the third with a style keyword such as `solid` or `dashed`.

```
margin:0;
}

h1
{
text-transform: uppercase;
padding-left: 20px;
margin-top:0;
margin-bottom:10px;
width: 520px;
border: 1px dashed #540907;|
}

p
{
line-height: 1.5em;
text-indent: .75em;
```

● When viewed in a browser, the heading has the border around it.

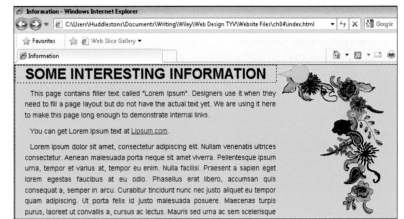

TIP

What are the possible values for the border style?

You can use any of the following for the style of the border.

Style	Description
none	No border is drawn.
hidden	Except in tables, this is the same as none. In tables, the property suppresses borders when used along with border-collapse.
solid	A single line.
double	A double line. The browser determines the space between lines.
dotted	A series of dots make up the border. The exact shape and position of the dots is up to the browser.
dashed	A series of dashes, with the exact position determined by the browser.
groove	A line with shading to create a slightly indented 3D effect. The shading is determined by the browser.
ridge	The opposite of groove, ridge uses shading to create a raised appearance.
inset	The browser shades two sides of the border to create the effect of the box being lowered below the page. As with other properties here, the exact shading is left to the browser.
outset	The opposite of inset, with the box apparently raised above the page.

CHAPTER 5

Advanced CSS

CSS provides many properties that allow you to fine-tune the look and feel of your site. In this chapter, you learn how to better target elements on your page and how to externalize your style sheet so that you can use it on multiple pages.

Style Multiple Elements

Often, designers need to apply an identical set of style properties to more than one element. For example, you may want all of your headings to use the same font family, share the same color, and have the same border applied. Using a single combined CSS selector, you can set all of these properties together, saving you initial development time as well as maintenance time in the future because you can alter the appearance of all of the elements by changing a single rule. Combined selectors are created by simply having a comma-separated list of elements as the selector.

Style Multiple Elements

1 In your editor, open a page that contains an embedded style sheet.

```
Index - Notepad          1
File  Edit  Format  View  Help
<!DOCTYPE html PUBLIC "-//W3C//DTD XHTML 1.0 Transitional//EN"
"http://www.w3.org/TR/xhtml1/DTD/xhtml1-transitional.dtd">
<html>
<head>
<title>Information</title>

<style type="text/css">

body
{
font-family: Arial, Helvetica, sans-serif;
font-size: 90%;
color: #540907;
background-color: #FFC955;
background-image:url("images/flowers.gif");
background-repeat: no-repeat;
background-position:550px 0;
margin:0;
}

h1
{
text-transform: uppercase;
padding-left: 20px;
```

2 Within the style sheet, type a list of elements to which you want to apply a style. Separate the elements with commas.

3 Press Enter.

4 Type {.

```
body
{
font-family: Arial, Helvetica, sans-serif;
font-size: 90%;
color: #540907;
background-color: #FFC955;
background-image:url("images/flowers.gif");
background-repeat: no-repeat;
background-position:550px 0;
margin:0;
}

h1, h2          2
{          4

h1
{
text-transform: uppercase;
padding-left: 20px;
margin-top:0;
margin-bottom:10px;
width: 520px;
border: 1px dashed #540907;
}
```

5 Type one or more style rules.

6 Type }.

```
body
{
font-family: Arial, Helvetica, sans-serif;
font-size: 90%;
color: #540907;
background-color: #FFC955;
background-image:url("images/flowers.gif");
background-repeat: no-repeat;
background-position:550px 0;
margin:0;
}

h1, h2
{
font-family: Georgia, "Times New Roman", Times, serif;
}

h1
{
text-transform: uppercase;
padding-left: 20px;
margin-top:0;
margin-bottom:10px;
width: 520px;
border: 1px dashed #540907;
}
```

● When you view your page in a Web browser, all of the specified elements share the same styles.

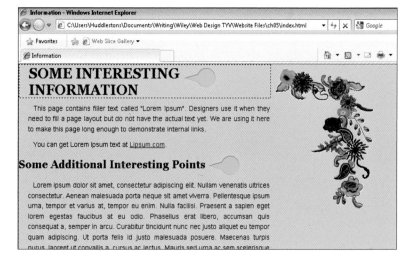

What if I want only some of the styles to apply to all of the elements?

You can use combined style declarations to apply styles to multiple elements, and then include separate rules to apply different styles to individual elements. For example, you could create a combined style similar to that shown in this section to set all of your headings to the same font and color, and then add individual style declarations for each heading level in which you set different font sizes.

Does the order in which I list the elements in a combined rule matter?

No. You can list them in any order. However, if you have both the combined selector and individual selectors for elements, and the individual selectors contain rules that contradict those in the combined selector, the rule that you want to apply must appear last in your style sheet.

Format Text with Spans

CSS formatting is applied to text by altering the appearance of the nearest HTML tag containing the text. For most work on your page, you can simply style whatever tag already exists, such as the paragraph. However, there will be times when you need to style a group of words or letters within a bigger block, and in particular style a portion of text that has no other tag around it. The <span> tag was added to HTML to solve this issue. The tag exists solely to provide you with an inline element to which you can apply styles.

Format Text with Spans

1 In your editor, open a page that contains an embedded style sheet.

1

```
index - Notepad
File  Edit  Format  View  Help
<!DOCTYPE html PUBLIC "-//W3C//DTD XHTML 1.0 Transitional//EN"
"http://www.w3.org/TR/xhtml1/DTD/xhtml1-transitional.dtd">
<html>
<head>
<title>Information</title>

<style type="text/css">

body
{
font-family: Arial, Helvetica, sans-serif;
font-size: 90%;
color: #540907;
background-color: #FFC955;
background-image:url("images/flowers.gif");
background-repeat: no-repeat;
background-position:550px 0;
margin:0;
}

h1, h2
{
font-family: Georgia, "Times New Roman", Times, serif;
}
```

2 Within the body text, type <span> before a word or words to which you want to apply a style.

3 After the text, type </span>.

```
</style>

</head>
<body>

<h1 id="top">Some Interesting Information</h1>
```
2   **3**
```
<p>This page contains filler text called <span>Lorem Ipsum</span>|. Designe
they need to
fill a page layout but do not have the actual text yet. We are using it he
page long enough to demonstrate internal links.</p>

<p>You can get Lorem Ipsum text at <a href="http://www.lipsum.com">Lipsum.

<h2>Some Additional Interesting Points</h2>

<p>Lorem ipsum dolor sit amet, consectetur adipiscing elit. Nullam venenat
consectetur. Aenean malesuada porta neque sit amet viverra. Pellentesque i
tempor et varius at, tempor eu enim. Nulla facilisi. Praesent a sapien ege
faucibus at eu odio. Phasellus erat libero, accumsan quis consequat a, sem
Curabitur tincidunt nunc nec justo aliquet eu tempor quam adipiscing. Ut p
justo malesuada posuere. Maecenas turpis purus, laoreet ut convallis a, cu
Mauris sed urna ac sem scelerisque lobortis. Nulla facilisis pharetra mi,
eros tristique a. Vivamus arcu diam, fringilla vitae iaculis eget, ullamco
Vivamus eu purus lorem. Aliquam erat volutpat. Vivamus interdum erat vel l
quis rutrum risus congue. Morbi consectetur, velit a sagittis aliquet, fel
sem, sed commodo est ante eleifend lectus. Vivamus auctor mattis nisi, con
magna tincidunt non. Morbi lacinia mauris ut orci pellentesque nec porttit
```

④ Within the style sheet, type span.

⑤ Press **Enter**.

⑥ Type {.

⑦ Type one or more style rules.

⑧ Press **Enter**.

⑨ Type }.

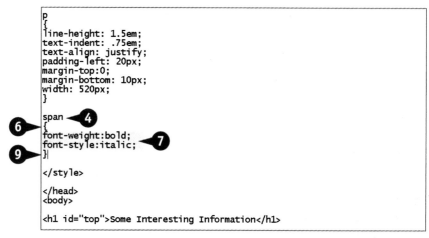

```
p
{
line-height: 1.5em;
text-indent: .75em;
text-align: justify;
padding-left: 20px;
margin-top:0;
margin-bottom: 10px;
width: 520px;
}

span ◄ 4
{ ◄ 6
font-weight:bold;
font-style:italic; ◄ 7
}| ◄ 9

</style>

</head>
<body>

<h1 id="top">Some Interesting Information</h1>
```

● When the page is viewed in the browser, the text wrapped within the span has the specified styles applied to it.

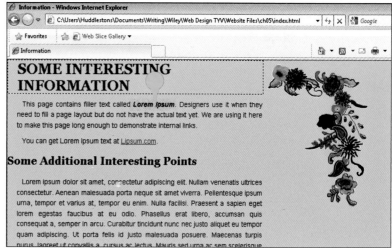

TIPS

How can I style different pieces of text differently?

You can wrap any text with the <span> tag. CSS provides for two special selectors — classes and IDs — that allow you to apply different styles to the individual instances of the same element. These two selectors are covered later in this chapter.

What happens if I add a <span> tag to my page but do not apply a style to it?

The <span> has no default formatting, so adding one to your page without a corresponding style does not affect the page's appearance at all. The <span> tag was specifically added to HTML as a way of applying styles where no other tag existed.

Group Elements with Divs

There may be times when you have a group of block elements that you need to style together. For example, the banner area at the top of your page may be made up of one or more images, a heading, and a set of links for your primary navigation. You can apply styles to these tags together by grouping them with the `<div>` tag. Like the `<span>` tag, `<div>` does not have any default formatting properties, and exists to allow you to logically group other tags into sections and then apply styles accordingly.

Group Elements with Divs

1 In your editor, open a page that contains an embedded style sheet.

2 Within the body of your document, type `<div>` before the first element you want to include in the group.

3 After the closing tag of the last element in the group, type `</div>`.

```
index - Notepad                    1
File Edit Format View Help
</head>
<body>

<h1 id="top">Some Interesting Information</h1>

<p>This page contains filler text called <span>Lorem Ipsum</span>. Designe
they need to fill a page layout but do not have the actual text yet. We ar
to make this page long enough to demonstrate internal links.</p>

<p>You can get Lorem Ipsum text at <a href="http://www.lipsum.com">Lipsum.

<h2>Some Additional Interesting Points</h2>

<div>
<p>Lorem ipsum dolor sit amet, consectetur adipiscing elit. Nullam venenat
consectetur. Aenean malesuada porta neque sit amet viverra. Pellentesque i
tempor et varius at, tempor eu enim. Nulla facilisi. Praesent a sapien ege
faucibus at eu odio. Phasellus erat libero, accumsan quis consequat a, sem
Curabitur tincidunt nunc nec justo aliquet eu tempor quam adipiscing. Ut p
justo malesuada posuere. Maecenas turpis purus, laoreet ut convallis a, cu
Mauris sed urna ac sem scelerisque lobortis. Nulla facilisis pharetra mi,
eros tristique a. Vivamus arcu diam, fringilla vitae iaculis eget, ullamco
Vivamus eu purus lorem. Aliquam erat volutpat. Vivamus interdum erat vel l
quis rutrum risus congue. Morbi consectetur, velit a sagittis aliquet, fel

<p>Morbi vehicula tristique tortor, et porttitor augue tempor in. Nullam n
Duis a diam odio. Mauris posuere vehicula lectus, nec faucibus tortor ultr
Cum sociis natoque penatibus et magnis dis parturient montes, nascetur rid
Integer imperdiet posuere purus sodales blandit. Donec sollicitudin gravid
convallis. Aenean luctus urna nec turpis iaculis eu posuere nisl mattis. N
iaculis neque. Nunc bibendum tempor lectus bibendum ultricies. Vivamus at
auctor rutrum. Curabitur id est eros, at gravida elit. Class aptent taciti
litora torquent per conubia nostra, per inceptos himenaeos. Cras nisl mass
vestibulum gravida, suscipit in justo. Quisque at orci lacus. Nulla facili
at nisl viverra blandit id id est. Aliquam viverra, nibh a luctus laoreet,
fringilla dolor, eu rhoncus nunc diam eget lorem. Donec vitae nunc libero,
mauris. Maecenas nec enim vitae nisl fermentum porttitor in ut ligula. </p

<p>Nullam id mauris eros. In vitae metus id lectus adipiscing tempor. Susp
Nunc et felis sit amet eros pretium porta. Quisque ac purus quis mauris ad
id sit amet purus. Quisque non gravida urna. Quisque tempus velit quis fel
placerat. In semper egestas fringilla. Sed cursus nisl vel augue egestas v
nibh facilisis. Nullam eu consectetur ante. Donec a tempus est. Donec quis
Nam libero felis, egestas quis malesuada vel, tristique congue tellus. Dui
consectetur a suscipit nec, condimentum eu dolor. Donec aliquam nisl nec l
at pharetra leo scelerisque. Nulla facilisi. Nullam semper, magna sit amet
purus arcu viverra nisi, et pellentesque lectus nulla sed est. Cras consec
hendrerit imperdiet, lectus magna cursus metus, a blandit tellus nisi in e

<p><a href="#top">Back to top</a></p>
</div>

</body>
```

4 Within the style sheet, type `div`.

5 Press `Enter`.

6 Type {.

7 Type one or more style rules.

8 Press `Enter`.

9 Type }.

● When the page is viewed in the browser, the elements wrapped within the div have the specified styles applied to them.

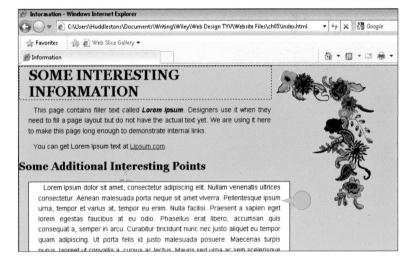

TIP

What is the difference between <div> and <span>?
The <span> tag is an inline element, meaning that it should only be used to wrap around pieces of text already contained within some other element, such as a paragraph or heading. The <div> tag, on the other hand, is a block-level element, so it should be used to wrap around those bigger elements. If you want to style a group of words in a paragraph, use <span>. If you want to style a group of paragraphs, use <div>.

Apply Styles with Classes

When you apply styles by using an element selector, the style affects every instance of that element on the page. Often, you want to target the style only at a few instances of the element, which can be done with a class selector and attribute. The class selector is used in your CSS to create a generic set of rules, whereas the matching class attribute is added to your HTML to specify to which tag the class' rules should be applied. In your CSS, the class name must begin with a period, but the period is not used in the attribute in HTML.

Apply Styles with Classes

1 In your editor, open a page that contains an embedded style sheet.

1
```
index - Notepad
File  Edit  Format  View  Help
<!DOCTYPE html PUBLIC "-//W3C//DTD XHTML 1.0 Transitional//EN"
"http://www.w3.org/TR/xhtml1/DTD/xhtml1-transitional.dtd">
<html>
<head>
<title>Information</title>

<style type="text/css">

body
{
font-family: Arial, Helvetica, sans-serif;
font-size: 90%;
color: #540907;
background-color: #FFC955;
background-image:url("images/flowers.gif");
background-repeat: no-repeat;
background-position:550px 0;
margin:0;
}

h1, h2
{
font-family: Georgia, "Times New Roman", Times, serif;
}
```

2 Within a tag to which you want to apply the style, type `class="?"`, replacing ? with a class name.

2
```
index - Notepad
File  Edit  Format  View  Help
faucibus at eu odio. Phasellus erat libero, accumsan quis consequat a, sem
Curabitur tincidunt nunc nec justo aliquet eu tempor quam adipiscing. Ut p
justo malesuada posuere. Maecenas turpis purus, laoreet ut convallis a, cu
Mauris sed urna ac sem scelerisque lobortis. Nulla facilisis pharetra mi,
eros tristique a. Vivamus arcu diam, fringilla vitae iaculis eget, ullamco
Vivamus eu purus lorem. Aliquam erat volutpat. Vivamus interdum erat vel l
quis rutrum risus congue. Morbi consectetur, velit a sagittis aliquet, fel
sem, sed commodo est ante eleifend lectus. Vivamus auctor mattis nisi, con
magna tincidunt non. Morbi lacinia mauris ut orci pellentesque nec porttit
imperdiet. </p>

<h3 class="contentSubhead">Subheading within the content</h3>

<p>Vesti   um sit amet tellus leo. Nulla tellus lorem, feugiat at pretium
vitae er   Duis tortor lectus, vehicula quis iaculis sit amet, gravida pe
turpis. Etiam sodales, erat at viverra vestibulum, purus magna auctor erat
risus lectus a nulla. Pellentesque habitant morbi tristique senectus et ne
fames ac turpis egestas. Nullam arcu metus, pellentesque a molestie sed, m
justo. Nam laoreet dapibus rutrum. Suspendisse eu sapien turpis. Quisque v
Nulla sagittis suscipit dignissim. Curabitur eget luctus nunc. Quisque eu
interdum nisi. Nunc sollicitudin nisi quis quam tristique egestas rhoncus
Maecenas felis mauris, facilisis et consequat ac, molestie sit amet neque.
sit amet lacus elementum auctor quis id justo. Maecenas egestas venenatis
volutpat dui fermentum id. Mauris dignissim erat eu orci auctor placerat.
risus, elementum id condimentum ac, eleifend vitae lacus. </p>
```

3 Within the style sheet, type a period and the class name you used in Step **2**.

4 Press Enter.

5 Type {.

6 Type one or more style rules.

7 Press Enter.

8 Type }.

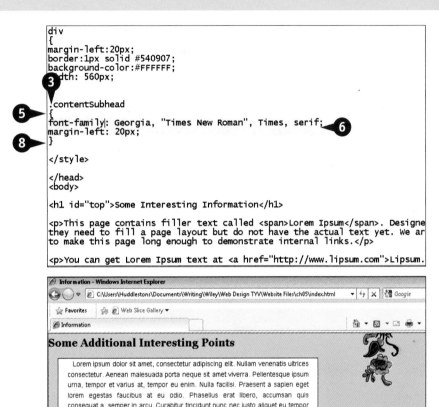

```
div
{
margin-left:20px;
border:1px solid #540907;
background-color:#FFFFFF;
  dth: 560px;


.contentSubhead
{
font-family: Georgia, "Times New Roman", Times, serif;
margin-left: 20px;
}

</style>

</head>
<body>

<h1 id="top">Some Interesting Information</h1>

<p>This page contains filler text called <span>Lorem Ipsum</span>. Designe
they need to fill a page layout but do not have the actual text yet. We ar
to make this page long enough to demonstrate internal links.</p>

<p>You can get Lorem Ipsum text at <a href="http://www.lipsum.com">Lipsum.
```

● When you view the page in the browser, the tag to which you added the class attribute has the style applied.

Some Additional Interesting Points

Lorem ipsum dolor sit amet, consectetur adipiscing elit. Nullam venenatis ultrices consectetur. Aenean malesuada porta neque sit amet viverra. Pellentesque ipsum urna, tempor et varius at, tempor eu enim. Nulla facilisi. Praesent a sapien eget lorem egestas faucibus at eu odio. Phasellus erat libero, accumsan quis consequat a, semper in arcu. Curabitur tincidunt nunc nec justo aliquet eu tempor quam adipiscing. Ut porta felis id justo malesuada posuere. Maecenas turpis purus, laoreet ut convallis a, cursus ac lectus. Mauris sed urna ac sem scelerisque lobortis. Nulla facilisis pharetra mi, vitae tincidunt eros tristique a. Vivamus arcu diam, fringilla vitae iaculis eget, ullamcorper nec leo. Vivamus eu purus lorem. Aliquam erat volutpat. Vivamus interdum erat vel lacus laoreet quis rutrum risus congue. Morbi consectetur, velit a sagittis aliquet, felis mauris tempus sem, sed commodo est ante eleifend lectus. Vivamus auctor mattis nisi, consequat congue magna tincidunt non. Morbi lacinia mauris id orci pellentesque nec porttitor dolor imperdiet.

Subheading within the content

Vestibulum sit amet tellus leo. Nulla tellus lorem, feugiat at pretium vitae,

TIPS

Are there rules for naming classes?

Yes. Class names must begin with a letter and can contain only letters, underscore characters, dashes, and numbers. Class names cannot contain spaces. Class names are also case-sensitive, so you need to be sure to use the same capitalization in the HTML attribute as you do in the style sheet.

Can I use the same class more than once on a page?

Yes. A single class can be applied to as many elements on the page as you want. You do not even need to apply it to the same element, so, for example, you could apply a class to a span and a paragraph in the same document without problem.

Apply Styles with IDs

Just as with a class, an ID selector allows you to create a generic set of style rules and then apply them to your page via the matching HTML attribute, ID. An important distinction, however, is that an ID selector can be applied only to a single tag on an HTML page, whereas a class selector can in theory be applied to as many elements on the page as you want. In your CSS, the ID selector must begin with a pound sign (#), but the sign is not repeated in the matching HTML attribute.

Apply Styles with IDs

1 In your editor, open a page that contains an embedded style sheet.

```
index - Notepad
File  Edit  Format  View  Help
<!DOCTYPE html PUBLIC "-//W3C//DTD XHTML 1.0 Transitional//EN"
"http://www.w3.org/TR/xhtml1/DTD/xhtml1-transitional.dtd">
<html>
<head>
<title>Information</title>

<style type="text/css">

body
{
font-family: Arial, Helvetica, sans-serif;
font-size: 90%;
color: #540907;
background-color: #FFC955;
background-image:url("images/flowers.gif");
background-repeat: no-repeat;
background-position:550px 0;
margin:0;
}

h1, h2
{
font-family: Georgia, "Times New Roman", Times, serif;
}
```

2 Within a tag to which you want to apply the style, type `id="?"`, replacing *?* with an ID.

```
index - Notepad
File  Edit  Format  View  Help
</style>

</head>
<body>

<h1 id="top">Some Interesting Information</h1>

<p>This page contains filler text called <span>Lorem Ipsum</span>. Designe
they need to fill a page layout but do not have the actual text yet. We ar
to make this page long enough to demonstrate internal links.</p>

<p>You can get Lorem Ipsum text at <a href="http://www.lipsum.com">Lipsum.

<h2>Some Additional Interesting Points</h2>

<div id="mainContent">
<p>Lorem ipsum dolor sit amet, consectetur adipiscing elit. Nullam venenat
consectetur. Aenean malesuada porta neque sit amet viverra. Pellentesque i
tempor et varius at, tempor eu enim. Nulla facilisi. Praesent a sapien ege
faucibus at eu odio. Phasellus erat libero, accumsan quis consequat a, sem
Curabitur tincidunt nunc nec justo aliquet eu tempor quam adipiscing. Ut p
justo malesuada posuere. Maecenas turpis purus, laoreet ut convallis a, cu
Mauris sed urna ac sem scelerisque lobortis. Nulla facilisis pharetra mi,
```

3 Within the style sheet, type a # and the ID you used in Step **2**.

4 Press Enter.

5 Type {.

6 Type one or more style rules.

7 Press Enter.

8 Type }.

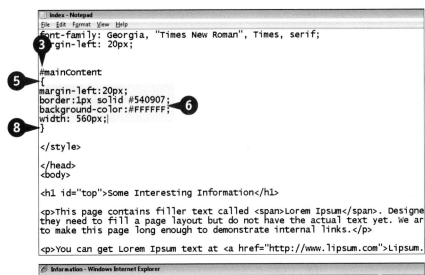

● When you view the page in the browser, the tag to which you added the ID attribute has the style applied.

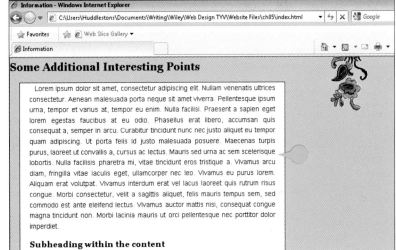

In Chapter 2, IDs were used as targets for links. Is this a different ID?
No. IDs can be used for several purposes, including targeting links and applying styles. They can also be used for JavaScript. A single element's ID can be used for any or all of these purposes on a single page.

What is the difference between an ID and a class?
The main difference between IDs and classes is that an ID must be unique on a page, whereas a class can be used repeatedly. IDs are also more specific than classes, so if an element has both an ID and a class applied with conflicting styles, the ID's styles take precedence over those of the class.

Use Contextual Selectors

A ny style can be applied anywhere on your page with the appropriate use of class or ID selectors, but at times this can become needlessly cumbersome. For example, if you wanted to apply a particular style to each item of a long list, you might need to add a class attribute to every one of the items. A simpler, cleaner solution is to use a contextual selector, which allows you to target an element based on its position within another element. With a contextual selector, you could apply the desired style to the list items by referencing their position within another element, such as a div with an ID.

Use Contextual Selectors

1 In your editor, open a page that contains an embedded style sheet.

1

```
Index - Notepad
File Edit Format View Help
<!DOCTYPE html PUBLIC "-//W3C//DTD XHTML 1.0 Transitional//EN"
"http://www.w3.org/TR/xhtml1/DTD/xhtml1-transitional.dtd">
<html>
<head>
<title>Information</title>

<style type="text/css">

body
{
font-family: Arial, Helvetica, sans-serif;
font-size: 90%;
color: #540907;
background-color: #FFC955;
background-image:url("images/flowers.gif");
background-repeat: no-repeat;
background-position:550px 0;
margin:0;
}

h1, h2
{
font-family: Georgia, "Times New Roman", Times, serif;
}
```

2 Within the style sheet, type a parent element or ID and its child element, separated by a space.

2

```
Index - Notepad
File Edit Format View Help

.contentSubhead
{
font-family: Georgia, "Times New Roman", Times, serif;
margin-left: 20px;
}

#mainContent
{
margin-left:20px;
border:1px solid #540907;
background-color:#FFFFFF;
width: 560px;
}

#mainContent p|

</style>

</head>
<body>

<h1 id="top">Some Interesting Information</h1>
```

3 Press Enter.

4 Type {.

5 Type one or more style rules to apply to the child element.

6 Press Enter.

7 Type }.

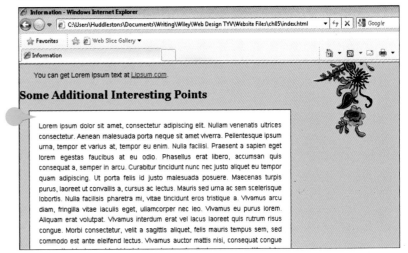

● When you view the page in the browser, the child element has the style applied to it.

TIPS

How complex can my contextual selectors be?
You can create contextual selectors as complex as you need. For example, if you wanted to apply a style to an image that was inside a paragraph, which in turn was inside a div with an ID of `content`, you could write `#content p img` and successfully target the image.

Do I need to use any special characters within the contextual selector?
No. A contextual selector is a list of selectors separated by spaces. A comma-separated list of selectors applies the style to each of the elements in the list, as shown earlier in this chapter.

Use Pseudo-Elements

A pseudo-element is a special selector type in CSS that allows you to target an element in special situations. For example, you can use the `:first-line` pseudo-element to apply a style only to the first line of an element, whereas the first-letter pseudo-element applies to the first character within the specified element. The pseudo-element is separated from the element by a colon, so to style the first line of a paragraph, you would use `p:first-line`. CSS also recognizes a before-and-after pseudo-element, but some browsers do not properly support them.

Use Pseudo-Elements

1 In your editor, open a page that contains an embedded style sheet.

```
index - Notepad
File  Edit  Format  View  Help
<!DOCTYPE html PUBLIC "-//W3C//DTD XHTML 1.0 Transitional//EN"
"http://www.w3.org/TR/xhtml1/DTD/xhtml1-transitional.dtd">
<html>
<head>
<title>Information</title>

<style type="text/css">

body
{
font-family: Arial, Helvetica, sans-serif;
font-size: 90%;
color: #540907;
background-color: #FFC955;
background-image:url("images/flowers.gif");
background-repeat: no-repeat;
background-position:550px 0;
margin:0;
}

h1, h2
{
font-family: Georgia, "Times New Roman", Times, serif;
}
```

2 Within the style sheet, type the name of an element.

3 Type a colon.

4 Type the pseudo-element you want to use.

```
index - Notepad
File  Edit  Format  View  Help

#mainContent
{
margin-left:20px;
border:1px solid #540907;
background-color:#FFFFFF;
width: 560px;
}

#mainContent p
{
text-indent:0;
padding-top: (3)x;
}

#mainContent p:first-line

</style>

</head>
<body>

<h1 id="top">Some Interesting Information</h1>
```

140

5 Press Enter.

6 Type {.

7 Type the styles you want to use.

8 Press Enter.

9 Type }.

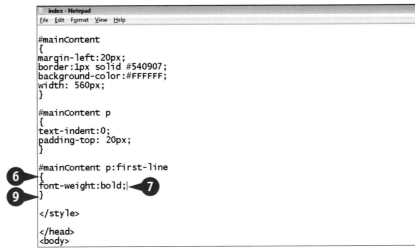

```
#mainContent
{
margin-left:20px;
border:1px solid #540907;
background-color:#FFFFFF;
width: 560px;
}

#mainContent p
{
text-indent:0;
padding-top: 20px;
}

#mainContent p:first-line
{
font-weight:bold;
}

</style>

</head>
<body>
```

● When you view the page in a browser, the style is applied based on the pseudo-element. In this example, the first line of text in the paragraphs is formatted in bold.

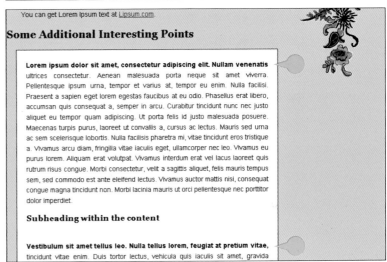

You can get Lorem Ipsum text at Lipsum.com.

Some Additional Interesting Points

Lorem ipsum dolor sit amet, consectetur adipiscing elit. Nullam venenatis ultrices consectetur. Aenean malesuada porta neque sit amet viverra. Pellentesque ipsum urna, tempor et varius at, tempor eu enim. Nulla facilisi. Praesent a sapien eget lorem egestas faucibus at eu odio. Phasellus erat libero, accumsan quis consequat a, semper in arcu. Curabitur tincidunt nunc nec justo aliquet eu tempor quam adipiscing. Ut porta felis id justo malesuada posuere. Maecenas turpis purus, laoreet ut convallis a, cursus ac lectus. Mauris sed urna ac sem scelerisque lobortis. Nulla facilisis pharetra mi, vitae tincidunt eros tristique a. Vivamus arcu diam, fringilla vitae iaculis eget, ullamcorper nec leo. Vivamus eu purus lorem. Aliquam erat volutpat. Vivamus interdum erat vel lacus laoreet quis rutrum risus congue. Morbi consectetur, velit a sagittis aliquet, felis mauris tempus sem, sed commodo est ante eleifend lectus. Vivamus auctor mattis nisi, consequat congue magna tincidunt non. Morbi lacinia mauris ut orci pellentesque nec porttitor dolor imperdiet.

Subheading within the content

Vestibulum sit amet tellus leo. Nulla tellus lorem, feugiat at pretium vitae, tincidunt vitae enim. Duis tortor lectus, vehicula quis iaculis sit amet, gravida

TIPS

To which elements can I apply pseudo-elements?
In theory, any element can take a pseudo-element. In practice, however, browsers tend to ignore the pseudo-element when it is not applied to text-based elements, such as paragraphs, lists, and table cells.

Can I apply pseudo-elements with ID or class selectors?
Yes. You simply replace the element name before the colon with the class or ID name. Therefore, `.intro:first-line` would style the first line of any element with the intro class, and `#mainArticle:first-line` would apply the style to an element with a `mainArticle` ID.

Use Pseudo-Classes

A pseudo-class can apply a style to an element based on its current state. The most commonly used pseudo-classes are used to style links in their five common states: normal, visited, hover, active, and focus. The `a:link` pseudo-class applies a style to a link in its normal state. The `a:visited` applies when you have visited the target of the link. The `a:hover` applies when the user mouses over the link, and `a:active` should apply when the link is selected — for example, when you are pressing your mouse down on it. Finally, `a:focus` defines a style to be shown when `Tab` is used to navigate the page.

Use Pseudo-Classes

1 In your editor, open a page that contains an embedded style sheet.

1

```
Index - Notepad
File  Edit  Format  View  Help
<!DOCTYPE html PUBLIC "-//W3C//DTD XHTML 1.0 Transitional//EN"
"http://www.w3.org/TR/xhtml11/DTD/xhtml11-transitional.dtd">
<html>
<head>
<title>Information</title>

<style type="text/css">

body
{
font-family: Arial, Helvetica, sans-serif;
font-size: 90%;
color: #540907;
background-color: #FFC955;
background-image:url("images/flowers.gif");
background-repeat: no-repeat;
background-position:550px 0;
margin:0;
}

h1, h2
{
font-family: Georgia, "Times New Roman", Times, serif;
}
```

2 Within the style sheet, type `a:link`.

3 Press `Enter`.

4 Type {.

5 Type the styles you want to apply to the link.

6 Press `Enter`.

7 Type }.

```
#mainContent p
{
text-indent:0;
padding-top: 20px;
}

#mainContent p:first-line
{
font-weight:bold;
}

a:link
{
font-weight:bold;
color:#540907;
}

</style>

</head>
<body>

<h1 id="top">Some Interesting Information</h1>
```

8 Repeat Steps **2** to **7**, creating style selectors for `a:visited, a:hover, a:active,` and `a:focus`.

```
a:link
{
font-weight:bold;
color:#540907;
}

a:visited
{
font-weight:bold;
color: #8A3D20;
}

a:hover
{
text-decoration:none;
color: #372F22;
}                          ◀ 8

a:active
{
text-decoration:none;
color: #372F22;
}

a:focus
{
text-decoration:none;
color: #372F22;
}

</style>
```

● When you view the page in a browser, the links should be styled based either on the styles used in the `a:link` or `a:visited` declarations. When you position your mouse pointer over the links, you should see the `a:hover` style.

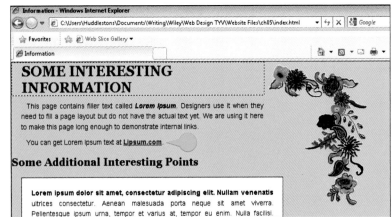

TIP

Are there other pseudo-classes beyond the ones for styling links?
CSS defines a first-child pseudo-class that allows you to apply a style to the element immediately following the one to which the style is applied. For example, styles applied with a selector `h2:first-child` would not apply to the heading, but instead to whatever element, most likely a paragraph, followed the heading.

Create an External Style Sheet

You can ensure that you maintain a consistent look and feel to your entire site as well as make it quite simple to modify your design site-wide by relying on one of the most powerful features of CSS: the ability to define styles independent of a particular document. By separating your content and presentation into distinct documents, you can apply the styles to as many HTML documents as you want. Changes to the external styles document can be reflected throughout all of your site's HTML pages. The external style sheet is saved as an independent document, most commonly using the .css file extension.

Create an External Style Sheet

1 In your editor, open a page that contains an embedded style sheet.

2 Select everything inside the `<style>` tag block.

3 Click **Edit**.

4 Click **Cut**.

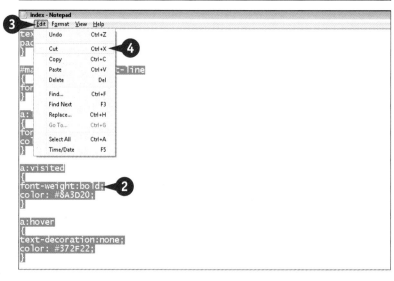

5 Open a new, blank file in your editor.

6 Click **Edit**.

7 Click **Paste**.

8 Save the document, using a .css extension.

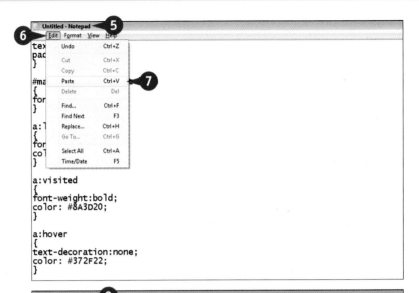

9 Return to the original page.

10 Delete the opening and closing style sheets.

The style sheet is removed from the HTML document and saved as an external document.

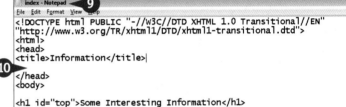

Where should I save the CSS file?
External style sheets can be saved anywhere within your Web site's root folder. Some designers like to create a special folder that contains all of their style sheets, whereas others simply place them in the root.

Can I put some of my styles in an external sheet and leave others as embedded styles?
Yes. In general, those styles that apply to all or most of your pages are placed in the external sheet, whereas styles that apply only to a single document might be kept in an embedded style sheet. See "Use the Cascade," later in this chapter, for another example of combining external and embedded styles.

Link a Style Sheet to a Page

O nce you move styles to an external style sheet, you must link the HTML page to the CSS document in order to reapply the styles. You can use the `<link>` tag to accomplish this. The `link` element takes three required attributes: `rel`, `type`, and `href`. The `rel` attribute specifies the relationship between this page and the style sheet, and most often is set to a value of `stylesheet`. The `type` attribute informs the browser as to which type of file it can expect when it requests the style sheet from the server, and is always `text/css`. Finally, the `href` attribute sets the path to the style sheet document.

Link a Style Sheet to a Page

1 In your editor, open a page to which you want to link the style sheet.

1

```
index - Notepad
File Edit Format View Help
<!DOCTYPE html PUBLIC "-//W3C//DTD XHTML 1.0 Transitional//EN"
"http://www.w3.org/TR/xhtml1/DTD/xhtml1-transitional.dtd">
<html>
<head>
<title>Information</title>

</head>
<body>

<h1 id="top">Some Interesting Information</h1>

<p>This page contains filler text called <span>Lorem Ipsum</span>. Designe
they need to fill a page layout but do not have the actual text yet. We ar
to make this page long enough to demonstrate internal links.</p>

<p>You can get Lorem Ipsum text at <a href="http://www.lipsum.com">Lipsum.

<h2>Some Additional Interesting Points</h2>

<div id="mainContent">
<p>Lorem ipsum dolor sit amet, consectetur adipiscing elit. Nullam venenat
consectetur. Aenean malesuada porta neque sit amet viverra. Pellentesque i
tempor et varius at, tempor eu enim. Nulla facilisi. Praesent a sapien ege
faucibus at eu odio. Phasellus erat libero, accumsan quis consequat a, sem
```

2 In the head section of the document, type `<link`.

```
index - Notepad
File Edit Format View Help
<!DOCTYPE html PUBLIC "-//W3C//DTD XHTML 1.0 Transitional//EN"
"http://www.w3.org/TR/xhtml1/DTD/xhtml1-transitional.dtd">
<html>
<head>
<title>Information</title>

<link

</head>
<body>

<h1 id="top">Some Interesting Information</h1>

<p>This page contains filler text called <span>Lorem Ipsum</span>. Designe
they need to fill a page layout but do not have the actual text yet. We ar
to make this page long enough to demonstrate internal links.</p>

<p>You can get Lorem Ipsum text at <a href="http://www.lipsum.com">Lipsum.

<h2>Some Additional Interesting Points</h2>

<div id="mainContent">
<p>Lorem ipsum dolor sit amet, consectetur adipiscing elit. Nullam venenat
consectetur. Aenean malesuada porta neque sit amet viverra. Pellentesque i
```

2

③ Type `type="text/css"`.

④ Type `rel="stylesheet"`.

⑤ Type `href="?" />`,
replacing *?* with a relative or
absolute path to the style
sheet.

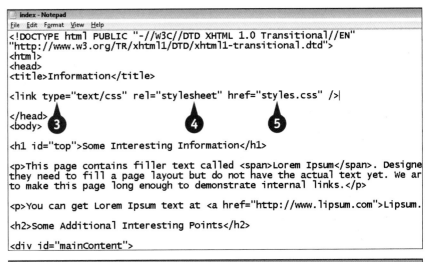

When you view the page in
a browser, the styles are
properly applied.

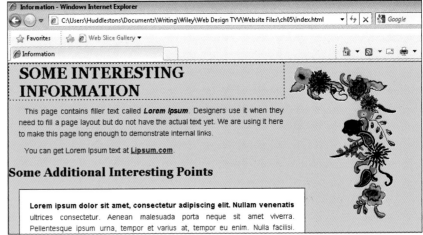

TIPS

Can I link to more than one style sheet?
Yes. A single page can be linked to as many style
sheets as you want. However, if there are conflicts
in the style declarations from one sheet to the next,
the sheet whose `<link>` tag is lowest in the order
applies.

Is there any other way to link to a style sheet?
Yes. Modern browsers support importing style sheets,
which can be done by placing an `@import`
command between `<style>` tags. The `@import`
command takes as its value the keyword `url`, with a
path to the CSS document in parentheses.

Use the Cascade

You can have CSS declarations in both an external style sheet and an embedded style sheet. In this case, the order of the cascade specifies that the embedded styles override conflicts with the external styles. This can be used to your advantage because it allows you to have page-specific formatting for select elements while still maintaining the overall look and feel of the site. You should understand that only those styles in direct conflict are overridden. As much as possible, the browser attempts to use both the external and embedded styles together.

Use the Cascade

1 Open a Web page that contains a link to an external style sheet.

```
index.html - Notepad          1
File Edit Format View Help
<!DOCTYPE html PUBLIC "-//W3C//DTD XHTML 1.0 Transitional//EN" "http://www
<html>
<head>
<title>Information</title>

<link type="text/css" rel="stylesheet" href="styles.css" />

</head>
<body>

<h1 id="top">Some Interesting Information</h1>

<p>This page contains filler text called <span>Lorem Ipsum</span>. Designe

<p>You can get Lorem Ipsum text at <a href="http://www.lipsum.com">Lipsum.

<h2>Some Additional Interesting Points</h2>

<div id="mainContent">
<p>Lorem ipsum dolor sit amet, consectetur adipiscing elit. Nullam venenat
entesque nec porttitor dolor imperdiet. </p>

<h3 class="contentSubhead">Subheading within the content</h3>
```

2 In the head of the document, type `<style type= "text/css">`.

```
index.html - Notepad
File Edit Format View Help
<!DOCTYPE html PUBLIC "-//W3C//DTD XHTML 1.0 Transitional//EN" "http://www
<html>
<head>
<title>Information</title>

<link type="text/css" rel="stylesheet" href="styles.css" />

<style type="text/css">

</head>
<body>

<h1 id="top">Some Interesting Information</h1>

<p>This page contains filler text called <span>Lorem Ipsum</span>. Designe

<p>You can get Lorem Ipsum text at <a href="http://www.lipsum.com">Lipsum.

<h2>Some Additional Interesting Points</h2>

<div id="mainContent">
<p>Lorem ipsum dolor sit amet, consectetur adipiscing elit. Nullam venenat
entesque nec porttitor dolor imperdiet. </p>
```

3 Add one or more declarations to the embedded style sheet.

4 Type `</style>`.

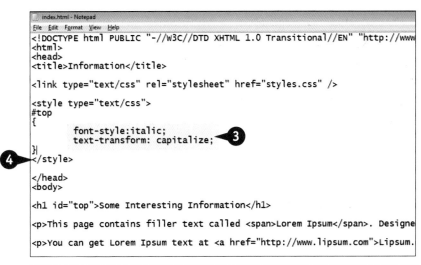

● When the page is viewed in a browser, the embedded style sheet's rule overrides conflicting rules on the linked style sheet.

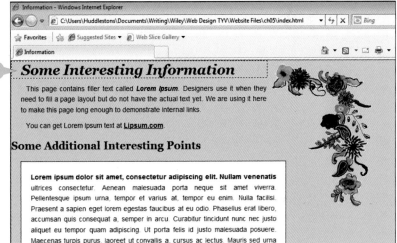

TIP

What factors determine which rules apply?

The most important factor in determining whether a style overrides another is specificity. That is, a declaration with a more specific selector overrides one with a less specific selector. ID selectors, for example, are very specific: They target one distinct element on a page. Class selectors are less specific, and element selectors less still. The relative proximity of a style declaration to its affected element is another factor in determining whether a particular rule is overridden.

CHAPTER 6

Laying Out Pages

CSS gives you the ability to create multicolumn layouts quickly and easily in your pages.

Laying out your page using CSS involves applying styles to elements grouped together with `<div>` tags, so before you can begin learning about the properties needed, you must create these groups and give them appropriate ID attributes. Before you began coding the page, you should have planned out the design of your site. Now, you will be referring back to that design. The site will likely have several logical sections — most pages will at least have a header, a body, and a footer, and many will also have one or more sidebars or additional columns. Each of these sections is represented by one of the groups you are creating with the `<div>` tags.

Set Up Your Page for CSS Layouts

1 In your editor, open a page that you want to use for layouts.

2 At the point at which you want to create a section, type `<div id=" ?">`, replacing *?* with an identifier for this section of the page.

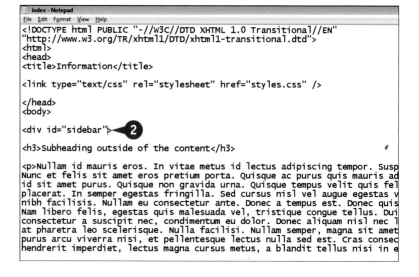

③ At the end of the section, type `</div>`.

④ Repeat Steps **2** and **3** to add additional `<div>` tags around other logical groups of elements on your page.

The page is divided into sections.

```
index - Notepad
File  Edit  Format  View  Help
<!DOCTYPE html PUBLIC "-//W3C//DTD XHTML 1.0 Transitional//EN"
"http://www.w3.org/TR/xhtml11/DTD/xhtml11-transitional.dtd">
<html>
<head>
<title>Information</title>

<link type="text/css" rel="stylesheet" href="styles.css" />

</head>
<body>

<div id="sidebar">

<h3>Subheading outside of the content</h3>

<p>Nullam id mauris eros. In vitae metus id lectus adipiscing tempor. Susp
Nunc et felis sit amet eros pretium porta. Quisque ac purus quis mauris ad
id sit amet purus. Quisque non gravida urna. Quisque tempus velit quis fel
placerat. In semper egestas fringilla. Sed cursus nisl vel augue egestas v
nibh facilisis. Nullam eu consectetur ante. Donec a tempus est. Donec quis
Nam libero felis, egestas quis malesuada vel, tristique congue tellus. Dui
consectetur a suscipit nec, condimentum eu dolor. Donec aliquam nisl nec l
at pharetra leo scelerisque. Nulla facilisi. Nullam semper, magna sit amet
purus arcu viverra nisi, et pellentesque lectus nulla sed est. Cras consec
hendrerit imperdiet, lectus magna cursus metus, a blandit tellus nisi in e

</div>
```

```
<p>Nullam id mauris eros. In vitae metus id lectus adipiscing tempor. Susp
Nunc et felis sit amet eros pretium porta. Quisque ac purus quis mauris ad
id sit amet purus. Quisque non gravida urna. Quisque tempus velit quis fel
placerat. In semper egestas fringilla. Sed cursus nisl vel augue egestas v
nibh facilisis. Nullam eu consectetur ante. Donec a tempus est. Donec quis
Nam libero felis, egestas quis malesuada vel, tristique congue tellus. Dui
consectetur a suscipit nec, condimentum eu dolor. Donec aliquam nisl nec l
at pharetra leo scelerisque. Nulla facilisi. Nullam semper, magna sit amet
purus arcu viverra nisi, et pellentesque lectus nulla sed est. Cras consec
hendrerit imperdiet, lectus magna cursus metus, a blandit tellus nisi in e

</div>

<div id="mainContent">

<h1 id="top">Some Interesting Information</h1>

<p>This page contains filler text called <span>Lorem Ipsum</span>. Designe
they need to fill a page layout but do not have the actual text yet. We ar
to make this page long enough to demonstrate internal links.</p>

<p>You can get Lorem Ipsum text at <a href="http://www.lipsum.com">Lipsum.
```

TIP

Can I have nested groups?
Yes. Many sites have nested sections or groups on the page. For example, you might want to place your main navigation within the header section. In this case, you would group the elements of the navigation with a `<div>` tag, and then include that group inside the header's `<div>` tag. You might also have logical groups in any of the other sections. You can nest groups as many levels deep as you need.

Float Elements

Perhaps the easiest method of creating multicolumn layouts involves using the CSS `float` property. When you apply a float to an element, you are saying that the content that follows the element in question can float next to it. In so doing, you can create columns in your content. The three values of float are `left`, `right`, and `none`. Applying `float:left` allows the element to float to the left of elements that follow it, and `float:right` allows the element to float to the right. Setting float to `none`, the default, removes the float.

Float Elements

1 In your editor, open a style sheet document that is linked to an HTML document.

Note: The following steps can also be done using an existing embedded style sheet.

1
```
styles - Notepad
File  Edit  Format  View  Help
text-indent:0;
padding-top: 20px;
}

#mainContent p:first-line
{
font-weight:bold;
}

a:link
{
font-weight:bold;
color:#540907;
}

a:visited
{
font-weight:bold;
color: #8A3D20;
}
```

2 In the style sheet, type #, followed by the ID of the element you want to float.

3 Press **Enter**.

4 Type {.

```
a:visited
{
font-weight:bold;
color: #8A3D20;
}

a:hover
{
text-decoration:none;
color: #372F22;
}

a:active
{
text-decoration:none;
color: #372F22;
}

a:focus
{
text-decoration:none;
color: #372F22;
}

#sidebar
{
```

5 Type `width: ?;`, replacing *?* with the size of the element. Be sure to include a unit of measurement such as `px`.

6 Press `Enter`.

7 Type `float: ?;`, replacing *?* with either `left` or `right`.

8 Press `Enter`.

9 Type `}`.

● When you view the page in your browser, the content that follows the element you floated appears either to the right or the left of it, depending on the value you chose in Step **7**. The layout may not look correct yet.

```
color: #8A3D20;
}

a:hover
{
text-decoration:none;
color: #372F22;
}

a:active
{
text-decoration:none;
color: #372F22;
}

a:focus
{
text-decoration:none;
color: #372F22;
}

#sidebar
{
width:150px;        5
float:left;
}|           9
```

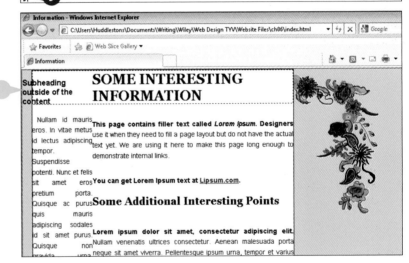

TIPS

Do I have to set a width?
Yes. By default, elements have a width of 100%, which does not leave any room for the elements that follow to float. Therefore, you must set a width on every element you want to float. You generally also set widths on the elements that follow the floated element to better control them.

Can I stop sections such as footers from floating?
Yes. You can create a style for your footer and add the CSS `clear:all` property, which tells the browser that that section should not float. You can also set `clear` to `left` or `right` to have it ignore a float on that particular side.

155

Chapter 4 discussed how you can add white space to your page by using the margin and padding properties. When you float a section of your page, you often need to set margins and padding on other sections in order to fix layout problems that the floats create. For example, if you float a short sidebar to the left of a long main column, the main column will wrap back to the left after the end of the sidebar. Applying a left margin to the column that equals or exceeds the width of the sidebar fixes the problem.

Use Margins and Padding to Fix Float Problems

1 In your editor, open a style sheet document linked to an HTML document.

Note: The following steps can also be done using an existing embedded style sheet.

```
styles - Notepad   1
File  Edit  Format  View  Help
text-align: justify;
padding-left: 20px;
margin-top:0;
margin-bottom: 10px;
}

span
{
font-weight:bold;
font-style:italic;
}

.contentSubhead
{
font-family: Georgia, "Times New Roman", Times, serif;
margin-left: 20px;
}

#mainContent
{
margin-left:20px;
border:1px solid #540907;
background-color:#FFFFFF;
width: 560px;
```

2 In the declaration that contains the float, type padding-right:"?" if you used float:left, or padding-left:"?" if you used float:right. Replace ? with an appropriate value for the padding.

```
a:hover
{
text-decoration:none;
color: #372F22;
}

a:active
{
text-decoration:none;
color: #372F22;
}

a:focus
{
text-decoration:none;
color: #372F22;
}

#sidebar
{
width:150px;
float:left;
padding-right: 20px;|
}
```

3 In the declaration for the other element, add `margin-left:"?"` or `margin-right:"?"` to create space between the elements. Replace *?* with an appropriate value for the margin, which needs to be at least the width of the floated element.

● When you view the HTML page in a browser, the problems created by the float are fixed.

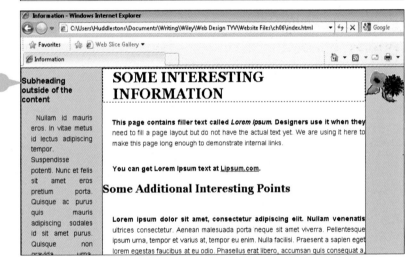

TIP

Why do I need to add a margin to the nonfloated element?
Floated elements are removed from the flow of the page; that is, other elements on the page may act as if the floated element was not where it is. Text correctly wraps around floated elements, but background colors and borders do not. Therefore, you need to add enough margin to the nonfloated element to force it out of the floated element's way.

You can use the CSS `height` property to specify the height of an element, but if you do so and then add more content than fits in the specified height, the browser may choose to either allow the content to flow out of the container to the detriment of your layout, or it might crop or not display the content. Unfortunately, different browsers handle this issue differently, so you cannot be sure how your page will look. The CSS `overflow` property allows you to control this behavior by adding a scrollbar as needed.

Work with Overflow

1 In your editor, open an existing document that contains content divided into groups and an embedded style sheet.

Note: The following steps can also be done using an existing external style sheet.

1
```
styles - Notepad
File  Edit  Format  View  Help
body
{
font-family: Arial, Helvetica, sans-serif;
font-size: 90%;
color: #540907;
background-color: #FFC955;
background-image:url("images/flowers.gif");
background-repeat: no-repeat;
background-position:730px 0;
margin:0;
}

h1, h2
{
font-family: Georgia, "Times New Roman", Times, serif;
}

h1
{
text-transform: uppercase;
padding-left: 20px;
margin-top:0;
margin-bottom:10px;
border: 1px dashed #540907;
```

2 In the declaration for the element you want to set overflow on, type `height: ?;`, replacing `?` with the height of the element. Be sure to include a unit of measurement such as `px`.

```
a:hover
{
text-decoration:none;
color: #372F22;
}

a:active
{
text-decoration:none;
color: #372F22;
}

a:focus
{
text-decoration:none;
color: #372F22;
}

#sidebar
{
width:150px;
float:left;
padding-right: 20px;
```
2 `height:500px;|`
```
}
```

③ On a new line, type
overflow:auto;.

```
a:hover
{
text-decoration:none;
color: #372F22;
}

a:active
{
text-decoration:none;
color: #372F22;
}

a:focus
{
text-decoration:none;
color: #372F22;
}

#sidebar
{
width:150px;
float:left;
padding-right: 20px;
height:500px;
③ overflow:auto;|
}
```

● When you view the HTML
page in a browser, the
element displays a scrollbar.

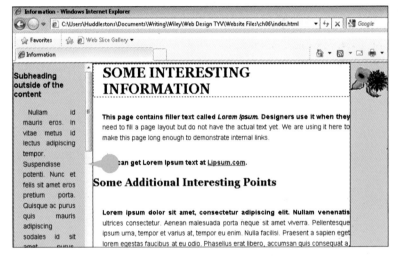

TIP

What are the other options available for overflow?
The other possible values for the overflow property are visible, hidden, and scroll. If you set it
to visible, content that does not fit in the box flows out of it, either overlapping other content or
forcing it down the page. A value of hidden crops the content, cutting it off at the bottom of the box.
The scroll value adds a scrollbar; the difference between scroll and auto is that in the former case,
the scrollbar is always visible, even if not needed, whereas in the later, the scrollbar appears only when
necessary.

CHAPTER 7

Adding Tables and Lists

HTML provides a set of tags that allow you to add tables to present complex data sets and lists to display items in numbered or bulleted list formats.

Tables allow you to present large blocks of data to your users in an organized fashion, such as phone lists, product specification grids, and calendars. HTML uses a set of three tags to define basic tables. The `<table>` tag defines the table itself. Each row of the table is defined by the table row tag, `tr`. Then each cell is created by use of the `td` element, which is short for table data. Each of these tags wraps around the other, so a `td` can appear only between the opening and closing `tr`, which must in turn appear within a `<table>` tag.

Add Data Tables

① In your editor, open a new HTML document that contains the basic HTML tags.

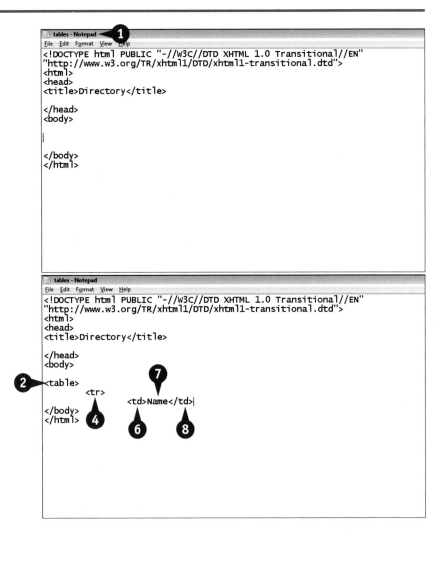

② Within the body, type `<table>`.

③ Press **Enter**.

④ Type `<tr>`.

⑤ Press **Enter**.

⑥ Type `<td>`.

⑦ Type the contents of the first cell of the table.

⑧ Type `</td>`.

Note: The code shown has been indented using **Tab**. This is not required, but highly recommended.

9 Repeat Steps **6** to **8** to add additional cells to the row.

10 Press `Enter`.

11 Type `</tr>`.

12 Repeat Steps **4** to **11** to add additional rows.

13 Press `Enter`.

14 Type `</table>`.

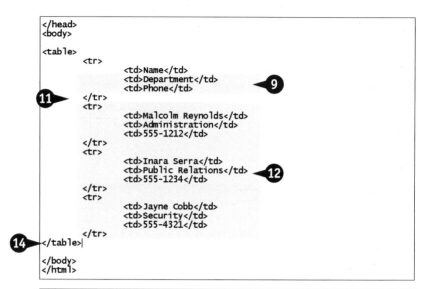

```
</head>
<body>

<table>
        <tr>
                <td>Name</td>
                <td>Department</td>
                <td>Phone</td>                    ◀ 9
11 ▶   </tr>
        <tr>
                <td>Malcolm Reynolds</td>
                <td>Administration</td>
                <td>555-1212</td>
        </tr>
        <tr>
                <td>Inara Serra</td>
                <td>Public Relations</td>          ◀ 12
                <td>555-1234</td>
        </tr>
        <tr>
                <td>Jayne Cobb</td>
                <td>Security</td>
                <td>555-4321</td>
        </tr>
14 ▶</table>|

</body>
</html>
```

● When viewed in a Web browser, the data is laid out in a basic tabular format.

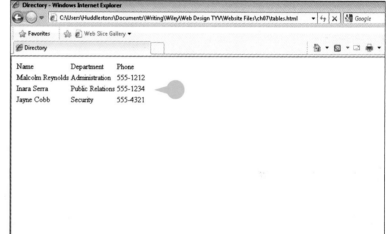

TIP

I have seen pages that use tables to create multicolumn layouts. Is this a good idea?
Not really. For years, before the adoption of CSS, tables provided the only feasible means by which multicolumn layouts could be approximated. However, using tables limits the editability of your page, adds considerably to the size of the page, and restricts the ability of search engines to effectively index your page and of disabled users to effectively use it. Therefore, tables should be limited to presenting tabular data only.

Because CSS styling relies on applying rules to elements on the page, designers are given a rich set of possibilities when styling tables thanks to the number of tags involved. With some creativity, tables can become one of the most visually exciting elements on a page. CSS properties that format text, such as font and color, can be applied to the text in cells. In addition, the `background-color` and `background-image` properties will work for tables, rows, or cells. You can also use CSS to add and format the border of the table.

Format Tables with CSS

1 In your editor, open a document that contains a table.

2 If necessary, add an opening and closing `<style>` tag to the head of the document.

Note: The steps below can also be done in an external style sheet.

1

```
tables - Notepad
File  Edit  Format  View  Help
<!DOCTYPE html PUBLIC "-//W3C//DTD XHTML 1.0 Transitional//EN"
"http://www.w3.org/TR/xhtml1/DTD/xhtml11-transitional.dtd">
<html>
<head>
<title>Directory</title>

<style type="text/css">

</style>

</head>
<body>

<table>
        <tr>
                <td>Name</td>
                <td>Department</td>
                <td>Phone</td>
        </tr>
        <tr>
                <td>Malcolm Reynolds</td>
                <td>Administration</td>
                <td>555-1212</td>
        </tr>
```

2

3 Within the style sheet, type `table`.

4 Press `Enter`.

5 Type {.

6 Press `Enter`.

7 Type `background-color: ?;`, replacing `?` with a valid color value.

```
tables - Notepad
File  Edit  Format  View  Help
<!DOCTYPE html PUBLIC "-//W3C//DTD XHTML 1.0 Transitional//EN"
"http://www.w3.org/TR/xhtml1/DTD/xhtml11-transitional.dtd">
<html>
<head>
<title>Directory</title>

<style type="text/css">

table
{
background-color: #FFC955;|

</style>

</head>
<body>

<table>
        <tr>
                <td>Name</td>
                <td>Department</td>
                <td>Phone</td>
        </tr>
        <tr>
```

3

5

7

8 Press Enter.

9 Type border: ? ? ?;, replacing ? with border width, style, and color values.

10 Press Enter.

11 Type }.

● When viewed in a browser, the table now has the specified background color, and the border is visible around the outside edge of the table.

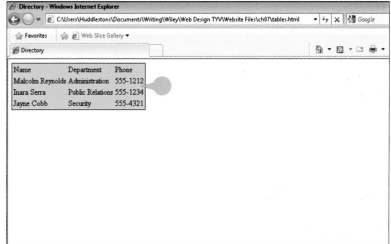

TIPS

Can I add borders to the individual cells?
Yes, by simply creating a CSS declaration that uses td as the selector and a border property as the rule. You may also want to add the border-collapse:collapse rule to the table declaration so that the cell border widths do not appear to be doubled.

Can I create alternating background colors for the rows?
Yes. You simply need to create two classes in your CSS, applying different background-colors to each. Then, add the appropriate class attribute to each alternate <tr> tag in your document.

165

Sometimes, you may need tables that do not follow a simple grid pattern. You may need tables that have cells that span more than one row or column. You can use the HTML `rowspan` and `colspan` attributes, both of which can be added to table cells, to accomplish this. Both take as their value an integer representing the number of cells to be spanned. A row that contains a `colspan` in one of its cells has a correspondingly lower number of overall cells, whereas a `rowspan` results in missing cells from an equal number of rows.

Create Complex Tables

1 In your editor, open a document that contains a table.

```
☐ tables - Notepad ◀ 1
File  Edit  Format  View  Help
<style type="text/css">

table
{
background-color: #FFC955;
border: 1px solid #540907;
}|

</style>

</head>
<body>

<table>
        <tr>
                <td>Name</td>
                <td>Department</td>
                <td>Phone</td>
        </tr>
        <tr>
                <td>Malcolm Reynolds</td>
                <td>Administration</td>
                <td>555-1212</td>
        </tr>
```

2 Within the table, type `<tr>`.

3 Press **Enter**.

4 Type `<td colspan="?">`, replacing *?* with the number of columns you want the cell to span.

5 Type the contents of the cell.

6 Type `</td>`.

```
<table>
        <tr>
                <td>Name</td>
                <td>Department</td>
                <td>Phone</td>
        </tr>
        <tr>
                <td>Malcolm Reynolds</td>
                <td>Administration</td>
                <td>555-1212</td>
        </tr>
        <tr>
                <td>Inara Serra</td>
                <td>Public Relations</td>
                <td>555-1234</td>
        </tr>
        <tr>
                <td>Jayne Cobb</td>
                <td>Security</td>
                <td>555-4321</td>
        </tr>
        <tr>
                <td colspan="3">Other Personnel</td>
</table>

</body>
</html>
```

7 Press `Enter`.

8 Type `</tr>`.

9 Add additional rows as needed to complete the table.

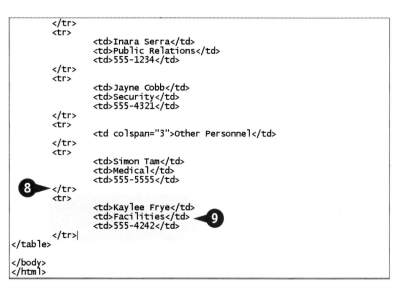

```
                </tr>
                <tr>
                        <td>Inara Serra</td>
                        <td>Public Relations</td>
                        <td>555-1234</td>
                </tr>
                <tr>
                        <td>Jayne Cobb</td>
                        <td>Security</td>
                        <td>555-4321</td>
                </tr>
                <tr>
                        <td colspan="3">Other Personnel</td>
                </tr>
                <tr>
                        <td>Simon Tam</td>
                        <td>Medical</td>
                        <td>555-5555</td>
                </tr>
                <tr>
                        <td>Kaylee Frye</td>
                        <td>Facilities</td>
                        <td>555-4242</td>
                </tr>
</table>

</body>
</html>
```

● When the page is viewed in a browser, the table cell stretches across the specified number of columns.

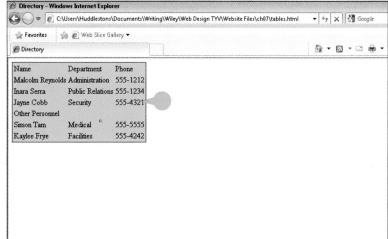

TIPS

Why is it necessary to delete additional cells from the row?

You need to be sure that your HTML tables always follow a grid. If a table had a total of four columns, and one cell in a row spans three columns, then that row should contain only one additional cell, because the other cell represents all three remaining cells.

How do I use rowspan?

The `rowspan` attribute works in essentially the same way as `colspan`. However, because you are having a cell that stretches vertically across multiple rows, you need to delete one cell from each affected row to maintain the overall grid.

Most tables require a row or column of headers to define for the user the data that row or column represents. Often, the data in the table is meaningless without headers. In HTML, you can represent this header information by using the <th> tag for those cells instead of <td>. You are therefore defining individual cells as headers, not entire rows or columns. Text within these header cells is formatted in bold and centered in the cell.

Add a Header Row

1 In your editor, open a document that contains an existing table.

2 Change the opening tag of a cell within the first row of the table from <td> to <th>.

3 Change the closing tag from </td> to </th>.

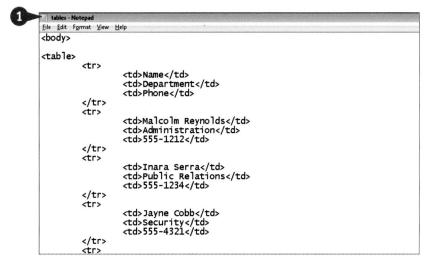

4 Repeat Steps **2** and **3** for each remaining cell in the row.

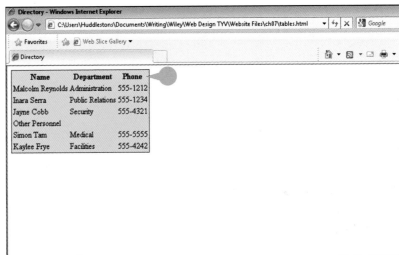

```
tables - Notepad
File  Edit  Format  View  Help
<body>

<table>
        <tr>
                <th>Name</th>
         4      <th>Department</th>
                <th>Phone</th>
        </tr>
        <tr>
                <td>Malcolm Reynolds</td>
                <td>Administration</td>
                <td>555-1212</td>
        </tr>
        <tr>
                <td>Inara Serra</td>
                <td>Public Relations</td>
                <td>555-1234</td>
        </tr>
        <tr>
                <td>Jayne Cobb</td>
                <td>Security</td>
                <td>555-4321</td>
        </tr>
        <tr>
```

● When you view the page in the browser, the header cells are bold and centered.

```
Directory - Windows Internet Explorer
C:\Users\Huddlestons\Documents\Writing\Wiley\Web Design TYV\Website Files\ch07\tables.html
Favorites      Web Slice Gallery
Directory
```

Name	Department	Phone
Malcolm Reynolds	Administration	555-1212
Inara Serra	Public Relations	555-1234
Jayne Cobb	Security	555-4321
Other Personnel		
Simon Tam	Medical	555-5555
Kaylee Frye	Facilities	555-4242

TIPS

Do the header cells have to be in the first row of the table?
No. For some tables, header cells in the left column make more sense. Others might have headers in both the first row and the left column, and still others might have multiple headers. You can use the <th> tag anywhere that it logically makes sense to have the header.

Can I have headers that are not bold or centered?
Yes. Simply create a CSS declaration for the <th> tag, and set font-weight:normal to override the bold and text-align:left to override the alignment. You could, of course, add other properties as well, perhaps setting the background color of the headers or making the font larger.

Most data tables are likely to be made up of two or three sections: a header at the top, a footer at the bottom, and the main body in between. HTML provides tags to denote these three sections: <thead>, <tbody>, and <tfoot>. These tags wrap around the rows that make up each section of the table. Each section can contain one or more rows, although the header and footer each rarely contain more than one. The three table section elements do not alter the default appearance of the table in the browser.

Add Table Sections

1 In your editor, open a Web page that contains a table.

2 Below the table element's opening tag, type <thead>.

3 Immediately following the final </tr> in the header, type </thead>.

1
```
tables.html - Notepad
File  Edit  Format  View  Help
<!DOCTYPE html PUBLIC "-//W3C//DTD XHTML 1.0 Transitional//EN" "http://www
<html>
<head>
<title>Directory</title>

<style type="text/css">

table
{
background-color: #FFC955;
border: 1px solid #540907;
}

</style>

</head>
<body>

<table>
    <thead>
        <tr>
            <th>Name</th>
            <th>Department</th>
            <th>Phone</th>
        </tr>
    </thead>
        <tr>
```
2 <thead>
3 </thead>

4 On the next line, type <tfoot>.

5 Type <tr>.

6 Type <td colspan="?">, replacing ? with a value equal to the number of columns in the table.

7 Add data for the footer.

```
<table>
    <thead>
        <tr>
            <th>Name</th>
            <th>Department</th>
            <th>Phone</th>
        </tr>
    </thead>
    <tfoot>
        <tr>
            <td colspan="3">All numbers are area code 999|
            <td>Malcolm Reynolds</td>
            <td>Administration</td>
            <td>555-1212</td>
        </tr>
        <tr>
            <td>Inara Serra</td>
            <td>Public Relations</td>
            <td>555-1234</td>
        </tr>
        <tr>
            <td>Jayne Cobb</td>
            <td>Security</td>
            <td>555-4321</td>
```

8 Type `</td>`.

9 Type `</tr>`.

10 Type `</tfoot>`.

11 On the next line, type `<tbody>`.

12 After the final `</tr>` of the table, type `</tbody>`.

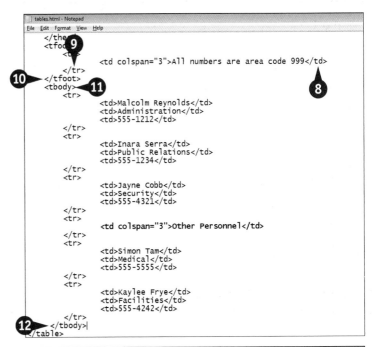

● When the page is viewed in the browser, you can see that the changes have not affected the table's appearance.

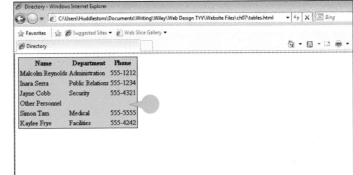

TIP

Why does the <tfoot> come before the <tbody> in the code?
The browser needs to know what the footer information is before it can properly lay out the table. Defining these sections out of order can be a bit confusing, and it may help to initially create the table in the more logical order, with the footer at the bottom, and then cut and paste those rows into the correct place when you are finished creating the table.

You will likely find many reasons to have lists on your pages. You may need to list the ingredients in a recipe or the materials required for a project or tutorial. The most common list, however, might be your navigation; after all, navigation could be said to simply be a list of links to the pages in your site. Perhaps the most common type of list on Web sites is an *unordered*, or bulleted, list. The list is defined via the `<ul>` tag, and each item is denoted by a list item tag, `<li>`.

Add an Unordered List

1 Open a new HTML document in your editor that contains the basic HTML structure tags.

Note: You can complete the following steps on an existing page if you want.

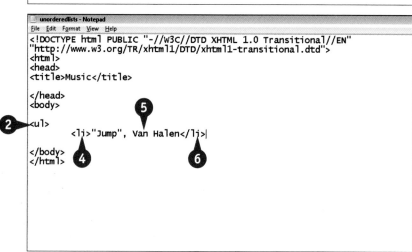

2 In the body of the document, type `<ul>`.

3 Press Enter.

4 Type `<li>`.

5 Type an item for the list.

6 Type `</li>`.

7 Press Enter.

Note: The code shown has been indented using Tab. This is not required, but highly recommended.

8 Repeat Steps **4** to **7** for each additional item in the list.

9 Press Enter.

10 Type `</ul>`.

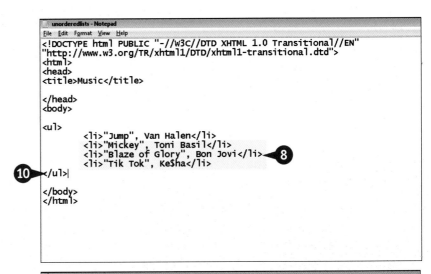

● When you view your page in a browser, the items appear in a bulleted list.

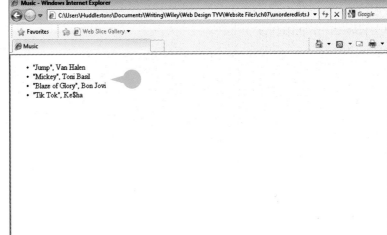

TIPS

Can I change the bullet?
Yes. CSS contains a set of properties for styling lists that includes the ability to change the bullet into any number of symbols, including your own images. Styling lists is covered later in this chapter.

Can I nest lists inside other lists?
Yes. Simply put a new `<ul>` and set of `<li>` tags as children of an `<li>` tag in the outer list. The nested list will be indented further and appear with a different bullet character.

Ordered or numbered lists are less common than unordered or bulleted lists, but are nonetheless quite useful on many sites. The ordered list uses an <ol> tag to define the overall list, but then relies on <li> tags to define the items, just as does the unordered list. Browsers automatically control the numbering of items of the list, so you can freely add, remove, and rearrange the items without needing to worry about the numbers themselves. Nested, ordered lists use different numbering schemes to differentiate them.

Add an Ordered List

1 Open a new or existing HTML document in your editor.

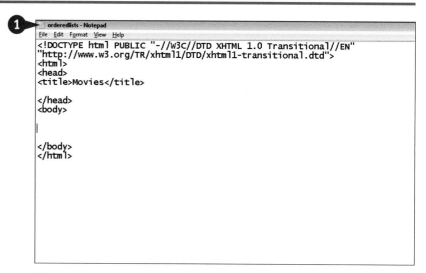

2 In the body of the document, type <ol>.

3 Press Enter.

4 Type <li>.

5 Type an item for the list.

6 Type </li>.

7 Press Enter.

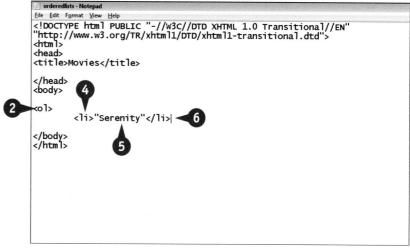

8 Repeat Steps **4** to **7** for each additional item in the list.

9 Press `Enter`.

10 Type `</ol>`.

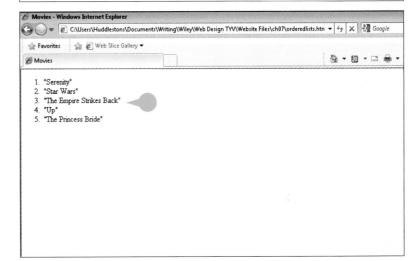

```
orderedlists - Notepad
File  Edit  Format  View  Help
<!DOCTYPE html PUBLIC "-//W3C//DTD XHTML 1.0 Transitional//EN"
"http://www.w3.org/TR/xhtml1/DTD/xhtml1-transitional.dtd">
<html>
<head>
<title>Movies</title>

</head>
<body>

<ol>
        <li>"Serenity"</li>
        <li>"Star Wars"</li>
        <li>"The Empire Strikes Back"</li>
        <li>"Up"</li>
        <li>"The Princess Bride"</li>
</ol>|

</body>
</html>
```

● When you view your page in a browser, the items appear in a numbered list.

```
Movies - Windows Internet Explorer
C:\Users\Huddlestons\Documents\Writing\Wiley\Web Design TYV\Website Files\ch07\orderedlists.htn
Favorites        Web Slice Gallery ▼
Movies

    1. "Serenity"
    2. "Star Wars"
    3. "The Empire Strikes Back"
    4. "Up"
    5. "The Princess Bride"
```

TIP

Can I use letters instead of numbers?
Yes. CSS allows you to change the list to appear using letters instead of numbers. In fact, upper- and lowercase Roman numerals, as well as letters in nine other languages, are supported. Be aware, however, that no standard specifies what letter should be used for the 27th item in a list if using the English alphabet, so you may get unpredictable results on long lists.

CSS provides several properties to style lists. Two very common properties are adjusting the indentation of the list items and changing the bullet type. You can use margins and padding to control or eliminate the indentation of the list. The CSS `list-style-type` property allows you to change the bullet for unordered lists. Possible values are `disc`, `square`, or `circle`. For numbered lists, you can use the property to change the numbering scheme. Some common values include `lower-roman` or `upper-roman` for Roman numerals, `lower-alpha` or `upper-alpha` for English alphabetic characters, and `decimal` or `decimal-leading-zero`.

Style Lists

① In your editor, open an HTML document that contains an unordered list.

② If necessary, add a set of `<style>` tags to the head of the document.

Note: The following steps can be completed in an external style sheet if you want.

①

```
unorderedlists - Notepad
File  Edit  Format  View  Help
<!DOCTYPE html PUBLIC "-//W3C//DTD XHTML 1.0 Transitional//EN"
"http://www.w3.org/TR/xhtml1/DTD/xhtml11-transitional.dtd">
<html>
<head>
<title>Music</title>

<style type="text/css">

                                                          ②

</style>

</head>
<body>

<ul>
        <li>"Jump", Van Halen</li>
        <li>"Mickey", Toni Basil</li>
        <li>"Blaze of Glory", Bon Jovi</li>
        <li>"Tik Tok", Ke$ha</li>
</ul>
```

③ Within the style sheet, type `ul`.

④ Press **Enter**.

⑤ Type `{`.

⑥ Press **Enter**.

⑦ Type `list-style-type: ?;`, replacing *?* with `disc`, `circle`, or `square`.

⑧ Press **Enter**.

⑤

```
unorderedlists - Notepad
File  Edit  Format  View  Help
<!DOCTYPE html PUBLIC "-//W3C//DTD XHTML 1.0 Transitional//EN"
"http://www.w3.org/TR/xhtml1/DTD/xhtml11-transitional.dtd">
<html>
<head>
<title>Music</title>

<style type="text/css">

ul  ③
{
list-style-type: square;  ⑦

</style>

</head>
<body>

<ul>
        <li>"Jump", Van Halen</li>
        <li>"Mickey", Toni Basil</li>
        <li>"Blaze of Glory", Bon Jovi</li>
        <li>"Tik Tok", Ke$ha</li>
</ul>

</body>
</html>
```

9 Type `margin-left: ?;`, replacing *?* with the amount of left margin you want to set.

10 Press **Enter**.

11 Type `padding-left: ?;`, replacing *?* with the amount of left padding you want to set.

12 Press **Enter**.

13 Type `}`.

● When you view the page in a browser, the list is no longer indented and the new bullet is used.

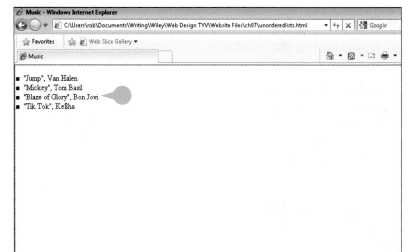

```
<style type="text/css">

ul
{
list-style-type: square;
margin-left:5px;
padding-left:5px;
}

</style>

</head>
<body>

<ul>
        <li>"Jump", Van Halen</li>
        <li>"Mickey", Toni Basil</li>
        <li>"Blaze of Glory", Bon Jovi</li>
        <li>"Tik Tok", Ke$ha</li>
</ul>

</body>
</html>
```

Music - Windows Internet Explorer

C:\Users\rob\Documents\Writing\Wiley\Web Design TYV\Website Files\ch07\unorderedlists.html

Favorites   Web Slice Gallery ▾

Music

■ "Jump", Van Halen
■ "Mickey", Toni Basil
■ "Blaze of Glory", Bon Jovi
■ "Tik Tok", Ke$ha

TIPS

Can I get rid of the bullet altogether, or use my own image?
You can eliminate the bullet by using `list-style-type:none;` in your style sheet. Custom images can be used with the `list-style-image: url(?);` rule, replacing *?* with a path to the image.

Why do I need to set both margin and padding to adjust the indentation?
Some browsers indent the list using the `margin` property, whereas others use the `padding` property. To make sure that your list indents in the same way on all browsers, you should always specify both, setting them to the same value.

Creating a Page Visually in Dreamweaver

Dreamweaver offers a wide range of powerful tools to simplify the process of creating Web pages, many enabling you to do so without typing code.

Introduction to Dreamweaver's Interface

s a part of Adobe's Creative Suite, Dreamweaver's interface is similar to Photoshop, Illustrator, and Fireworks. The Dreamweaver interface is made up of three basic elements: the menu bar, the panels, and the main workspace. The panels allow you to add elements to the page, control your site's file structure, and modify items you have inserted. When you first launch Dreamweaver, the main workspace displays the Welcome screen. Once you open a document, most of the panels become activated to allow you to use them.

Menu Bar

The menus provide access to Dreamweaver's commands.

Workspace Menu

You can switch between a variety of workspaces, or panel layouts, using the options presented here.

Panels

The primary functionality of the program can be accessed from these panels. Double-click the title of a panel to open or collapse it.

Properties Panel

This panel displays the properties of the currently selected objects, and changes depending on the type of object selected.

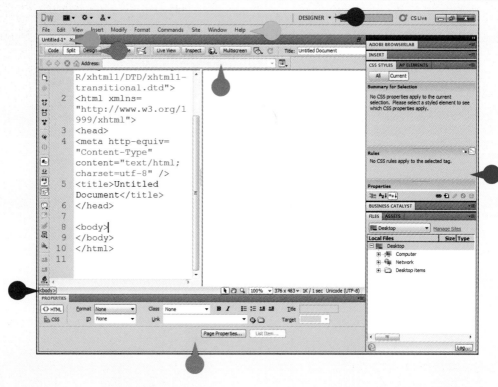

Tag Chooser

Quickly select specific HTML elements in your document by clicking them.

Browser Navigation Bar

While using Dreamweaver's Live view feature, you can navigate to pages or sites just as you would in a normal browser.

Toolbar

Switch between Dreamweaver's views or add a title to your document using these tools.

Document Tabs

Switch between open documents using these tabs.

Define a Site in Dreamweaver

Y̶ou will primarily use Dreamweaver to create and edit Web sites — collections of related pages. Although you can work with individual pages, you will find that many advanced features become available only when you define a site. Earlier, in your site planning, you will have created a single root folder to hold all of your site's files. At its simplest, defining a site in Dreamweaver allows you to tell the program where these files are. Later, you can configure additional settings to upload files to your Web host.

Define a Site in Dreamweaver

1 Click **Site**.

2 Click **New Site**.

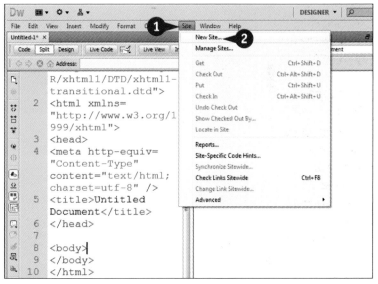

The Site Setup dialog box appears.

3 Type a name for your site.

4 Either type the path or browse to the folder on your hard drive that contains your site's files.

5 Click **Save**.

The site is created.

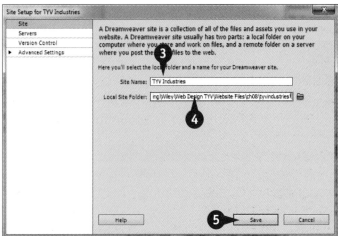

Create a New Document

A s with other programs, you can create a new document in Dreamweaver by selecting **New** from the File menu. If you have no documents open, you can also create a new document from the Welcome screen. Dreamweaver contains a set of starter pages that you can use to jumpstart your designs. The starter pages use CSS for layout, freeing you from having to implement the CSS code yourself. You can also select the DOCTYPE you want to use for your document, and link it to an external style sheet.

Create a New Document

1 Click **File**.

2 Click **New**.

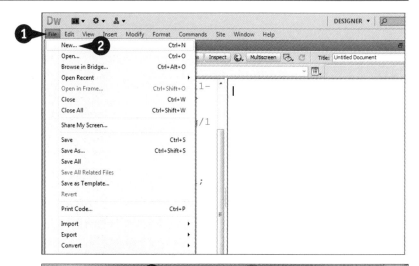

The New Document dialog box appears.

3 Select **Blank Page**.

4 Select **HTML**.

5 Select a layout.

6 Click **Create**.

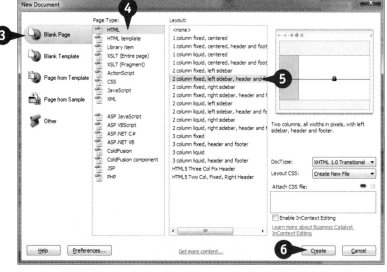

The Save Style Sheet File As dialog box appears.

7 Type a name for your style sheet.

8 Click **Save**.

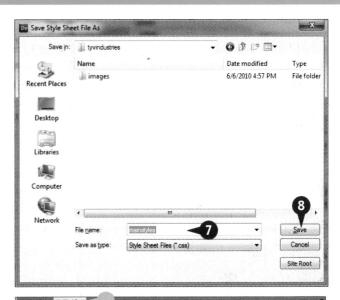

● The new document is created.

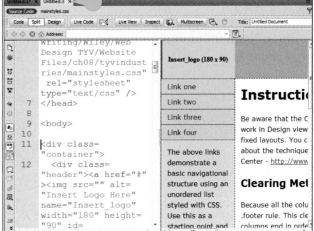

TIP

What are the differences between the starter page layouts?
The starter page layouts provided include one-, two-, or three-column pages. Fixed layouts use pixel dimensions for the layout, meaning that the page does not expand or collapse as your users resize their browser window. The liquid layouts, on the other hand, use percentages for the widths, so the layouts change to fit the screen size. Some of the layouts also contain areas for headers and footers.

Replace the Logo Placeholder

Sometimes, you need to design the layout of the page before you receive the content, including the images. Dreamweaver includes a feature called an image placeholder that allows you to place the HTML <img> tag on your page and then easily replace it later with the actual image. When you receive the final image, you can use the Properties panel at the bottom of the screen to point to the correct image. The starter pages that come with Dreamweaver include a placeholder image in the header designed to allow you to quickly add your own logo.

Replace the Logo Placeholder

1 Double-click the logo placeholder.

The Select Image Source dialog box appears.

2 Navigate to your images directory.

3 Select your logo.

4 Click **OK**.

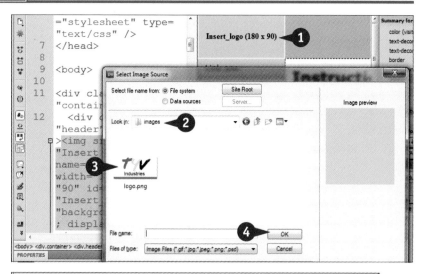

● The logo appears on the page.

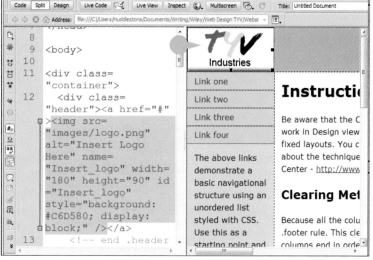

Replace the Main Content

The main content in the starter pages includes instructions on how to use them. Although you can read over these instructions, you will want to remove this content and replace it with your own. This content can consist of anything you would normally place on Web pages, be it headings, paragraphs, lists, or additional images. The starter pages contain several headings that you can replace with your own, or they can be deleted if you do not need them. You can select the text and type over it to keep the existing tags in place, or delete the selected text to remove the headings.

Replace the Main Content

1 Select the Instructions header.

2 Type your own main header.

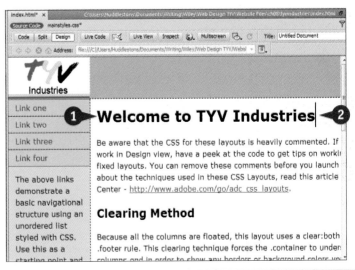

3 Select the remaining content in the main section.

4 Type your own content, or paste it from another source.

The sample content is replaced with your content.

Replace the Content in the Sidebar and Footer

The starter pages consist of three basic layouts for the main content. There are one-column, two-column, and three-column layouts. The two- and three-column layouts contain one or two sidebars for you to add additional content. Many of the layouts also contain a footer area, often used for copyright notices. Rather than type the new content, you can copy and paste it from other sources. Be aware, however, that if you copy and paste from a word processor or other program that formats text, some or all of that formatting may be copied with the text.

Replace the Content in the Sidebar and Footer

1 Select the text in the sidebar.

2 Type your own content, or paste it from another source.

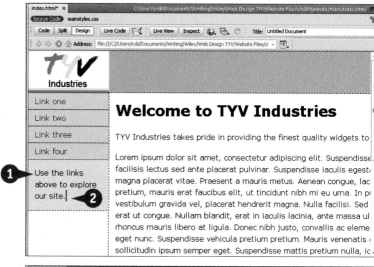

3 Select the content in the footer.

4 Replace it with your own content.

Note: To insert the copyright symbol, select **Insert, HTML, Special Characters**, and **Copyright**.

The content in the sidebar and footer is replaced.

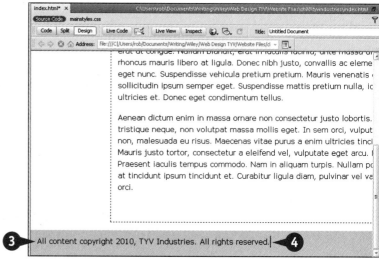

Add Navigation

Dreamweaver's starter pages include a set of sample navigation links that can be quickly converted into your site's primary navigation in the sidebars. These sidebars have a list styled to look like navigation buttons. You can simply replace the placeholder text and add hyperlinks to create your navigation. Hyperlinks can be added in Dreamweaver by entering the address to which you want the link to point in the Properties panel. Part of the style sheet's specification for the list is that links are not underlined.

Add Navigation

1 Select **Link one**.

2 Type the text you want to use for your first link.

3 On the Properties panel, replace the # in the Link text box with the address to your page.

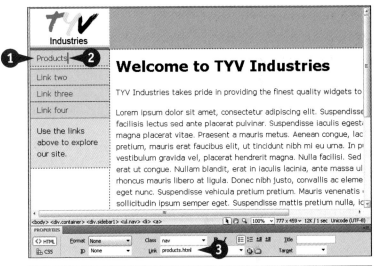

4 Repeat Steps **1** to **3** for each remaining link on the page.

5 If you need more than four links, press Enter.

6 Type the new link text.

7 On the Properties panel, type an address in the Link text box.

8 Press Enter.

The navigation is created.

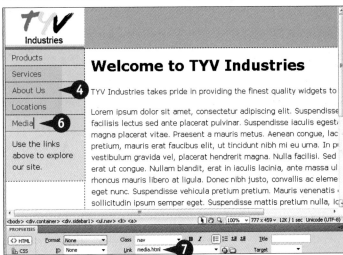

Add Images

You can add images to your page using Dreamweaver's Insert panel, which allows you to simply navigate to the PNG, GIF, or JPEG image on your hard drive. Images should already be located somewhere within your site's folder, ideally in a directory devoted solely to images. If you navigate to an image outside of your root, Dreamweaver asks if you want to move it into your site. It then copies the image into the directory that you specify. When you insert the image, Dreamweaver prompts you for alternate text. This provides a text description of the image for people with disabilities.

Add Images

1 Click the spot on the page where you want to place an image.

2 Double-click **Insert**.

The Insert panel opens.

3 Click **Images:Image**.

4 Click **Image**.

The Select Image Source dialog box appears.

5 Navigate to the folder that contains your image.

6 Select the image.

7 Click **OK**.

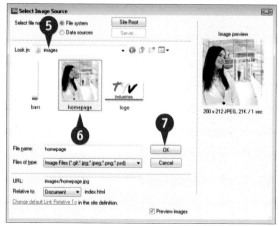

The Image Tag Accessibility
Attributes dialog box
appears.

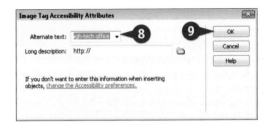

8 Type a description of the
image in the Alternate Text
box.

9 Click **OK**.

● The image is inserted into
the page.

TIPS

Do I need to provide alternate text for every image?
Screen readers — devices used by blind users — read the alternate text when they encounter images on Web pages, so you should always provide descriptive text for every image you insert.

Can I resize an image in Dreamweaver?
Yes, you can enter a new width and height in the Properties panel. Be aware, however, that this merely adds HTML code to change the size, and is not as effective as using an image-editing tool for resizing.

Insert a Photoshop Image

As a part of Adobe's Creative Suite, Dreamweaver includes features specifically designed to work with other Creative Suite tools. Normally, images created in Photoshop and saved using its native PSD format cannot be inserted into Web pages, but Dreamweaver actually allows you to select a PSD file when you use the Insert Image feature. When you select a PSD, Dreamweaver automatically prompts you for optimization settings, and saves a copy of the image in your site's folder as a JPEG, GIF, or PNG.

Insert a Photoshop Image

1 Click the spot on your page where you want to insert the image.

2 Click **Images:Image**.

The Select Image Source dialog box appears.

3 Navigate to the folder that contains your Photoshop PSD image.

4 Select the image.

5 Click **OK**.

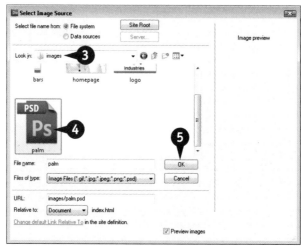

The Image Preview dialog box appears.

6 Select a desired format.

7 Select desired optimization settings.

8 Click **File**.

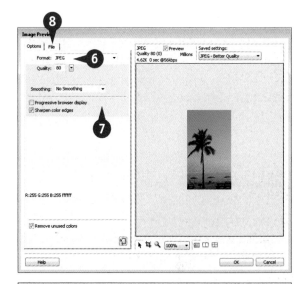

The File tab appears.

9 Set a desired scale, or enter width and height settings.

10 Click **OK**.

Dreamweaver prompts you to save the image.

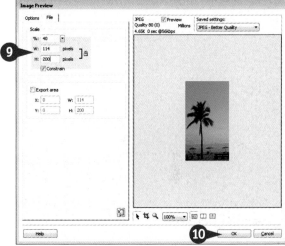

TIPS

Can I insert images created in other image-editing tools?

You can use any editor to create the images for your Web site. However, you must use that editor to save the image as a GIF, JPEG, or PNG before inserting it into Dreamweaver. Only Photoshop images may be inserted directly.

When I set the size in the Image Preview dialog box, am I actually resizing the image?

Yes. Unlike setting an image size in Dreamweaver's Properties panel, the Image Preview dialog box actually resizes the image based on the values you specify.

continued ▶

Insert a Photoshop Image (continued)

Once you have selected a Photoshop image and selected its optimization settings, you can determine where on your site you wish to save the image, set its alternate text, and insert it into the page. At this point, inserting the image works the same as inserting any other image on your page. In fact, that is what you are doing: the original PSD is not being added to your image, but rather, you are inserting the optimized JPG, GIF or PNG.

Insert a Photoshop Image (continued)

The Save Web Image dialog box appears.

11 Navigate to the folder within your site into which you want to save the image.

12 Enter a filename for the image.

13 Click **Save**.

The Image Tag Accessibility Attributes dialog box appears.

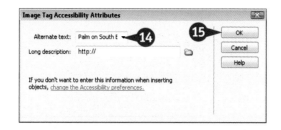

14 Enter a description of the image.

15 Click **OK**.

● The image is inserted into the page.

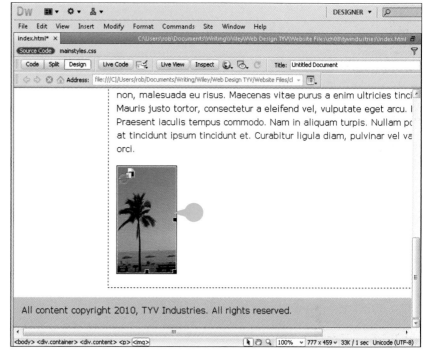

All content copyright 2010, TYV Industries. All rights reserved.

TIPS

Has Dreamweaver modified my original Photoshop image?
No. Dreamweaver has created a new version of your image, saved as a JPEG, GIF, or PNG, depending on what format you selected. Your original PSD file is not moved or changed in any way.

Can any Photoshop image be imported this way?
Yes. All Photoshop images, no matter how complex, can be imported directly into Dreamweaver using this technique.

Edit a Photoshop Image in Dreamweaver

When you directly insert a Photoshop image into Dreamweaver, a link back to the original source PSD file is maintained, which allows you to edit the image and have the image in your Web page update automatically. The image displays an icon in its top left corner indicating that it is from a Photoshop image, and also indicating whether or not the version you currently see on the page corresponds to the most recent version of the Photoshop image. If you alter the PSD, this icon changes, but you can simply click the Synch button on the Properties panel to update the image.

Edit a Photoshop Image in Dreamweaver

1 Click an image on your page that was inserted from a Photoshop PSD file.

2 On the Properties panel, click the **Edit** button (🖻).

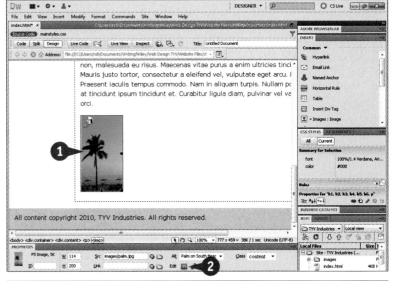

The original PSD image is opened in Photoshop.

3 Make any desired edits to the image in Photoshop.

4 Click **File**.

5 Click **Save**.

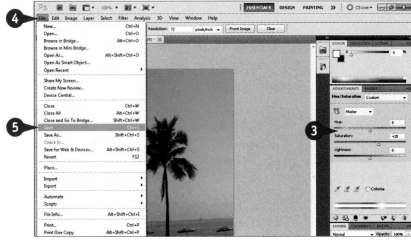

6 Return to Dreamweaver.

● The image indicates that the original asset has been modified.

7 Click the **Update from Original** button (⬚).

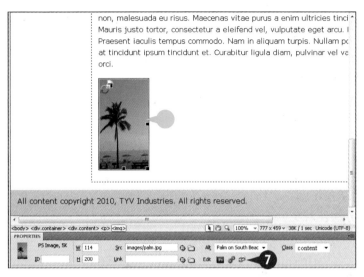

● The image updates, using all of the original optimization settings.

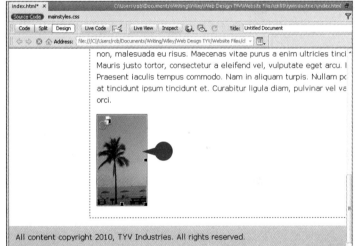

TIPS

Can I change the optimization settings?
Yes. Click the **Edit Image Settings** button (⬚) on the Properties panel to reopen the Image Preview dialog box and change the settings. Dreamweaver overwrites the copy of the image with a new image using the new settings.

What happens if I move or rename the original PSD image?
You can relink the original PSD image in Dreamweaver by browsing to the new location using the Original field on the Properties panel.

Modify CSS

Dreamweaver uses CSS by default for all formatting you do on the page. Its CSS panel provides a single location for you to manage your site's styles. From the panel, you can view the CSS currently in use in your page, either by seeing all of the selectors in a list or by viewing the rules that currently apply to the element or object you have selected. Either way, you can modify existing properties or add new ones. Throughout the process, Dreamweaver presents you with lists of options, minimizing the amount of typing you need to do.

Modify CSS

1 In Design view, click the element you want to style.

● You can use the Tag Chooser at the bottom of the Design window to make a more precise selection.

2 Click **Current**.

3 Click the value of an existing property.

4 Select a new value.

This example changes the background color of the header to white.

5 Click **Add Property**.

6 Select the property you want to add.

7 Set its value.

This example adds a background image to the header.

● The style sheet is modified. Design view updates to display the changed property.

TIPS

Does Dreamweaver correctly display all styles?
Unfortunately, Dreamweaver's Design view does not always display complex CSS styles accurately, particularly when it comes to using CSS layouts. You can preview your page in a browser or use Live view to see how the page will really look.

Is there an easy way to tell what styles are being applied to an element?
Yes. When you select an area on the page, the Code Navigator appears as a small ship's wheel icon (⊛). You can click the icon to see a display of all of the styles currently applied to that area of the page, and you can click a style listed to edit it.

Add New Styles

In addition to modifying existing styles, Dreamweaver makes it easy to add new styles to elements on pages. The New CSS Style button at the bottom of the CSS panel opens a dialog box that you can use to set the desired selector. Then, you are presented with another dialog box that contains most CSS properties, organized into categories. Most of these properties are presented with drop-down lists that allow you to choose the value you want to use from available defaults. Once you finish setting up the rules, you can click OK to have the style added to your style sheet.

Add New Styles

1 Click or select an element on the page to which you want to add a style.

2 On the CSS Styles panel, click the **New CSS Rule** button (🖹).

The New CSS Rule dialog box opens.

3 Choose the type of selector you want to use.

4 Type the name of the selector.

5 Choose whether you want the style added to an existing external style sheet, a new external style sheet, or embedded on the page.

6 Click **OK**.

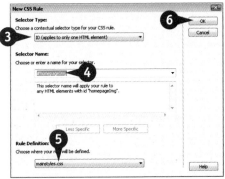

The CSS Rule Definition dialog box appears.

7 Select a category.

8 Apply the desired settings.

In this example, the image has a float property applied, allowing the text to wrap around it.

9 Click **OK**.

● The new style is created and applied to the page.

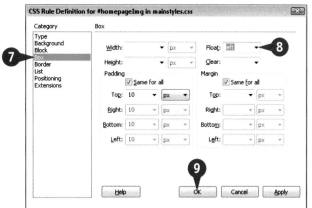

TIPS

How do I apply a class or ID to elements on the page?
You can apply class or ID styles to elements by selecting the element in Design view, and then selecting the desired class from the Class or ID drop-down menu on the Properties panel.

How do I apply styles to pieces of text?
You can select a portion of your text and then choose an appropriate class from the Class drop-down menu on the Properties panel. Dreamweaver automatically adds a `<span>` tag to your code.

Preview the Page Using Live View

Dreamweaver's Live view uses a real browser rendering engine to display your page exactly as it would appear in a browser, without requiring you to leave the program. The rendering engine used in Live view is the same as that used by Apple's Safari and Google's Chrome browser, among others. You can follow hyperlinks and navigate through your site in Live view, but you cannot edit your page in Live view. However, you can use Dreamweaver's Split view to look at your page in Live view while you view — and edit — the source code.

Preview the Page Using Live View

1 On the toolbar, click **Live View**.

The page appears in Live view.

2 Click **Design**.

The page returns to Design view.

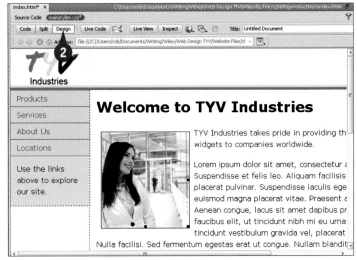

Preview the Page in a Browser

Live view is helpful for testing pages, but you should remember that it only mirrors the display of the page in Safari and Chrome. Although most of the time, if your page looks correct in Live view, it will be correct in other browsers, you should still view your page in other browsers, such as Microsoft's Internet Explorer and Mozilla Firefox, because you may still find issues with the display that need to be fixed. Remember, however, that pixel-perfect rendering consistency across browsers is virtually impossible, so you only need to be sure that the page looks good in all browsers, not that it looks precisely the same.

Preview the Page in a Browser

1 From the toolbar, click the **Preview/Debug in Browser** button ().

2 Select the browser you want to use to view your page.

The page appears in the selected browser.

Preview the Page in Other Browsers Using BrowserLab

One of the biggest challenges facing designers is the need to test on multiple browsers across multiple operating systems. This may well be cost-prohibitive, because it at a minimum requires that you have computers that run both Windows and the Macintosh OS. Even then, you can have problems, because you can run only one version of Internet Explorer on a machine. BrowserLab is an online service Adobe provides that allows you to view your page in a large set of browsers, including ones you do not have on your system.

Preview the Page in Other Browsers Using BrowserLab

1 Double-click **Adobe Browserlab** to open the panel.

2 Click **Preview**.

BrowserLab launches.

3 Click **Try BrowserLab**.

The Sign Up for CS Live dialog box appears.

④ Click **Next**.

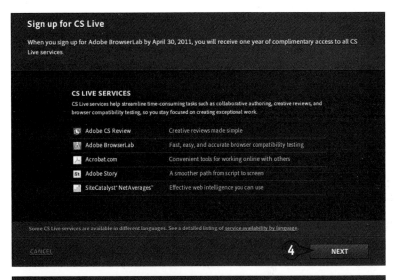

⑤ Enter your Adobe ID and password, or click the **Create Adobe ID** button to create an account.

⑥ Click **Sign In**.

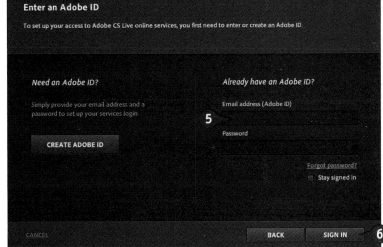

TIPS

Is BrowserLab free?

BrowserLab is one of the CS Live services Adobe offers. Those who register for an account by April 30, 2011 receive one free year; after that, a monthly fee applies.

What are the other CS Live services?

CS Live also includes CS Review for online reviewing of documents; Adobe Story, a script writing utility; SiteCatalyst NetAverages, to view site statistics; and Acrobat.com, which enables online document creation, online meetings, and more. You can get more information on CS Live at www.adobe.com/products/creativesuite/cslive/.

continued ▶

Once you have an account and log into BrowserLab, you can use it to test your page in the various browsers it offers. As of this writing, BrowserLab automatically loads your page in seven browsers: Firefox 3.0 for Mac, Safari 3.0 for Mac, Internet Explorer 6.0 for Windows, Firefox 3.6 for Mac, Chrome 3.0 for Windows, Internet Explorer 7.0 for Windows, and Internet Explorer 8.0 for Windows. You can also choose to have it load your page in a variety of other browsers. As the browser market changes, Adobe may adjust the browsers it offers in BrowserLab.

Preview the Page in Other Browsers Using BrowserLab (continued)

The Sign In dialog box appears.

7 Type your username and password.

BrowserLab loads the page from Dreamweaver. The Firefox 3.0 – OS X page appears.

8 Click the **View** button down arrow.

● A list of other browsers appears.

9 Select another browser.

● The page loads in another browser.

TIPS

Can I view pages in more than one browser at a time?

Yes. Click the **View** button to switch to a 2-Up view to see the page in two browsers side by side, or **Onion Skin** to see them superimposed on one another.

Where can I get more information on using BrowserLab?

Click the **Home** button at the top of the screen to see system updates and access pages that provide tips and tricks on using BrowserLab.

CHAPTER 9

Adding Interactivity and Multimedia

Interactivity and multimedia can easily set your site apart from others.

Whether you add JavaScript, Flash, or video, interactivity can add a new

dimension to your site.

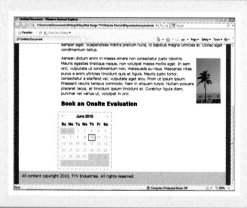

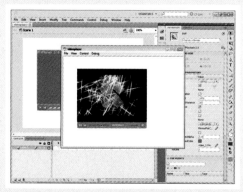

Introduction to JavaScript and Ajax

In the early days of the Web, a need arose to allow designers to provide some sort of interactivity for their users. Netscape, at the time the developer of the most popular browser, created a lightweight scripting language for that purpose. Named JavaScript, it was first introduced with the Netscape 2 browser in 1996. Although attempts were made to create competing languages, eventually every browser manufacturer adopted JavaScript in its browsers. The European Computer Manufacturers Association maintains a standardized version, known more formally as ECMAScript.

Writing JavaScript

JavaScript is text-based, and can be written in any text editor. Almost all editors designed for writing Web pages, whether they are code-based or visual editors, likely provide help in the form of code hints and syntax highlighting for JavaScript.

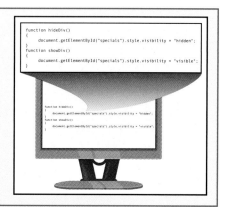

Running JavaScript

In order to run, your JavaScript code must be interpreted by an application. In most cases, the application being used to run it will be a Web browser. However, many other applications support JavaScript in some form today, so you might also encounter it being used elsewhere.

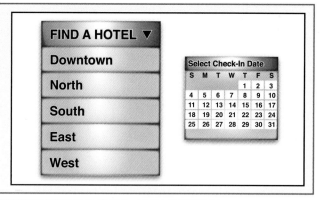

Browser Support

Every major modern browser offers full support of JavaScript. Microsoft's Internet Explorer officially supports ECMAScript, but this in effect means support of JavaScript. You can safely assume that, unless your user has specifically disabled it, all browsers will run your scripts.

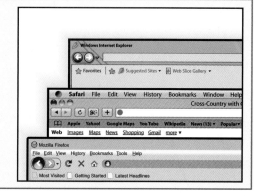

JavaScript Is Not Java

Java is a very powerful object-oriented programming language from Sun Microsystems, whereas JavaScript is a scripting language. Except for the name, they in fact have absolutely nothing in common. Although beginning Web designers commonly confuse the two, care should be taken not to because no help is available for Java that would be useful for JavaScript programming, and vice versa.

JavaScript and HTML

JavaScript allows developers to achieve many effects not offered by HTML. For example, HTML form controls are extremely limited, and offer little in the way of validation mechanisms to ensure that the data being entered is what is expected. JavaScript allows developers to write as complicated a validation scheme as they need on top of the form. JavaScript can also work in conjunction with CSS to achieve advanced visual effects such as drop-down menus, accordion effects, and much more.

Ajax

Ajax was developed as a way to allow designers and developers to extend the capabilities offered by HTML and CSS. Most Ajax development is done through prebuilt JavaScript libraries, saving you time in having to rewrite code. The better, more widely adopted libraries focus on good usability and accessibility, and also provide many features such as the ability for JavaScript to refresh only a portion of a Web page. The extremely popular Google Maps application is an example of Ajax.

JavaScript Libraries

Today, many libraries of JavaScript functions exist that enable developers to implement complex scripting effects while requiring that they write little or no script themselves. These libraries free developers from having to spend time coding and debugging applications, and allow them instead to focus on the end-user experience.

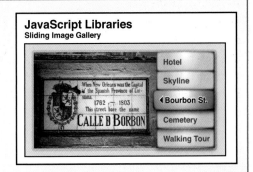

Embed JavaScript in HTML

JavaScript code can either be embedded directly within an HTML page or written in a separate text file that is then linked to the page. You can embed JavaScript by adding a `<style>` tag to your page. The tag is unique in HTML in that it is the only tag that can be legally placed in either the `<head>` or the `<body>` of the document. The tag takes a required `type` attribute, which is always set to a value of `text/javascript`. Be sure to remember the closing script tag because the browser will fail to show anything on the page without it.

Embed JavaScript in HTML

1 Open an HTML document in your editor.

```
index - Notepad
File  Edit  Format  View  Help
<!DOCTYPE html PUBLIC "-//W3C//DTD XHTML 1.0 Transitional//EN"
"http://www.w3.org/TR/xhtml1/DTD/xhtml1-transitional.dtd">
<html xmlns="http://www.w3.org/1999/xhtml">
<head>
<meta http-equiv="Content-Type" content="text/html; charset=utf-8" />
<title>Untitled Document</title>
<link href="mainstyles.css" rel="stylesheet" type="text/css" />

</head>

<body>

<div class="container">
   <div class="header"><a href="#"><img src="images/logo.png" alt="Insert
name="Insert_logo" width="180" height="90" id="Insert_logo" style="backgr
display:block;" /></a>
     <!-- end .header --></div>
   <div class="sidebar1">
     <ul class="nav">
       <li><a href="products.html">Products</a></li>
       <li><a href="services.html">Services</a></li>
       <li><a href="about.html">About Us</a></li>
```

2 Within the `<head>` section, type `<script`.

```
index - Notepad
File  Edit  Format  View  Help
<!DOCTYPE html PUBLIC "-//W3C//DTD XHTML 1.0 Transitional//EN"
"http://www.w3.org/TR/xhtml1/DTD/xhtml1-transitional.dtd">
<html xmlns="http://www.w3.org/1999/xhtml">
<head>
<meta http-equiv="Content-Type" content="text/html; charset=utf-8" />
<title>Untitled Document</title>
<link href="mainstyles.css" rel="stylesheet" type="text/css" />
<script |
</head>

<body>

<div class="container">
   <div class="header"><a href="#"><img src="images/logo.png" alt="Insert
name="Insert_logo" width="180" height="90" id="Insert_logo" style="backgr
display:block;" /></a>
     <!-- end .header --></div>
   <div class="sidebar1">
     <ul class="nav">
       <li><a href="products.html">Products</a></li>
       <li><a href="services.html">Services</a></li>
       <li><a href="about.html">About Us</a></li>
```

3 Type `type="text/javascript">`.

4 Press `Enter` twice.

```
index - Notepad
File  Edit  Format  View  Help
<!DOCTYPE html PUBLIC "-//W3C//DTD XHTML 1.0 Transitional//EN"
"http://www.w3.org/TR/xhtml1/DTD/xhtml1-transitional.dtd">
<html xmlns="http://www.w3.org/1999/xhtml">
<head>
<meta http-equiv="Content-Type" content="text/html; charset=utf-8" />
<title>Untitled Document</title>
<link href="mainstyles.css" rel="stylesheet" type="text/css" />
<script type="text/javascript">

|
</head>               3

<body>

<div class="container">
    <div class="header"><a href="#"><img src="images/logo.png" alt="Insert
name="Insert_logo" width="180" height="90" id="Insert_logo" style="backgr
display:block;" /></a>
        <!-- end .header --></div>
    <div class="sidebar1">
        <ul class="nav">
            <li><a href="products.html">Products</a></li>
```

5 Type `</script>`.

The code to embed JavaScript is added to the page.

```
index - Notepad
File  Edit  Format  View  Help
<!DOCTYPE html PUBLIC "-//W3C//DTD XHTML 1.0 Transitional//EN"
"http://www.w3.org/TR/xhtml1/DTD/xhtml1-transitional.dtd">
<html xmlns="http://www.w3.org/1999/xhtml">
<head>
<meta http-equiv="Content-Type" content="text/html; charset=utf-8" />
<title>Untitled Document</title>
<link href="mainstyles.css" rel="stylesheet" type="text/css" />
<script type="text/javascript">
</script> |
</head>

<body>

<div class="container">
    <div class="header"><a href="#"><img src="images/logo.png" alt="Insert
name="Insert_logo" width="180" height="90" id="Insert_logo" style="backgr
display:block;" /></a>
        <!-- end .header --></div>
    <div class="sidebar1">
        <ul class="nav">
            <li><a href="products.html">Products</a></li>
```

TIP

Will my JavaScript always work?

Every modern browser fully supports JavaScript. However, all browsers also provide users with the option to disable it. Although only a very small percentage of users will ever disable JavaScript, you need to be sure to provide a backup if your script is mission-critical; that is, if your user will be unable to effectively use your site without it. For example, if you are using JavaScript to create drop-down menus for navigation, be sure to provide normal text links as well.

Write a Function

M ost JavaScript code is encapsulated into functions. A *function* is a common programming construct that allows you to combine a set of related code together into a single block. Functions allow you to reuse the same code repeatedly in your script, saving you from having to write, and debug, multiple similar blocks. In JavaScript, functions are also important because any code contained in a script block but not inside a function executes as soon as the page loads. By placing your code in a function, you can delay the code's execution.

Write a Function

1 In your editor, open a page that contains a `<script>` tag block.

1

```
index - Notepad
File  Edit  Format  View  Help
<!DOCTYPE html PUBLIC "-//W3C//DTD XHTML 1.0 Transitional//EN"
"http://www.w3.org/TR/xhtml1/DTD/xhtml1-transitional.dtd">
<html xmlns="http://www.w3.org/1999/xhtml">
<head>
<meta http-equiv="Content-Type" content="text/html; charset=utf-8" />
<title>Untitled Document</title>
<link href="mainstyles.css" rel="stylesheet" type="text/css" />
<script type="text/javascript">

</script> |
</head>

<body>

<div class="container">
  <div class="header"><a href="#"><img src="images/logo.png" alt="Insert
name="Insert_logo" width="180" height="90" id="Insert_logo" style="backgr
display:block;" /></a>
    <!-- end .header --></div>
  <div class="sidebar1">
    <ul class="nav">
      <li><a href="products.html">Products</a></li>
```

2 Within the script, type function.

3 Type a name for your function.

4 Type a pair of parentheses.

2 **4**

```
index - Notepad
File  Edit  Format  View  Help
<!DOCTYPE html PUBLIC "-//W3C//DTD XHTML 1.0 Transitional//EN"
"http://www.w3.org/TR/xhtml1/DTD/xhtml1-transitional.dtd">
<html xmlns="http://www.w3.org/1999/xhtml">
<head>
<meta http-equiv="Content-Type" content="text/html; charset=utf-8" />
<title>Untitled Document</title>
<link href="mainstyles.css" rel="stylesheet" type="text/css" />
<script type="text/javascript">

function hideDiv()|

</script>
</head>

<body>

<div class="container">
  <div class="header"><a href="#"><img src="images/logo.png" alt="Insert
name="Insert_logo" width="180" height="90" id="Insert_logo" style="backgr
display:block;" /></a>
    <!-- end .header --></div>
  <div class="sidebar1">
```

3

5 Press Enter.

6 Type an opening curly brace.

7 Press Enter twice.

```
index - Notepad
File  Edit  Format  View  Help
<!DOCTYPE html PUBLIC "-//W3C//DTD XHTML 1.0 Transitional//EN"
"http://www.w3.org/TR/xhtml1/DTD/xhtml1-transitional.dtd">
<html xmlns="http://www.w3.org/1999/xhtml">
<head>
<meta http-equiv="Content-Type" content="text/html; charset=utf-8" />
<title>Untitled Document</title>
<link href="mainstyles.css" rel="stylesheet" type="text/css" />
<script type="text/javascript">

function hideDiv()
{


</script>
</head>

<body>

<div class="container">
  <div class="header"><a href="#"><img src="images/logo.png" alt="Insert
name="Insert_logo" width="180" height="90" id="Insert_logo" style="backgr
display:block;" /></a>
      <!-- end .header --></div>
```

8 Type a closing curly brace.

Note: Some editors, such as Dreamweaver CS5, may automatically insert the closing curly brace.

The function code is added to your page.

```
index - Notepad
File  Edit  Format  View  Help
<!DOCTYPE html PUBLIC "-//W3C//DTD XHTML 1.0 Transitional//EN"
"http://www.w3.org/TR/xhtml1/DTD/xhtml1-transitional.dtd">
<html xmlns="http://www.w3.org/1999/xhtml">
<head>
<meta http-equiv="Content-Type" content="text/html; charset=utf-8" />
<title>Untitled Document</title>
<link href="mainstyles.css" rel="stylesheet" type="text/css" />
<script type="text/javascript">

function hideDiv()
{
}

</script>
</head>

<body>

<div class="container">
  <div class="header"><a href="#"><img src="images/logo.png" alt="Insert
name="Insert_logo" width="180" height="90" id="Insert_logo" style="backgr
display:block;" /></a>
      <!-- end .header --></div>
```

TIPS

What is the purpose of the parentheses and curly braces?

More complicated functions can have data passed to them as arguments or parameters. The data a function expects to be passed to it is included within the parentheses. The curly braces are used throughout the language to denote a block of code. In the case of a function, they denote the code that makes up the function.

Are there restrictions on what I can name the function?

Yes. Function names must begin with a letter, and can contain only letters, numbers, and underscores. They cannot contain spaces or any other special characters. JavaScript is case-sensitive. It does not matter what case you use for your functions, but you must be consistent.

Change the Visibility of an Object

JavaScript is known as an *object-based* language. Basically, this means that your script relies on calling and modifying programmatic objects, the most common of which is `document`, an object that represents the Web page itself. The `document` object in turn contains a common function or method, `getElementById()`, which returns an element on your page with the given ID. Using this element, you can change CSS styles via the `style` object, including the `visibility` property to show and hide elements. Thus, the line `document.getElementById("content").style.visibility = "hidden"` would hide an element on the page that contained an ID attribute set to `content`.

Change the Visibility of an Object

1 In your editor, open a document that contains a script block.

1

```
index - Notepad
File  Edit  Format  View  Help
<!DOCTYPE html PUBLIC "-//W3C//DTD XHTML 1.0 Transitional//EN"
"http://www.w3.org/TR/xhtml1/DTD/xhtml1-transitional.dtd">
<html xmlns="http://www.w3.org/1999/xhtml">
<head>
<meta http-equiv="Content-Type" content="text/html; charset=utf-8" />
<title>Untitled Document</title>
<link href="mainstyles.css" rel="stylesheet" type="text/css" />
<script type="text/javascript">

</script> |
</head>

<body>

<div class="container">
  <div class="header"><a href="#"><img src="images/logo.png" alt="Insert
name="Insert_logo" width="180" height="90" id="Insert_logo" style="backgr
display:block;" /></a>
    <!-- end .header --></div>
  <div class="sidebar1">
    <ul class="nav">
      <li><a href="products.html">Products</a></li>
      <li><a href="services.html">Services</a></li>
      <li><a href="about.html">About Us</a></li>
```

2 In the document's body, type `<div id="?">`, replacing *?* with an ID.

3 Type some text.

4 Type `</div>`.

```
  <div class="sidebar1">
    <ul class="nav">
      <li><a href="products.html">Products</a></li>
      <li><a href="services.html">Services</a></li>
      <li><a href="about.html">About Us</a></li>
      <li><a href="locations.html">Locations</a></li>
    </ul>
    <p> Use the links above to explore our site.</p>
  <!-- end .sidebar1 --></div>
    <div class="content">
    <div id="specials">
          For a limited time, all our widgets are 25% off!
    </div>|
        <h1>Welcome to TYV Industries</h1>
        <p><img src="images/homepage.jpg" alt="Woman in high-tech office" nam
width="200" height="212" id="homepageImg" />TYV Industries takes pride ir
finest quality widgets to companies worldwide.</p>
        <p>Lorem ipsum dolor sit amet, consectetur adipiscing elit. Suspendis
leo. Aliquam facilisis lectus sed ante placerat pulvinar. Suspendisse iac
urna, quis euismod magna placerat vitae. Praesent a mauris metus. Aenean
sit amet dapibus pretium, mauris erat faucibus elit, ut tincidunt   nibh
purus purus, tincidunt vestibulum gravida vel, placerat   hendrerit magna
Sed fermentum egestas erat ut congue. Nullam   blandit, erat in iaculis ]
massa ultricies lorem, ac rhoncus mauris   libero at ligula. Donec nibh ;
ac elementum id, interdum eget   nunc. Suspendisse vehicula pretium prett
venenatis ornare nibh, sit   amet sollicitudin ipsum semper eget. Suspend
pretium nulla, id   dapibus magna ultricies et. Donec eget condimentum te
```

5 In the script, type
`function hideDiv()`.

6 Press Enter.

7 Type {.

```
index - Notepad
File Edit Format View Help
<!DOCTYPE html PUBLIC "-//W3C//DTD XHTML 1.0 Transitional//EN"
"http://www.w3.org/TR/xhtml1/DTD/xhtml1-transitional.dtd">
<html xmlns="http://www.w3.org/1999/xhtml">
<head>
<meta http-equiv="Content-Type" content="text/html; charset=utf-8" />
<title>Untitled Document</title>
<link href="mainstyles.css" rel="stylesheet" type="text/css" />
<script type="text/javascript">

function hideDiv()
{


</script>
</head>

<body>

<div class="container">
  <div class="header"><a href="#"><img src="images/logo.png" alt="Insert
name="Insert_logo" width="180" height="90" id="Insert_logo" style="backgr
display:block;" /></a>
    <!-- end .header --></div>
```

8 Type `document.
getElement
ById("?").style.
visibility =
"hidden";`, replacing *?*
with the ID you used in
Step **2**.

9 Press Enter.

10 Type }.

The function to hide the
content is created.

```
index - Notepad
File Edit Format View Help
<!DOCTYPE html PUBLIC "-//W3C//DTD XHTML 1.0 Transitional//EN"
"http://www.w3.org/TR/xhtml1/DTD/xhtml1-transitional.dtd">
<html xmlns="http://www.w3.org/1999/xhtml">
<head>
<meta http-equiv="Content-Type" content="text/html; charset=utf-8" />
<title>Untitled Document</title>
<link href="mainstyles.css" rel="stylesheet" type="text/css" />
<script type="text/javascript">

function hideDiv()
{
    document.getElementById("specials").style.visibility = "hidden";
}

</script>
</head>

<body>

<div class="container">
  <div class="header"><a href="#"><img src="images/logo.png" alt="Insert
name="Insert_logo" width="180" height="90" id="Insert_logo" style="backgr
display:block;" /></a>
    <!-- end .header --></div>
```

TIPS

Can I set any style sheet property?
Yes. The style object allows you to modify any CSS
property. You could for example change the
background color to red by typing `document.
getElementById("content").style.
background-color = "FF0000"`.

**Where can I find more information on
JavaScript's objects?**
You can find a wealth of information on the Web.
Rather than rely on any one particular Web site, you
can use your favorite search engine to find current
details. *HTML, XHTML, and CSS: Your visual blueprint
for designing effective Web pages* (Wiley, 2008) has a
chapter that covers the topic in more detail as well.

continued ▶

If you encapsulate your JavaScript in a function, you must explicitly call the function in order for it to run. JavaScript can be called via either browser events such as the page loading, or through user events such as moving the mouse over something or clicking. HTML has a set of event attributes available to match these actions. For example, if you want JavaScript to execute when the user clicks a link, you can add the `onclick` attribute to the link. The attribute's value will be set to the name of the function you want to call.

Change the Visibility of an Object (continued)

⑪ Type `function showDiv()`.

⑫ Press `Enter`.

⑬ Type `{` and press `Enter`.

⑭ Type `document.getElementById("?").style.visibility = "visible";`, replacing `?` with the ID you used in Step 2.

⑮ Press `Enter`.

⑯ Type `}`.

⑰ In the body, type `<a href="javascript:void"`.

⑱ Type `onclick="hideDiv()">`.

⑲ Type descriptive text for the link.

⑳ Type `</a>`.

```
index - Notepad
File  Edit  Format  View  Help
<!DOCTYPE html PUBLIC "-//W3C//DTD XHTML 1.0 Transitional//EN"
"http://www.w3.org/TR/xhtml1/DTD/xhtml1-transitional.dtd">
<html xmlns="http://www.w3.org/1999/xhtml">
<head>
<meta http-equiv="Content-Type" content="text/html; charset=utf-8" />
<title>Untitled Document</title>
<link href="mainstyles.css" rel="stylesheet" type="text/css" />
<script type="text/javascript">

function hideDiv()
{
    document.getElementById("specials").style.visibility = "hidden";
}

function showDiv()
{
    document.getElementById("specials").style.visibility = "visible";
}

</script>
</head>

<body>

<div class="container">
  <div class="header"><a href="#"><img src="images/logo.png" alt="Insert
```

```
<div class="container">
  <div class="header"><a href="#"><img src="images/logo.png" alt="Insert
name="Insert_logo" width="180" height="90" id="Insert_logo" style="backgr
display:block;" /></a>
  <!-- end .header --></div>
    <div class="sidebar1">
      <ul class="nav">
        <li><a href="products.html">Products</a></li>
        <li><a href="services.html">Services</a></li>
        <li><a href="about.html">About Us</a></li>
        <li><a href="locations.html">Locations</a></li>
      </ul>
      <p> Use the links above to explore our site.</p>
    <!-- end .sidebar1 --></div>
    <div class="content">
      <a href="javascript:void" onclick="hideDiv">Hide Specials</a>
      <div id="specials">
          For a limited time, all our widgets are 25% off!
      </div>
      <h1>Welcome to TYV Industries</h1>
      <p><img src="images/homepage.jpg" alt="woman in high-tech office" nam
width="200" height="212" id="homepageImg" />TYV Industries takes pride in
finest quality widgets to companies worldwide.</p>
        <p>Lorem ipsum dolor sit amet, consectetur adipiscing elit. Suspendis
leo. Aliquam facilisis lectus sed ante placerat pulvinar. Suspendisse iac
urna, quis euismod magna placerat vitae. Praesent a mauris metus. Aenean
```

21 In the body, type `<a href="javascript: void"`.

22 Type `onclick= "showDiv()">`.

23 Type descriptive text for the link.

24 Type `</a>`.

● When viewed in a browser, the content is visible. When you click the "hide" link, the content disappears. When you click the "show" link, the content reappears.

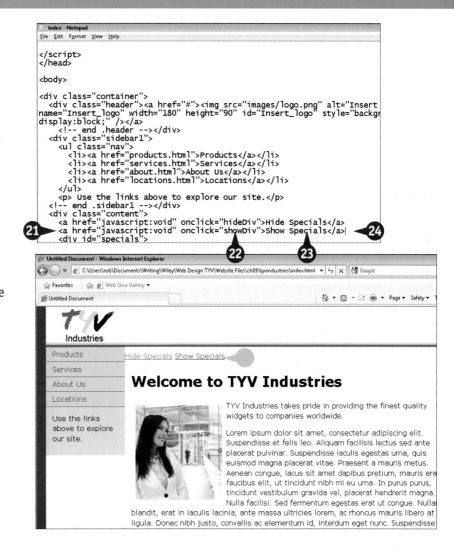

TIP

What does javascript:void; do in the href attribute?
In order to have a valid anchor tag, you need an `href` attribute. However, in this example you do not want the user to leave the page when they click the link, but instead merely to trigger the script. The `javascript:void` code essentially tells the browser to ignore the `href` attribute when the user clicks the link. Many tutorials suggest adding a pound sign (#) instead, but some browsers reload the page when you click that link, so `javascript:void` is safer.

Create a Menu Using Spry

Spry is an Ajax framework from Adobe. Unlike many other frameworks, Spry focuses mostly on visual components and effects, although it does have the ability to read and interpret XML and HTML data files. You can use Spry with almost no code if you use Dreamweaver, because Spry functionality is included directly in the program. However, Adobe does make the Spry framework openly available for anyone to download and use if desired. One of the commonly used Spry widgets is its Menu Bar, which creates an interactive menu with flyout submenus.

Create a Menu Using Spry

① In Dreamweaver, open an existing or new document.

② On the Insert panel, click **Common**.

③ Click **Spry**.

The Insert panel opens to show the Spry widgets.

④ If necessary, scroll down on the panel and click **Spry Menu Bar**.

Note: If you are prompted to save your document at this point, click **Yes**.

⑤ Select whether you want a vertical or a horizontal menu (◎ changes to ◉).

⑥ Click **OK**.

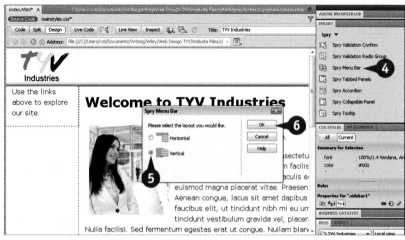

The menu is added to the page.

7 Click **Spry Menu Bar: MenuBar1**.

The Property Inspector displays the menu bar properties.

8 Replace Item 1 with descriptive text.

9 Type an address for the Item 1 link.

10 If desired, replace 1.1 to 1.3 with descriptive text and appropriate links; you can also use the minus button to remove them.

11 Repeat Steps **8** to **10** for the remaining links.

● When the page is viewed in a Web browser, you can navigate between the tabs.

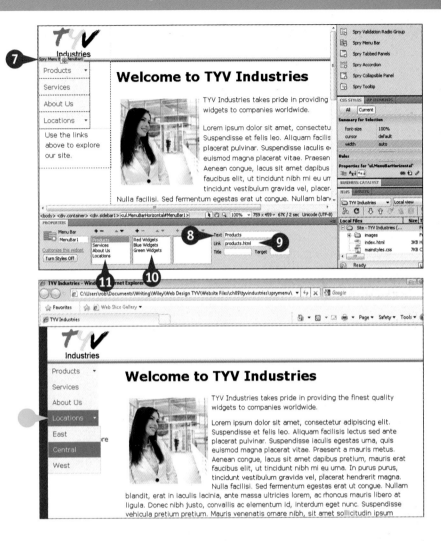

TIPS

Can I add more menu items?
Yes. You can click on the blue bar across the top of the tabbed panels widget and then use the Properties panel at the bottom of the screen to add and remove menu and submenu items.

Can I change the appearance of the menus?
Yes. The menu's appearance is completely controlled by CSS. Your CSS Styles panel displays a SpryMenuBar.css document that contains all of the style rules for the widget.

Create a Calendar Control with YUI

Internet search provider Yahoo! has developed a set of Ajax widgets. Yahoo! makes these widgets freely available on their Web site at http://developer.yahoo.com/yui/. From here, you can get the code for the widgets, read technical documentation, and get help and troubleshooting tips. Instead of having you download files, the YUI components allow you to link to the necessary JavaScript files, using the `src` attribute of the `<script>` tag. One particularly useful and easy-to-implement widget is the calendar control. The calendar appears in a monthly format, and allows users to move back and forth to see past or future dates.

Create a Calendar Control with YUI

1 In your editor, open an existing document or create a new one.

2 In the head section, type `<link rel= "stylesheet" type= "text/css" href= "http://yui.yahoo apis.com/2.8.1/build/ calendar/assets/ skins/sam/calendar. css">`.

3 Type `<script src= "http://yui. yahooapis.com/2.8.1/ build/yahoo-dom- event/yahoo-dom- event.js"></script>`.

4 Type `<script src= "http://yui.yahoo apis.com/2.8.1/build/ calendar/calendar- min.js"></script>`.

5 In the body section, type `<div class=" yui-skin-sam">`.

6 Type `<div id="cal1 Container"></div>`.

7 Type `</div>`.

8 At the bottom of the code, type `<script type="text/javascript">`.

9 Type `var call = new YAHOO.widget.Calendar("call Container");`.

10 Press `Enter`.

11 Type `call.render();`.

12 Press `Enter`.

13 Type `</script>`.

• When the page is viewed in the browser, the calendar appears.

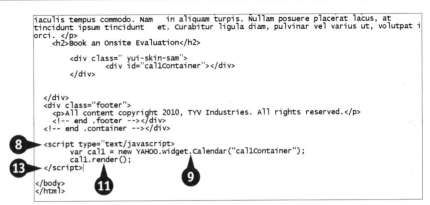

TIP

Can I customize the calendar?

Yes. You can set parameters such as the default date for the calendar, the range of dates to be displayed, and more using configuration settings in the JavaScript. You can also create calendars that display more than one month at a time and a navigator to jump to a specific date. The calendar's appearance can be controlled via CSS. All of these settings are described on the calendar's home page at http://developer.yahoo.com/yui/calendar/.

Create an Image Gallery with jQuery

Another extremely popular and extremely versatile Ajax library is jQuery. Originally developed by John Resig, it was released in 2006 and has quickly become one of the most-used JavaScript libraries available. It is free and open source. A particularly popular implementation of jQuery involves creating image sliders, or animated image galleries. The Nivo Slider is particularly easy to use because it involves simply downloading a JavaScript file and creating an unordered list of images. With any image slider, you should first ensure that all of your images are the same size.

Create an Image Gallery with jQuery

1 In your Web browser, navigate to http://nivo.dev7studios.com.

2 At the bottom of the page, click **Download**.

The File Download dialog box appears.

3 When prompted, click **Save**.

The file is downloaded.

4 Open the folder that you downloaded from the site.

5 In Windows, click **Extract all files**.

On a Mac, you can simply double-click the file to extract it.

6 Navigate to your Web site's folder.

7 Click **Extract**.

The files are extracted.

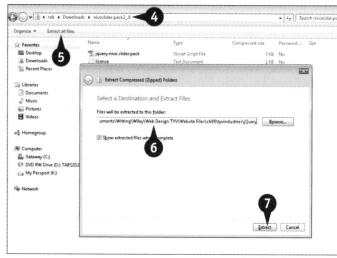

222

8 In your editor, open an existing file or create a new one.

9 In the head section, type `<link rel="stylesheet" href="nivo-slider.css" type="text/css" media="screen" />`.

10 Type `<script src="http://ajax.googleapis.com/ajax/libs/jquery/1.4.2/jquery.min.js" type="text/javascript"></script>`.

11 Type `<script src="jquery.nivo.slider.pack.js" type="text/javascript"></script>`.

8
```
index - Notepad
File Edit Format View Help
<!DOCTYPE html PUBLIC "-//W3C//DTD XHTML 1.0 Transitional//EN"
"http://www.w3.org/TR/xhtml1/DTD/xhtml1-transitional.dtd">
<html xmlns="http://www.w3.org/1999/xhtml">
<head>
<meta http-equiv="Content-Type" content="text/html; charset=utf-8" />
<title>jQuery Example</title>

<link rel="stylesheet" href="nivo-slider.css" type="text/css" media="screen" />

</head>

<body>


</body>
</html>
```
9

10
```
index - Notepad
File Edit Format View Help
<!DOCTYPE html PUBLIC "-//W3C//DTD XHTML 1.0 Transitional//EN"
"http://www.w3.org/TR/xhtml1/DTD/xhtml1-transitional.dtd">
<html xmlns="http://www.w3.org/1999/xhtml">
<head>
<meta http-equiv="Content-Type" content="text/html; charset=utf-8" />
<title>jQuery Example</title>

<link rel="stylesheet" href="nivo-slider.css" type="text/css" media="screen" />

<script src="http://ajax.googleapis.com/ajax/libs/jquery/1.4.2/jquery.min.js"
type="text/javascript"></script>

<script src="jquery.nivo.slider.pack.js" type="text/javascript"></script>
```
11
```
</head>

<body>
```

TIP

Can I use jQuery locally, without linking to the script?
Yes. You can go to http://jquery.com and download the code base yourself. This can be particularly useful if you need to develop and test your pages in situations where you may not have an active Internet connection. The jQuery Web site also includes extensive documentation on the library, tutorials on using it, and a discussion area where you can connect with other jQuery users for additional help.

continued ▶

Create an Image Gallery with jQuery (continued)

A concern anytime you use JavaScript is what will happen to your page if a user disabled scripting in his browser. The Nivo slider uses a simple set of HTML <img> tags with a <div> to display the images, so this script degrades nicely — the user with scripting disabled will simply see the images on the page without the animated effect. The same is true for disabled users. Blind users relying on a screen reader will hear the page as if the script did not exist, so they will be given the alternate text for the images.

Create an Image Gallery with jQuery (continued)

⑫ In the body, type <div id="slider">.

⑬ Type <img src="?" alt="?" />, replacing the first ? with the path to the first image you want for the slider, and the second with appropriate alternate text for the image.

⑭ Repeat Step **13** for each additional image you want to display in the slider.

⑮ Type </div>.

⑯ In the head section, below the other script tags, type <script type="text/javascript">.

⑰ Press Enter.

⑱ Type $(window).load(function() {.

```
<meta http-equiv="Content-Type" content="text/html; charset=utf-8" />
<title>jQuery Example</title>

<link rel="stylesheet" href="nivo-slider.css" type="text/css" media="screen" />

<script src="http://ajax.googleapis.com/ajax/libs/jquery/1.4.2/jquery.min.js"
type="text/javascript"></script>

<script src="jquery.nivo.slider.pack.js" type="text/javascript"></script>

</head>
<body>
<div id="slider">

<img src="images/jqueryimg1.jpg" alt="North Coast of Grand Cayman" />
<img src="images/jqueryimg2.jpg" alt="Old Sailing Ship off Grand Cayman"
<img src="images/jqueryimg3.jpg" alt="Lamp post and surf board on Grand Cayman" />
<img src="images/jqueryimg4.jpg" alt="Cruise ship and rainbow off Grand Cayman" />
</div>|

</body>
</html>
```

```
Index - Notepad
File  Edit  Format  View  Help
<!DOCTYPE html PUBLIC "-//W3C//DTD XHTML 1.0 Transitional//EN"
"http://www.w3.org/TR/xhtml1/DTD/xhtml1-transitional.dtd">
<html xmlns="http://www.w3.org/1999/xhtml">
<head>
<meta http-equiv="Content-Type" content="text/html; charset=utf-8" />
<title>jQuery Example</title>

<link rel="stylesheet" href="nivo-slider.css" type="text/css" media="screen" />

<script src="http://ajax.googleapis.com/ajax/libs/jquery/1.4.2/jquery.min.js"
type="text/javascript"></script>

<script src="jquery.nivo.slider.pack.js" type="text/javascript"></script>

<script type="text/javascript">

$(window).load(function() {

</script>

</head>
<body>
<div id="slider">
```

19 Type $('#slider').
nivoSlider();.

20 Type });.

21 Press Enter.

22 Type </script>.

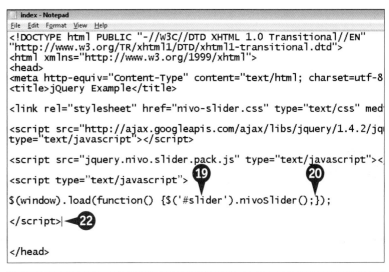

● When viewed in the browser, the image slider is visible.

TIPS

Are there other configuration options available?
Yes. The slider allows you to set the animated effect, the speed of the animation, the appearance of the buttons that allow the user to navigate through the images manually, and more by setting additional parameters in the script. All of these are detailed on the Nivo slider home page at http://nivo.dev7studios.com/.

Is there a limit to the size of images I can use?
No. As long as all of the images are the same size, the slider works with any size images. Keep in mind, however, that all of the images load when the page first loads, so you need to take that into account when setting up your images.

Create Animation Using Flash Professional

Flash has for years been the de facto standard for Web animation. Advertising, games, and video are just a few of its many uses. Although Adobe currently makes several tools that can create Flash-based content, Flash Professional CS5 is the one most familiar and easiest to learn for designers. Its interface closely matches that of other tools in Adobe's Creative Suite. To create simple animation, you begin by drawing shapes on the stage, using tools similar to those found in Illustrator. Then, you convert those shapes to *symbols* — reusable objects that can be animated.

Create Animation Using Flash Professional

1 From the Flash Welcome screen, click **ActionScript 3.0**.

A new document opens.

2 Click the **Rectangle** tool (▣).

Note: You can press and hold your mouse button on the tool to see a menu of other shape tools.

3 On the Properties panel, click **Fill Color**.

4 Select a color.

5 Click and drag on the stage to create the shape.

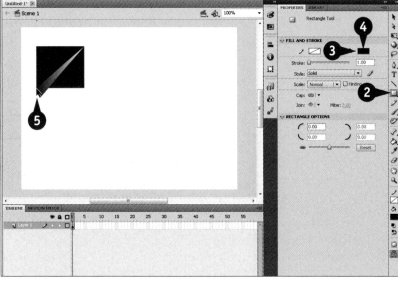

6 Click the **Selection** tool (![selection tool icon]).

7 Double-click the shape to select its fill and stroke.

8 Click **Modify**.

9 Click **Convert to Symbol**.

The Convert to Symbol dialog box opens.

10 Enter a name for the symbol.

11 Select **Movie Clip**.

12 Click **OK**.

The shape is converted to a symbol and ready to be animated.

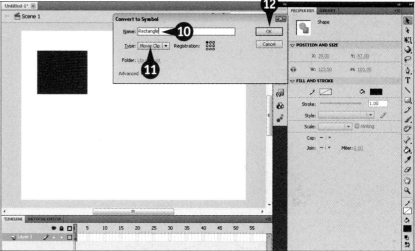

TIP

What is a Movie Clip?

Flash supports three types of symbols: Movie Clips, Buttons, and Graphics. Movie Clips are the most commonly used because they are the most versatile. Buttons provide for user interaction by allowing you to change their appearance when the user mouses over and clicks the button. Graphics are the most basic type of symbol, but are rarely used because they have significant limitations not shared by Movie Clips.

continued ▶

Flash animates objects in much the same way animation is achieved in traditional film: by moving an object slightly in a series of frames, and then playing those frames back quickly enough to fool the eye into believing the object is moving. Flash includes a process known as *tweening* where you, as the designer, need only specify the starting and ending points of the animation. Flash handles positioning the shape in each frame in between. By default, a tween lasts for 24 frames, the equivalent of one second, but you can adjust its length using the Timeline panel.

Create Animation Using Flash Professional (continued)

13 Right-click (**Control**+click) the symbol on the stage.

14 Select **Create Motion Tween**.

● The tween is created. The Timeline panel displays the tween over 24 frames.

15 On the stage, move the shape to the point at which you want the animation to end.

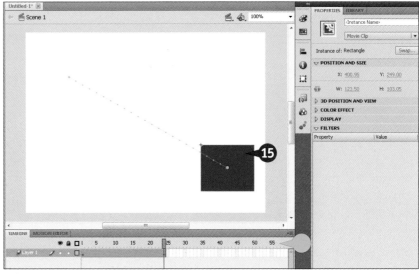

16 Click and drag the right edge of the tween on the Timeline to extend or shorten its duration.

17 Press **Ctrl**+**Enter** (**Control**+ **Enter**).

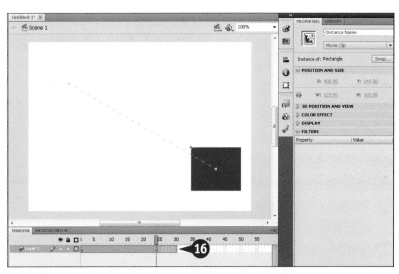

● The test window opens and shows the animation.

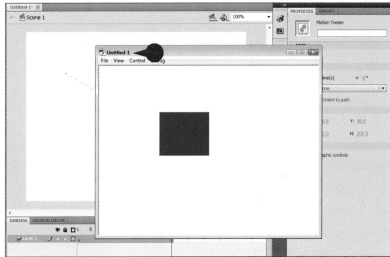

TIPS

Can I prevent the animation from looping?
Yes. Flash contains a powerful scripting language known as ActionScript that allows you complete control over your movie. ActionScript allows you to add code to do everything from stopping the movie from looping to much more complex functions such as loading external, server-based content. *ActionScript: Your visual blueprint for creating interactive projects in Flash CS4 Professional* (Wiley, 2009) guides you through the language.

What does the line with the dots on the stage represent?
When you create a tween, Flash draws the line on the stage to show you the path the shape will take. The dots represent each frame. You can drag this line to bend if you want your shape to follow a curved path.

Publish a Flash Movie

When you complete your Flash movie, you must publish it in order to add it to your Web site. When you publish, Flash converts the movie from the editing format, FLA, to the published format, SWF. The SWF is the file that you add to your HTML document. Note, however, that SWF is not an editable format, so you should be sure to save the FLA file because you will have to return to it later if you want to make changes. The changed file must then be republished as an SWF.

Publish a Flash Movie

1 In Flash Professional, open an existing Flash movie.

2 Click **File**.

3 Click **Publish Settings**.

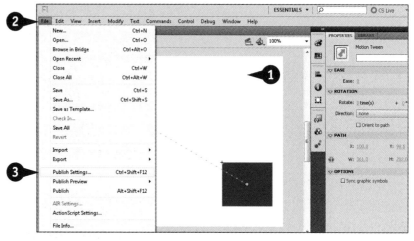

The Publish Settings dialog box opens.

4 If necessary, enter a filename for the SWF.

Note: Because this file will be linked to your Web page, be sure that the filename follows Web page naming rules, as outlined in Chapter 1.

5 Remove the check mark next to HTML (☑ changes to ☐).

6 Click **Publish**.

The file is published.

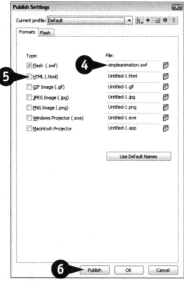

Add a Flash Movie to Your Page in Dreamweaver

Once you have published an SWF file, you can embed it into your HTML page. A popular means by which Flash movies can be added to a page is via the JavaScript SWFObject library. SWFObject allows you to embed your movie, but also provides Flash Player detection to ensure that users who do not have the correct version of Player are prompted to download it. It further allows you to add alternate content to display on your page in case your user does not or cannot install Flash Player. Dreamweaver's Insert panel includes an option to insert a Flash movie into your page that uses SWFObject.

Add a Flash Movie to Your Page in Dreamweaver

1 In Dreamweaver, open an existing page or create a new one.

2 On the Insert panel, click **Media**.

3 Click **SWF**.

The Select SWF dialog box opens.

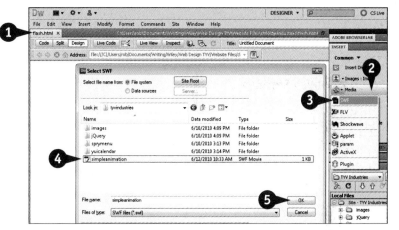

4 Select the SWF file you want to insert.

5 Click **OK**.

● The movie is inserted into the page.

● You can click the **Play** button on the Properties panel to preview your movie.

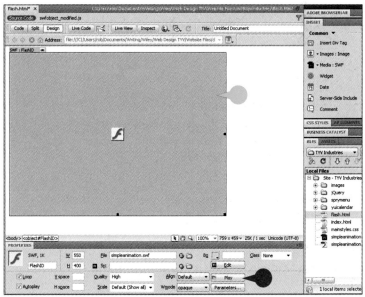

Convert a Video to Flash Video

Many sites today include video. Although shooting and producing video is a skill in and of itself, placing the video on the Web is not difficult, thanks to Flash. Flash video is the most popular video format found on the Web today, and is used on thousands of sites including YouTube and Facebook. The video format your camera uses will not be compatible with Flash Player, so the first step in getting video onto your Web site is to convert it to the Flash Video format. The Adobe Media Encoder, included free with any of the Creative Suite editions, performs this task for you.

Convert a Video to Flash Video

1 Open the Adobe Media Encoder.

In Windows, click **Start**, **All Programs**, the folder in which your Adobe programs reside, and then **Adobe Media Encoder**.

On a Mac, use Finder to open your Applications folder and then select **Adobe Media Encoder**.

2 Click **Add**.

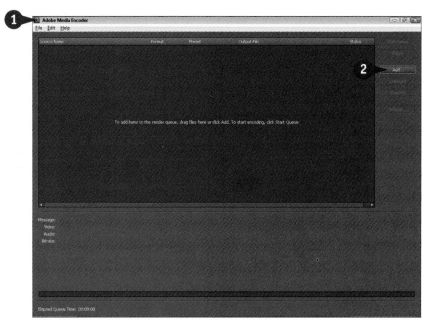

The Open dialog box appears.

3 Navigate to the folder that contains your video file.

4 Select the video you want to convert.

5 Click **Open**.

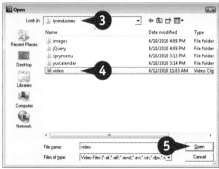

6 Click the **Format** drop-down and select **FLV/F4V**.

7 Ensure that the Output File location is correct.

8 Click **Start Queue**.

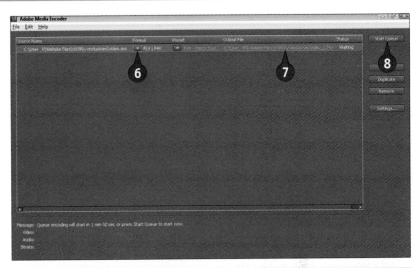

● The video encoding process begins. A preview of the video plays while it encodes.

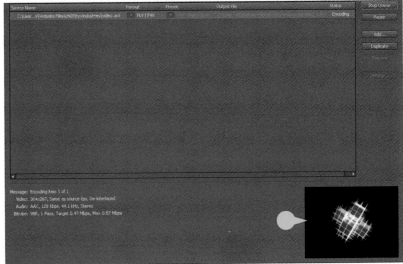

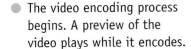

TIPS

What can I use to edit my video?

Many video-editing programs exist. Professional video editors often rely on Apple's FinalCut Pro and Adobe's Premiere Pro. Adobe also sells Premiere Elements, a simpler version of Premiere Pro for hobbyist and home users. Many open-source, free editors also exist.

What format does my video need to be in before I encode?

The Media Encoder supports almost all common, popular video formats. If you are taking video directly from your camera, it will likely be MPG, MOV, AVCHD, or AVI, all of which are supported. Final Cut's and Premiere's native formats are not, but both can export to formats such as AVI and MOV that are.

Add Flash Video Using Flash Professional

Once you have a video encoded to the FLV or F4V format, you can use the FLVPlayback component to add your video to your Flash movie. Components are prepackaged widgets available in Flash to simplify common yet complex tasks. The Components panel lists all of the available components, which can be easily dragged onto the stage. The Property Inspector can then be used to configure the parameters of the component. The FLVPlayback component needs only one parameter: the location of the FLV or F4V video.

Add Flash Video Using Flash Professional

1 In Flash Professional, open an existing document or create a new one.

2 Open the Components panel by clicking its icon (⊞).

The Components panel opens.

3 If necessary, click the arrow to open the Video folder.

4 Drag the FLVPlayback 2.5 component to the stage.

The component is added to the stage.

5 Click the pencil icon (✐) next to source.

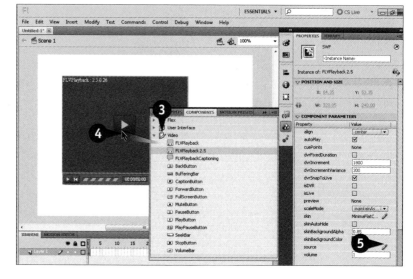

The Content Path dialog box appears.

6 Enter the path to the video file.

Note: You can also click the file folder () and navigate to the file.

7 Click **OK**.

The component is set to play the video.

8 Press Ctrl+Enter (Control+Enter).

● The movie opens in the text window.

9 Click the **Play** button (▶).

The video plays.

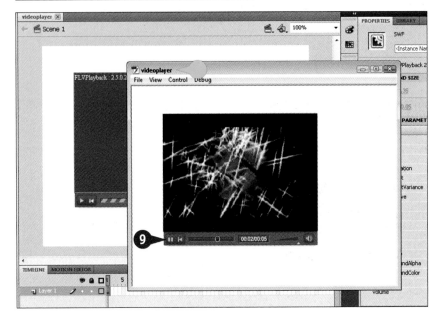

TIPS

Can I modify the playback controls?

Flash includes a set of skins, or playback controls, for the component. You can use the Property Inspector to select different controls by clicking the pencil icon (✎) next to skin and then choosing a different skin in the dialog box that appears.

Do I simply need to publish my movie for my video to work?

You must publish your movie to create the SWF, but you should be sure when you upload your files to your Web server that you upload not only the SWF and container HTML files, but also the FLV or F4V video as well.

Add Video with HTML5

Although the next version of HTML is not due to be released as a full standard for at least a decade, some browsers are already adopting parts of it. In particular, support for HTML5's ability to play video directly in the browser, without the need for a plug-in such as Flash, is becoming more popular. Unfortunately, browsers currently support a few different implementations of video, so you must encode your video in at least two different formats for it to work. Once the video is encoded, you can simply use the `<video>` tag and its child `<source>` tag in your page.

Add Video with HTML5

1 In your editor, open an existing Web page or create a new one.

2 In the body of the document, type `<video>`.

3 Press Enter.

1
```
htmI5video - Notepad
File  Edit  Format  View  Help
<!DOCTYPE html>
<html>
<head>
<meta http-equiv="Content-Type" content="text/html; charset=utf-8" />
<title>HTML5 Video</title>

</head>

<body>
```
2 `<video>`
```

</body>
</html>
```

4 Type `<source src="?" type="video/ ogg" codecs="theora, vorbis" >`, replacing *?* with the path to the video.

5 Press Enter.

```
htmI5video - Notepad
File  Edit  Format  View  Help
<!DOCTYPE html>
<html>
<head>
<meta http-equiv="Content-Type" content="text/html; charset=utf-8" />
<title>HTML5 Video</title>

</head>

<body>

<video>
```
4 `<source src="oggvideo.dv" type="video/ogg" codecs="theora, vorbis" >`
```

</body>
</html>
```

6 Type `<source src="?"
type="video/mp4"
codecs="avc1.42E01E,
mp4a.40.2">`, replacing *?*
with the path to the video.

7 Press Enter.

8 Type `</video>`.

● When viewed in Firefox,
Safari, or Chrome browsers,
the video plays.

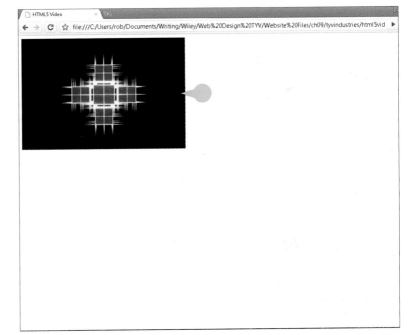

TIPS

What browsers support HTML5 video?

As of mid-2010, Firefox 3.5, Opera 10.5, and Chrome 5 support video using the OGG codec, and Chrome, Safari, and the browsers in the iPhone, iPad, and Android mobile devices support video using the H.264 codec. Currently, Internet Explorer does not support HTML5 video, but IE9, due out in late 2010, will.

What is a codec?

A *codec* is the means by which video is encoded. HTML5 currently does not support a particular codec, hence the need to have multiple copies of the video. A very detailed explanation of codecs, along with step-by-step instructions for converting video to OGG and H.264, can be found at http://diveintohtml5.org/video.html.

Making Sites Accessible

In order to reach the widest possible audience for your site, you need to take into consideration those users who may have physical or cognitive disabilities that would impede their ability to effectively use your site.

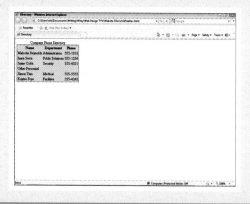

Understanding Web Standards

Although HTML was invented by a single person, Tim Berners-Lee, its development was fairly quickly turned over to a relatively informal, ad-hoc community. Many in the community had different ideas as to where the language should go. Thus, by the late 1990s, the language was an at-times-confusing mixture of structural and presentational code, with a dose of browser-specific tags mixed in. Hoping to solve this issue, a group of prominent designers and developers banded together to begin a push for Web standards, hoping to return to the original ideal of being able to write a page once and have it appear consistently everywhere.

Semantics

HTML was originally envisioned as a language that would describe the logical structure of a page; that is, it would provide developers with the ability to define headings, paragraphs, lists, and the like. An important aspect of the Web standards movement is to get designers back to this ideal. Semantic design focuses on using the HTML tag that makes the most sense logically for the text in question, rather than the older common practice of using the tag that displayed the text the way the designer wanted.

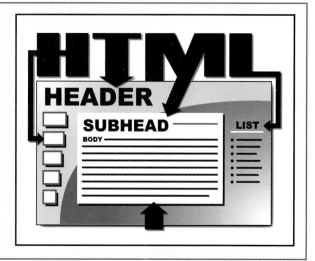

Separating Content, Presentation, and Behavior

Instead of attempting to mix the content of the page, its presentation, and its behavior in a single document, designers who adhere to Web standards can separate each into logical documents: HTML pages for the content, CSS for the presentation, and JavaScript for behavior. Doing so makes each document easier to write, easier to maintain, and easier to reuse later.

Progressive Enhancement

Someday, we may reach the long-sought goal of having browsers that all display pages the same. Today, however, we have a mixture of browsers with different capabilities. Progressive enhancement allows you to have a basic page that appears on all browsers, and then added features such as JavaScript menus that appear on browsers that support it. This way, those with browsers with richer features get a better experience, but everyone can access the content.

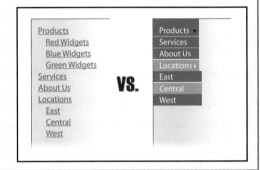

Validation

From the beginning, browsers have been designed to ignore bad code. When they encounter an HTML tag they do not recognize, they simply ignore it. Thus, you do not get errors when you have mistakes on your page. Validation offers a solution: By using a free online service such as http://validator.w3.org, you can check your page to be sure that you are using proper code.

Good Code Solves Display Issues

Many beginners labor under the misconception that because browsers do not display errors for bad or invalid HTML, writing good code does not matter. Unfortunately, not displaying errors does not mean that the browsers do not have problems with bad code. More often than not, browser display issues, even those seemingly caused by CSS, can be solved by simply ensuring that your HTML is correct.

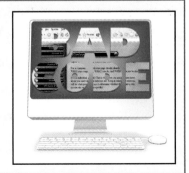

Understanding Web Accessibility

Businesses, generally speaking, do not like to turn away potential customers. However, many do just that on their Web sites when they fail to recognize that significant numbers of users may have disabilities that limit their ability to navigate the Web in the ways that nondisabled users can. Navigation that can be accessed only with a mouse, video or audio content without captioning, needlessly complex layouts, and nonsemantic markup all pose challenges to disabled users. Ignoring accessibility on your Web site can at least drive away customers, and may subject you to legal penalties.

Visual Impairment

Because the Web is a primarily visual medium, visual impairment is perhaps the most important disability to consider when building your site. From total blindness to very poor eyesight, those with visual impairments use software applications called *screen readers* to navigate on their computers. Visually impaired users rely almost exclusively on their keyboards to navigate within their machine because they obviously cannot use a mouse or other pointer device.

Hearing Impairment

Hearing disabilities, of course, become an issue only if your site contains audio content, usually in videos. You need to ensure that any content delivered through audio channels is also available in a nonaudio format, either through closed captioning or similar technologies or through a text transcript of the audio.

Color Blindness

A very significant percentage of people, mostly men, suffer from some degree of color blindness. Although extreme cases involve the complete inability to see color, most people suffer from some lesser degree of color blindness whereby they are simply unable to distinguish between certain shades of color, or even see differences between colors if they lack sufficient contrast.

Cognitive Disabilities

Those with cognitive disabilities, such as learning disorders or dyslexia, will have a difficult time understanding your site's content unless you take these disabilities into consideration and create content that can be easily understood.

Mobility Impairment

Although a lot of Web professionals now understand, and take into consideration, visual impairment, many still ignore mobility impairments. They mistakenly believe that as long as a person can see, they can use any Web site. However, many people with mobility impairments lack the full use of their hands, which in turn means that they cannot use a mouse.

Numbers Math
Shapes and areas
Angles and geometry
Handeling data
Algebra

Accessibility Is N[ot] ...

A common myth is tha[t] ...
pages is difficult and [...]
accessibility from the [...]
development process [...]
you will discover that [...]
mostly accessible without any additional work, and
thus you incur little additional development cost.

[Accessibility] and the Law

[...]ns have laws requiring that Web
[...]ccessible. In the United States, for
[...]endment to the Rehabilitation Act,
[...]red to as Section 508, requires
[...]es be made accessible, and a
growing body of legal precedent is forcing private
industry to follow suit. Be sure to check your local
and federal regulations to see what requirements
might apply in your area.

Benefits to Nondisabled Users

Almost everything you do to make your site accessible also benefits your users who do
not have disabilities. Videos with closed captions can be viewed by users in busy office
environments who cannot turn on speakers. Pages with logical layouts and well-written
content are easier for everyone to follow and understand. Menus that do not require
mousing over small targets are easier to follow.

Accessibility and Search Engines

Google has sometimes been called the largest blind user on the Web. The
search engine and its competitors do not care what your page looks like.
Accessible sites are those that provide clear, well-written, logically organized
content, which are precisely the same things search engines look for in
cataloging sites. Therefore, accessible pages are more likely to get good
search engine rankings than nonaccessible sites.

Add Captions and Summaries to Tables

To ensure accessibility for your site, you should never use tables to lay out your page. However, you can and should use tables for tabular data. You can also use the `<caption>` tag to display a caption or title immediately above the table. Screen readers for the blind linearize the table, meaning they read it top to bottom. A summary, inserted into the opening `<table>` tag, provides users with an overview of the table's structure and its contents to help them make sense of what they hear.

Add Captions and Summaries to Tables

1 In your editor, open an HTML page that includes a table.

```
tables - Notepad
File  Edit  Format  View  Help

<table>
        <tr>
                <th>Name</th>
                <th>Department</th>
                <th>Phone</th>
        </tr>
        <tr>
                <td>Malcolm Reynolds</td>|
                <td>Administration</td>
                <td>555-1212</td>
        </tr>
        <tr>

                <td>Inara Serra</td>
                <td>Public Relations</td>
                <td>555-1234</td>
        </tr>
        <tr>

                <td>Jayne Cobb</td>
                <td>Security</td>
                <td>555-4321</td>
        </tr>
        <tr>
```

2 Immediately after the opening `<table>` tag, type `<caption>?</caption>`, replacing *?* with an appropriate caption or title for your table.

```
tables - Notepad
File  Edit  Format  View  Help

<table>
<caption>Company Phone Directory</caption>|
        <tr>
                <th>Name</th>
                <th>Department</th>
                <th>Phone</th>
        </tr>
        <tr>
                <td>Malcolm Reynolds</td>
                <td>Administration</td>
                <td>555-1212</td>
        </tr>
        <tr>

                <td>Inara Serra</td>
                <td>Public Relations</td>
                <td>555-1234</td>
        </tr>
        <tr>

                <td>Jayne Cobb</td>
                <td>Security</td>
                <td>555-4321</td>
        </tr>
        <tr>
```

3 Within the opening
`<table>` tag, type
`summary=" ?"`, replacing *?*
with a summary of the table's
structure and contents.

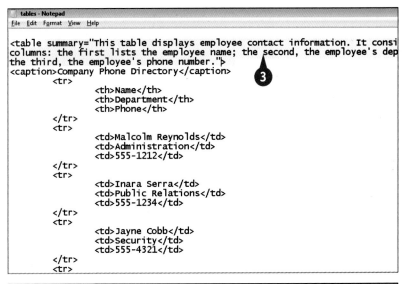

```
tables - Notepad
File  Edit  Format  View  Help

<table summary="This table displays employee contact information. It consi
columns: the first lists the employee name; the second, the employee's dep
the third, the employee's phone number.">
<caption>Company Phone Directory</caption>
        <tr>
                <th>Name</th>
                <th>Department</th>
                <th>Phone</th>
        </tr>
        <tr>

                <td>Malcolm Reynolds</td>
                <td>Administration</td>
                <td>555-1212</td>
        </tr>
        <tr>

                <td>Inara Serra</td>
                <td>Public Relations</td>
                <td>555-1234</td>
        </tr>
        <tr>

                <td>Jayne Cobb</td>
                <td>Security</td>
                <td>555-4321</td>
        </tr>
        <tr>
```

● When viewed in a Web
browser, the table's headers
appear, along with the
caption. The summary does
not appear.

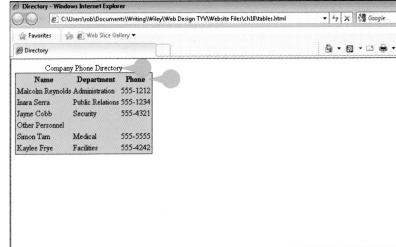

Company Phone Directory

Name	Department	Phone
Malcolm Reynolds	Administration	555-1212
Inara Serra	Public Relations	555-1234
Jayne Cobb	Security	555-4321
Other Personnel		
Simon Tam	Medical	555-5555
Kaylee Frye	Facilities	555-4242

TIPS

Why can I not see my table's summary?
The summary is one of the very few things you add
to your code for accessibility that exists purely for
disabled users, specifically the visually impaired.
Users with a screen reader hear the summary, but it
does not appear anywhere on the page.

Can I change the appearance of the caption?
Yes, with CSS. It is important to make sure that your
page without CSS makes logical sense. Once
it does, you are free to style it to appear however
you want.

Create Accessible Table Headings

Complex tables may contain multiple heading rows or columns, or might have headings in both rows and columns. As a sighted user, you can constantly reference the headings by looking back at them. A visually impaired user with a screen reader, however, cannot do this and so may become confused as the table is linearized and read back. Fortunately, HTML provides a solution with its headers and ID attributes. You can add IDs to each header cell, and then reference that ID in the scope attribute of the cells. When the screen reader reads the page, it references the relevant headers before reading the content of each cell.

Create Accessible Table Headings

1 In your editor, open a page that contains a table.

2 If necessary, convert `<td>` tags to `<th>` tags for any cells that serve as headings.

```
tables - Notepad                           1
File  Edit  Format  View  Help
<table summary="This table displays employee contact information. It consi
columns: the first lists the employee name; the second, the employee's dep
third, the employee's phone number.">
<caption>Company Phone Directory</caption>
        <tr>
                <th>Name</th>
      2 →      <th>Department</th>
                <th>Phone</th>
        </tr>
        <tr>
                <td>Malcolm Reynolds</td>
                <td>Administration</td>
                <td>555-1212</td>
        </tr>
        <tr>|
                <td>Inara Serra</td>
                <td>Public Relations</td>
                <td>555-1234</td>
        </tr>
        <tr>
                <td>Jayne Cobb</td>
                <td>Security</td>
                <td>555-4321</td>
```

3 Add an ID attribute with an appropriate, logical value to each `<th>` tag.

4 In the `<td>` tag, type `headers="?"`, replacing *?* with the ID of the header for that cell.

```
tables - Notepad
File  Edit  Format  View  Help
<table summary="This table displays employee contact information. It consi
columns: the first lists the employee name; the second, the employee's dep
third, the employee's phone  3 nber.">
<caption>Company Phone Dire  try</caption>
        <tr>
                <th id="nameheader">Name</th>
                <th id="departmentheader">Department</th>
                <th id="phoneheader">Phone</th>
        </tr>                          4
        <tr>
                <td headers="nameheader">Malcolm Reynolds</td>
                <td>Administration</td>
                <td>555-1212</td>
        </tr>
        <tr>
                <td>Inara Serra</td>
                <td>Public Relations</td>
                <td>555-1234</td>
        </tr>
        <tr>
                <td>Jayne Cobb</td>
                <td>Security</td>
                <td>555-4321</td>
```

5 Repeat Step 4 for each additional cell.

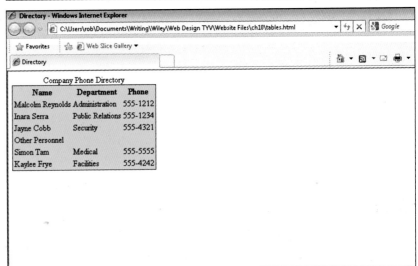

```
tables - Notepad
File  Edit  Format  View  Help
<table summary="This table displays employee contact information. It consi
columns: the first lists the employee name; the second, the employee's dep
third, the employee's phone number.">
<caption>Company Phone Directory</caption>
        <tr>
                <th id="nameheader">Name</th>
                <th id="departmentheader">Department</th>
                <th id="phoneheader">Phone</th>
        </tr>
        <tr>
                <td headers="nameheader">Malcolm Reynolds</td>
                <td headers="departmentheader">Administration</td>
                <td headers="phoneheader">555-1212</td>
        </tr>
        <tr>
                <td headers="nameheader">Inara Serra</td>
                <td headers="departmentheader">Public Relations</td>
                <td headers="phoneheader">555-1234</td>
        </tr>
        <tr>
                <td headers="nameheader">Jayne Cobb</td>
                <td headers="departmentheader">Security</td>
                <td headers="phoneheader">555-4321</td>
```

The table is made more accessible. When viewed in a Web browser, the table shows no visual change.

Company Phone Directory

Name	Department	Phone
Malcolm Reynolds	Administration	555-1212
Inara Serra	Public Relations	555-1234
Jayne Cobb	Security	555-4321
Other Personnel		
Simon Tam	Medical	555-5555
Kaylee Frye	Facilities	555-4242

TIP

Can I reference more than one heading for a single cell, such as for tables with both column and row headings?

Yes. You can provide a space-separated list of the heading IDs. For example, if you have a row heading with an ID of `product` and column heading `June`, you could write `<td headers="product June">`. The order in which you list the heading IDs is irrelevant.

Create Accessible Navigation

Under normal circumstances, a visually impaired user's screen reader reads through the page chronologically. Because most sites have the main navigation at or near the top of the document, above the main content, users must endure having all of the links read to them for each and every page, which can quickly become annoying. The solution, a skip navigation link, is simple to implement. Add a descriptive ID attribute to the main content, and provide a link just before the navigation to that spot on the page.

Create Accessible Navigation

1 Open a page in your editor.

2 In the element that wraps around the main content, or the main content's first element, add a descriptive ID attribute if one does not already exist.

3 Near the top of the page, type `<a href="#?">`, replacing ? with the ID value you added in Step **2**.

```
index - Notepad                                          1
File  Edit  Format  View  Help
<body>

<div class="container">
    <div class="header"><a href="#"><img src="images/logo.png" alt="Insert L
name="Insert_logo" width="180" height="90" id="Insert_logo" style="backgro
display:block;" /></a>
        <!-- end .header --></div>
    <div class="sidebar1">
        <ul class="nav">
            <li><a href="products.html">Products</a></li>
            <li><a href="services.html">Services</a></li>
            <li><a href="about.html">About Us</a></li>
            <li><a href="locations.html">Locations</a></li>
        </ul>
        <p> Use the links above to        lore our site.</p>
    <!-- end .sidebar1 --></div>
    <div class="content" id="mainSection">
        <h1>Welcome to TYV Industries</h1>
        <p><img src="images/homepage.jpg" alt="Woman in high-tech office" name
width="200" height="212" id="homepageImg" />TYV Industries takes pride in
finest quality widgets to companies worldwide.</p>
```

```
index - Notepad
File  Edit  Format  View  Help
<head>
<meta http-equiv="Content-Type" content="text/html; charset=utf-8" />
<title>Untitled Document</title>
<link href="mainstyles.css" rel="stylesheet" type="text/css" />
</head>

<body>

<div class="container">
<a href="#mainSection">|
    <div class="header"><a href="#"><img src="images/logo.png" alt="Insert L
name="Insert_logo" width="180" height="90" id="Insert_logo" style="backgro
display:block;" /></a>
        <!-- end .header --></div>
    <div class="sidebar1">
        <ul class="nav">
            <li><a href="products.html">Products</a></li>
            <li><a href="services.html">Services</a></li>
            <li><a href="about.html">About Us</a></li>
            <li><a href="locations.html">Locations</a></li>
        </ul>
        <p> Use the links above to explore our site.</p>
    <!-- end .sidebar1 --></div>
```

248

④ Type Skip navigation.

⑤ Type </a>.

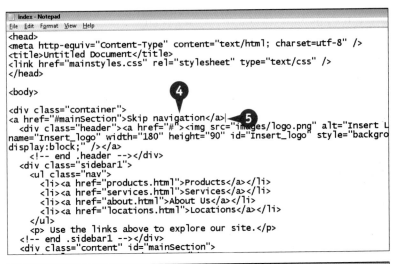

● When viewing the page in a browser, you can click the **Skip navigation** link to jump to the main content.

TIP

Can I hide the skip navigation link?

Yes. You can use CSS, positioning the link off the page through a negative text-indent property or absolute positioning. However, many accessible advocates point out that the link can add not just to the accessibility of the page, but also to its usability. Some users simply prefer to use their keyboards instead of their mouses, and face the same problem of having to repeatedly tab through the navigation on pages to reach the content.

Adding Forms to Your Site

Many Web sites include forms to collect information. Sites use forms to allow users to register for accounts, purchase products, log in, change passwords, and much more. HTML provides a set of tags for creating these forms.

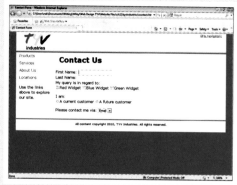

Create a Form

A form in HTML consists of a group of form controls wrapped in a `<form>` tag. The tag takes two common attributes: `action` and `method`. The value of `action` is a URL to a page that contains the code necessary to process the form's data. The `method` attribute accepts one of two values. Setting the value to `get` instructs the browser to send the form's data by appending it to the action's URL, whereas the value `post` has the browser send the data as part of the background information it normally sends to the server.

Create a Form

1 In your editor, open a new or existing HTML document into which you want to add a form.

2 Within the body, type `<form`.

```
<body>
<div class="container">
<a href="#mainSection" id="skipnav">Skip navigation</a>
    <div class="header"><a href="#"><img src="images/logo.png" alt="In
name="Insert_logo" width="180" height="90" id="Insert_logo" style="b
display:block;" /></a>
        <!-- end .header --></div>
        <div class="sidebar1">
            <ul class="nav">
                <li><a href="products.html">Products</a></li>
                <li><a href="services.html">Services</a></li>
                <li><a href="about.html">About Us</a></li>
                <li><a href="locations.html">Locations</a></li>
            </ul>
            <p> Use the links above to explore our site.</p>
        <!-- end .sidebar1 --></div>
        <div class="content" id="mainSection">
            <h1>Contact Us</h1>

                <form |

        <!-- end .content --></div>
        <div class="footer">
            <p>All content copyright 2010, TYV Industries. All rights reserv
            <!-- end .footer --></div>
        <!-- end .container --></div>
</body>
</html>
```

1

2

3 Type `action="?"`, replacing *?* with the path to the file that will process your form.

Note: See Chapter 12 for more information on writing scripts to process forms.

```
<div class="container">
<a href="#mainSection" id="skipnav">Skip navigation</a>
    <div class="header"><a href="#"><img src="images/logo.png" alt="In
name="Insert_logo" width="180" height="90" id="Insert_logo" style="b
display:block;" /></a>
        <!-- end .header --></div>
        <div class="sidebar1">
            <ul class="nav">
                <li><a href="products.html">Products</a></li>
                <li><a href="services.html">Services</a></li>
                <li><a href="about.html">About Us</a></li>
                <li><a href="locations.html">Locations</a></li>
            </ul>
            <p> Use the links above to explore our site.</p>
        <!-- end .sidebar1 --></div>
        <div class="content" id="mainSection">
            <h1>Contact Us</h1>

                <form action="processform.php" |

        <!-- end .content --></div>
        <div class="footer">
            <p>All content copyright 2010, TYV Industries. All rights reserv
            <!-- end .footer --></div>
        <!-- end .container --></div>
</body>
</html>
```

3

④ Type `method=" ?"`,
replacing *?* with either `get`
or `post`.

⑤ Type `>`.

⑥ Press **Enter** twice.

```
<div class="container">
<a href="#mainSection" id="skipnav">Skip navigation</a>
   <div class="header"><a href="#"><img src="images/logo.png" alt="Inser
name="Insert_logo" width="180" height="90" id="Insert_logo" style="back
display:block;" /></a>
      <!-- end .header --></div>
   <div class="sidebar1">
      <ul class="nav">
         <li><a href="products.html">Products</a></li>
         <li><a href="services.html">Services</a></li>
         <li><a href="about.html">About Us</a></li>
         <li><a href="locations.html">Locations</a></li>
      </ul>
      <p> Use the links above to explore our site.</p>
   <!-- end .sidebar1 --></div>
   <div class="content" id="mainSection">
      <h1>Contact Us</h1>

         <form action="processform.php" method="post" >|◀━❺

      <!-- end .content --></div>
      <div class="footer">
                                    ❹
         <p>All content copyright 2010, TYV Industries. All rights reserved.
         <!-- end .footer --></div>
      <!-- end .container --></div>
</body>
</html>
```

⑦ Type `</form>`.

The form container is created
on the page.

```
<div class="container">
<a href="#mainSection" id="skipnav">Skip navigation</a>
   <div class="header"><a href="#"><img src="images/logo.png" alt="Inser
name="Insert_logo" width="180" height="90" id="Insert_logo" style="back
display:block;" /></a>
      <!-- end .header --></div>
   <div class="sidebar1">
      <ul class="nav">
         <li><a href="products.html">Products</a></li>
         <li><a href="services.html">Services</a></li>
         <li><a href="about.html">About Us</a></li>
         <li><a href="locations.html">Locations</a></li>
      </ul>
      <p> Use the links above to explore our site.</p>
   <!-- end .sidebar1 --></div>
   <div class="content" id="mainSection">
      <h1>Contact Us</h1>

         <form action="processform.php" method="post" >

         </form>|◀━❼

      <!-- end .content --></div>
      <div class="footer">
         <p>All content copyright 2010, TYV Industries. All rights reserved.
         <!-- end .footer --></div>
      <!-- end .container --></div>
</body>
```

TIP

Which method should I use?

The default method is `get`. However, using `get` has many disadvantages, so the World Wide Web
Consortium has for some time officially recommended that all forms use `post` as their method. Today,
almost all sites except search engines use `post` for their forms. Search engines continue to use `get`
because that method allows users to bookmark the results page of a form. Most Web scripting languages
handle the data differently, so your choice of methods will likely be dictated by the script you write.

Add a Text Field

The most common form control by far is the single-line text field. You can add a text field to your page through the HTML `<input>` tag. As you will see, however, most of the form controls use that tag, so you also need to provide a `type` attribute, set to a value of `text`. Also required is a `name` attribute, the value of which is used by the server-side script in processing this field. The `name` attribute's value should be a single, descriptive word that begins with a letter and contains only letters, numbers, and underscore characters.

Add a Text Field

1 In your editor, open an HTML document that contains a `<form>` tag.

2 Between the opening and closing form tags, type text as a label for the field.

```
<div class="container">
<a href="#mainSection" id="skipnav">Skip navigation</a>
  <div class="header"><a href="#"><img src="images/logo.png" alt="Inser
name="Insert_logo" width="180" height="90" id="Insert_logo" style="back
display:block;" /></a>
    <!-- end .header --></div>
  <div class="sidebar1">
    <ul class="nav">
      <li><a href="products.html">Products</a></li>
      <li><a href="services.html">Services</a></li>
      <li><a href="about.html">About Us</a></li>
      <li><a href="locations.html">Locations</a></li>
    </ul>
    <p> Use the links above to explore our site.</p>
  <!-- end .sidebar1 --></div>
  <div class="content" id="mainSection">
    <h1>Contact Us</h1>

      <form action="processform.php" method="post" >

      First Name: |

      </form>

    <!-- end .content --></div>
```

3 Type `<input`.

4 Type `type="text"`.

```
<body>

<div class="container">
<a href="#mainSection" id="skipnav">Skip navigation</a>
  <div class="header"><a href="#"><img src="images/logo.png" alt="Insert
name="Insert_logo" width="180" height="90" id="Insert_logo" style="backgr
display:block;" /></a>
    <!-- end .header --></div>
  <div class="sidebar1">
    <ul class="nav">
      <li><a href="products.html">Products</a></li>
      <li><a href="services.html">Services</a></li>
      <li><a href="about.html">About Us</a></li>
      <li><a href="locations.html">Locations</a></li>
    </ul>
    <p> Use the links above to explore our site.</p>
  <!-- end .sidebar1 --></div>
  <div class="content" id="mainSection">
    <h1>Contact Us</h1>

      <form action="processform.php" method="post" >

      First Name: <input type="text" |

      </form>
```

5 Type `name="?"`, replacing *?* with a name for the field.

6 Type `/>`.

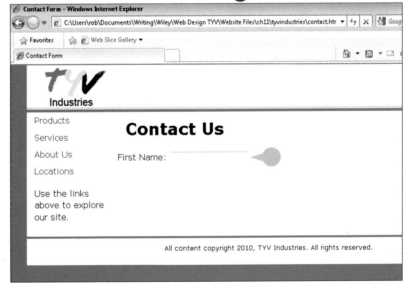

```
<div class="container">
<a href="#mainSection" id="skipnav">Skip navigation</a>
  <div class="header"><a href="#"><img src="images/logo.png" alt="Insert
name="Insert_logo" width="180" height="90" id="Insert_logo" style="backgr
display:block;" /></a>
    <!-- end .header --></div>
  <div class="sidebar1">
    <ul class="nav">
      <li><a href="products.html">Products</a></li>
      <li><a href="services.html">Services</a></li>
      <li><a href="about.html">About Us</a></li>
      <li><a href="locations.html">Locations</a></li>
    </ul>
    <p> Use the links above to explore our site.</p>
  <!-- end .sidebar1 --></div>
  <div class="content" id="mainSection">
    <h1>Contact Us</h1>

      <form action="processform.php" method="post" >

      First Name: <input type="text" name="firstname" />|
      
      </form>
```

● The text field appears and is editable when the page is viewed in a browser.

TIPS

Can I change the size of the field?

Yes. You can use the HTML `size` attribute to set the field's width. The attribute takes as its value a number, theoretically set to the number of characters that will display in the field. You can also use the CSS `width` property. See Chapter 4 for more about CSS.

Can I restrict how much text a user can add to the field?

Yes. Adding the `maxlength` attribute of the `<input>` tag restricts the user to entering only the specified number of characters into the field. You can also specify a `value` attribute to prepopulate the field with text.

Add a Label

Whi le simple text placed next to the field can serve as a label for form fields, you should always wrap the text in an HTML <label> tag. The tag can either be wrapped around both the label text and the form field, or it can wrap around the text by itself. Either way, you should also add an ID attribute to the field, and a for attribute to the label, with a value set to the field's ID. This creates a logical association between the field and the label, regardless of whether the label tags include the field or not.

Add a Label

1 In your editor, open an HTML page that contains a form tag set and at least one form control.

```
<body>

<div class="container">
<a href="#mainSection" id="skipnav">Skip navigation</a>
    <div class="header"><a href="#"><img src="images/logo.png" alt="Inser
name="Insert_logo" width="180" height="90" id="Insert_logo" style="bac
display:block;" /></a>
    <!-- end .header --></div>
    <div class="sidebar1">
      <ul class="nav">
        <li><a href="products.html">Products</a></li>
        <li><a href="services.html">Services</a></li>
        <li><a href="about.html">About Us</a></li>
        <li><a href="locations.html">Locations</a></li>
      </ul>
      <p> Use the links above to explore our site.</p>
    <!-- end .sidebar1 --></div>
    <div class="content" id="mainSection">
      <h1>Contact Us</h1>

        <form action="processform.php" method="post" >

        First Name: <input type="text" name="firstname" />

        </form>
```

1

2 Within the field's tag, type id=" ?", replacing ? with a descriptive identifier for the field.

```
<body>

<div class="container">
<a href="#mainSection" id="skipnav">Skip navigation</a>
    <div class="header"><a href="#"><img src="images/logo.png" alt="Inser
name="Insert_logo" width="180" height="90" id="Insert_logo" style="bac
display:block;" /></a>
    <!-- end .header --></div>
    <div class="sidebar1">
      <ul class="nav">
        <li><a href="products.html">Products</a></li>
        <li><a href="services.html">Services</a></li>
        <li><a href="about.html">About Us</a></li>
        <li><a href="locations.html">Locations</a></li>
      </ul>
      <p> Use the links above to explore our site.</p>
    <!-- end .sidebar1 --></div>
    <div class="content" id="mainSection">
      <h1>Contact Us</h1>

        <form action="processform.php" method="post" >

        First Name: <input type="text" name="firstname" id="firstname"

        </form>
```

2

3 Before the text being used as the field's label, type `<label for=" ?">`, replacing *?* with the ID you used in Step **2**.

4 After the label text, type `</label>`.

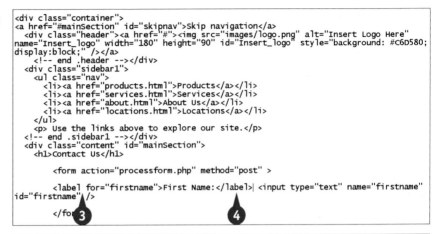

```
<div class="container">
<a href="#mainSection" id="skipnav">Skip navigation</a>
  <div class="header"><a href="#"><img src="images/logo.png" alt="Insert Logo Here"
name="Insert_logo" width="180" height="90" id="Insert_logo" style="background: #C6D580;
display:block;" /></a>
     <!-- end .header --></div>
  <div class="sidebar1">
     <ul class="nav">
       <li><a href="products.html">Products</a></li>
       <li><a href="services.html">Services</a></li>
       <li><a href="about.html">About Us</a></li>
       <li><a href="locations.html">Locations</a></li>
     </ul>
     <p> Use the links above to explore our site.</p>
  <!-- end .sidebar1 --></div>
  <div class="content" id="mainSection">
     <h1>Contact Us</h1>

        <form action="processform.php" method="post" >

        <label for="firstname">First Name:</label>| <input type="text" name="firstname"
id="firstname" />

        </fo
```

When viewed in the browser, the form appears as it did before.

All content copyright 2010, TYV Industries. All rights reserved.

TIP

If it does not change the appearance of the form, why should I use the <label> tag?
Using the tag improves the accessibility of the form, because screen readers for blind users can more easily associate the text with the form field if the tag is present. The tag also simplifies styling the form's labels because they will all have a consistent tag that can be used as a selector in your CSS. Modern browsers allow users to click on labels if they are in the tag to place the cursor in the form field.

Add Check Boxes

Instead of having your users enter information, you can provide them with a set of choices. When you want to allow users to select from a group of choices, and allow them to potentially select more than one choice, you can use check boxes. In HTML, check boxes use the `<input>` tag, but with the `type` attribute set to `checkbox`. Like text fields, check boxes need a `name` attribute, but they also require a value. A set of check boxes should all have the same name, but different values. If you are using labels, each also needs a unique ID.

Add Check Boxes

1 In your editor, open an HTML page that contains a `<form>` tag set.

2 Type `<input type="checkbox"`.

3 Type `name=" ?"`, replacing ? with a descriptive name for the set of check boxes.

```
<ul class="nav">
   <li><a href="products.html">Products</a></li>
   <li><a href="services.html">Services</a></li>
   <li><a href="about.html">About Us</a></li>
   <li><a href="locations.html">Locations</a></li>
</ul>
<p> Use the links above to explore our site.</p>
<!-- end .sidebar1 --></div>                                    1
<div class="content" id="mainSection">
   <h1>Contact Us</h1>

      <form action="processform.php" method="post" >

         <label for="firstname">First Name:</label> <input type="text" name="firstname"
id="firstname" /><br />

         <label for="lastname">Last Name:</label> <input type="text" name="lastname"
id="lastname" /><br />

         <p>My query is in regard to:<br />
  2      <input type="checkbox" name="widgets" |
         </p>
                                              3
      </form>
```

4 Type `value=" ?"`, replacing ? with a value for this check box.

5 Type `id=" ?"`, replacing ? with an appropriate ID value.

6 Type `/>`.

```
<ul class="nav">
   <li><a href="products.html">Products</a></li>
   <li><a href="services.html">Services</a></li>
   <li><a href="about.html">About Us</a></li>
   <li><a href="locations.html">Locations</a></li>
</ul>
<p> Use the links above to explore our site.</p>
<!-- end .sidebar1 --></div>
<div class="content" id="mainSection">
   <h1>Contact Us</h1>

      <form action="processform.php" method="post" >

         <label for="firstname">First Name:</label> <input type="text" name="firstname"
id="firstname" /><br />

         <label for="lastname">Last Name:</label> <input type="text" name="lastname"
id="lastname" /><br />

         <p>My query is in regard to:<br />
         <input type="checkbox" name="widgets" value="redwidget" id="redwidget" />|
         </p>
                                        4          5          6
      </form>
```

7 Within the form, type
`<label for="?">`,
replacing *?* with the ID you
added in Step **5**.

8 Type label text and
`</label>`.

9 Repeat Steps **2** to **8** to add
additional check boxes.

Note: Be sure that all of the
`name` attributes are the same.

● When the page is viewed in
the browser, the check boxes
appear. Any or all of them
may be selected at the same
time.

```
    </ul>
    <p> Use the links above to explore our site.</p>
 <!-- end .sidebar1 --></div>
  <div class="content" id="mainSection">
    <h1>Contact Us</h1>

        <form action="processform.php" method="post" >

        <label for="firstname">First Name:</label> <input type="text" name="firstname"
id="firstname" /><br />

        <label for="lastname">Last Name:</label> <input type="text" name="lastname"
id="lastname" /> />

        <p>My query is in regard to:<br />
        <input type="checkbox" name="widgets" value="redwidget" id="redwidget" /><label
for="redwidget">Red Widget</label>

        <input type="checkbox" name="widgets" value="bluewidget" id="bluewidget" /><label
for="bluewidget">Blue Widget</label>

        <input type="checkbox" name="widgets" value="greenwidget"
id="greenwidget" /><label for="greenwidget">Green Widget</label>|
        </p>

    </form>
```

All content copyright 2010, TYV Industries. All rights reserved.

TIPS

**Can I have check boxes that are prechecked when
the page loads?**
Yes. Each check box accepts an optional checked
attribute, which preselects the check box when
added. If you are using HTML, you can simply add
`checked` to the tag; XHTML, on the other hand,
requires that attributes have values, so you must
write `checked="checked"` to precheck a box in
XHTML.

How can I lay out my check boxes?
If you want to have each check box on its own line,
you can simply add an HTML line break tag, `<br>`,
after each one. Alternately, you can use CSS layout
properties. See Chapter 6 for more about CSS layout
properties.

Add Radio Buttons

A set of mutually exclusive options can be added to your page through radio buttons. In code, radio buttons and check boxes are almost identical: Both use the `<input>` tag, and both require `name` and `value` attributes. As with check boxes, a set of radio buttons need to all have the same name. The only difference is that the `type` value is now set to `radio`. Also, users can select as many check boxes as they want, but they can select only a single radio button within a group. As soon as a second button is chosen, the prior one deselects.

Add Radio Buttons

① In your editor, open an HTML page that contains a form.

② Type `<input type="radio".`

③ Type `name=" ?"`, replacing `?` with a descriptive name for the set of radio buttons.

```
<form action="processform.php" method="post" >

    <label for="firstname">First Name:</label> <input type="text" name=
id="firstname" /><br />

    <label for="lastname">Last Name:</label> <input type="text" name="l
id="lastname" /><br />

    <p>My query is in regard to:<br />
    <input type="checkbox" name="widgets" value="redwidget" id="redwidg
for="redwidget">Red Widget</label>

    <input type="checkbox" name="widgets" value="bluewidget" id="bluewi
for="bluewidget">Blue Widget</label>

    <input type="checkbox" name="widgets" value="greenwidget"
id="greenwidget" /><label for="greenwidget">Green Widget</label>
    </p>

    <p>I am:<br />
    <input type="radio" name="status" |
    </p>

</form>
```

④ Type `value=" ?"`, replacing `?` with a value for this radio button.

⑤ Type `id=" ?"`, replacing `?` with an appropriate ID value.

⑥ Type `/>`.

```
<form action="processform.php" method="post" >

    <label for="firstname">First Name:</label> <input type="text" name=
id="firstname" /><br />

    <label for="lastname">Last Name:</label> <input type="text" name="l
id="lastname" /><br />

    <p>My query is in regard to:<br />
    <input type="checkbox" name="widgets" value="redwidget" id="redwidg
for="redwidget">Red Widget</label>

    <input type="checkbox" name="widgets" value="bluewidget" id="bluewi
for="bluewidget">Blue Widget</label>

    <input type="checkbox" name="widgets" value="greenwidget"
id="greenwidget" /><label for="greenwidget">Green Widget</label>
    </p>

    <p>I am:<br />
    <input type="radio" name="status" value="current" id="current" />|
    </p>

</form>
```

7 Within the form, type `<label for="?">`, replacing *?* with the ID you used in Step **5**.

8 Type label text and `</label>`.

9 Repeat Steps **2** to **8** to add additional radio buttons.

Note: Be sure that all of the `name` attributes are the same.

- When the page is viewed in the browser, the radio buttons appear. Only one of them may be selected at the same time.

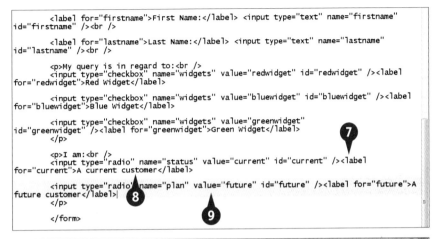

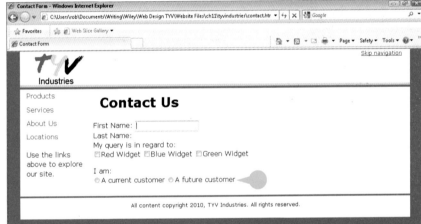

All content copyright 2010, TYV Industries. All rights reserved.

TIP

How can I force my user to select one of the radio buttons?
Like check boxes, radio buttons take an optional `checked` value to preselect one. However, a user can deselect the check box without selecting another, thus submitting the form with no check boxes selected. If you preselect a radio button, your user can deselect it only by choosing another button in the group. Thus, preselecting a radio button with the `checked` attribute in essence forces your user to select at least one of the buttons.

Create a Drop-Down List

You can create a drop-down list in HTML with a combination of the `<select>` tag and its child `<option>` tags. The `<select>` tag contains the name and, if necessary, the ID. Each choice within the drop-down is provided with an `<option>` tag. The text that appears in the list is simply the text within the `<option>` tag. If you want to have a slightly different value be submitted to the server from that which the user sees, you can optionally add a `value` attribute to the tag. A select list can contain as many options as you need.

Create a Drop-Down List

1 In your editor, open an HTML page that contains a form.

2 Within the form, type `<label for="?">`, replacing *?* with the ID you plan to use for the list.

3 Type label text and `</label>`.

```
            <input type="checkbox" name="widgets" value="greenwidget"
   id="greenwidget" /><label for="greenwidget">Green Widget</label>
            </p>

            <p>I am:<br />
            <input type="radio" name="status" value="current" id="current" /><la
   for="current">A current customer</label>

            <input type="radio" name="plan" value="future" id="future" /><label
   future customer</label>
            </p>

            <p><label for="contact">Please contact me via:</label>|
            </p>

            </form>

      <!-- end .content --></div>
      <div class="footer">
         <p>All content copyright 2010, TYV Industries. All rights reserved.</p>
         <!-- end .footer --></div>
      <!-- end .container --></div>
   </body>
   </html>
```

1

2

3

4 Type `<select name="?"`, replacing *?* with a descriptive name for the list.

5 Type `id="?"`, replacing *?* with the value you used for the attribute in Step **2**.

6 Type `>`.

```
            <input type="checkbox" name="widgets" value="greenwidget"
   id="greenwidget" /><label for="greenwidget">Green Widget</label>
            </p>

            <p>I am:<br />
            <input type="radio" name="status" value="current" id="current" /><la
   for="current">A current customer</label>

            <input type="radio" name="plan" value="future" id="future" /><label
   future customer</label>
            </p>

            <p><label for="contact">Please contact me via:</label>
            <select name="contact" id="contact">|
            </p>

            </form>

      <!-- end .content --></div>
      <div class="footer">
         <p>All content copyright 2010, TYV Industries. All rights reserved.</p>
         <!-- end .footer --></div>
      <!-- end .container --></div>
   </body>
   </html>
```

4

5

6

262

7 Type `<option>`.

8 Type the text to display in the list, followed by `</option>`.

9 Repeat Steps **7** and **8** to add additional options.

10 Type `</select>`.

```
        <p>I am:<br />
        <input type="radio" name="status" value="current" id="current"
for="current">A current customer</label>

        <input type="radio" name="plan" value="future" id="future" /><
future customer</label>
        </p>

        <p><label for="contact">Please contact me via:</label>
        <select name="contact" id="contact">
            <option>Email</option>
            <option>Phone</option>
            <option>Mail</option>
        </select>|
        </p>

        </form>

    <!-- end .content --></div>
    <div class="footer">
        <p>All content copyright 2010, TYV Industries. All rights reserved
        <!-- end .footer --></div>
    <!-- end .container --></div>
</body>
</html>
```

● When the page is viewed in the browser, the drop-down list appears in the form.

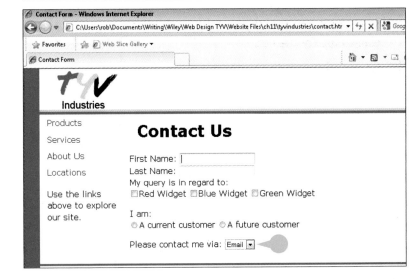

TIPS

Can I allow my user to select more than one option at a time?

Yes. You can add the `multiple` attribute to the `<select>` tag. In HTML, you simply type `multiple`; in XHTML, you need to write `multiple="multiple"`. You can also add a `size` attribute, with a `value` set to the number of options you want to have the list show without scrolling.

How can I choose more than one option when I have the multiple attribute set?

You can press and hold **Shift** to select multiple contiguous options. For noncontiguous selection, you can press and hold **Ctrl** on Windows or **⌘** on a Mac. You should provide these instructions on your page for your users.

Insert a Text Area

HTML allows you to provide your user with the ability to enter large blocks of text with the `<textarea>` tag. Like every other form control, the tag has a required `name` attribute. The default display size of the field varies between browsers, but the tag also accepts `rows` and `cols` attributes to set the size, where the former sets the field's height and the latter its width. The `<textarea>` tag is a container tag, and thus has a required closing tag. If you want to prepopulate the field with some default text, the text will appear between the opening and closing tags.

Insert a Text Area

1 In your editor, open an HTML page that contains a form.

2 Within the form, type `<label for="?">`, replacing ? with the ID you plan to use for the list.

3 Type label text and `</label>`.

4 Type `<br />`.

```
                <input type="checkbox" name="widgets" value="greenwidget"
id="greenwidget" /><label for="greenwidget">Green Widget</label>
                </p>

                <p>I am:<br />
                <input type="radio" name="status" value="current" id="current" />
for="current">A current customer</label>

                <input type="radio" name="plan" value="future" id="future" /><lab
future customer</label>
                </p>

                <p><label for="contact">Please contact me via:</label>
                <select name="contact" id="contact">
                    <option>Email</option>
                    <option>Phone</option>
                    <option>Mail</option>
                </select>
                </p>

                <p>
                <label for="comments">Additional comments:</label><br />|
                </p>

                </form>
```

5 Type `<textarea name="?"`, replacing ? with a descriptive name for the field.

6 Type `id="?"`, replacing ? with the ID value you used in Step **2**.

```
                <input type="checkbox" name="widgets" value="greenwidget"
id="greenwidget" /><label for="greenwidget">Green Widget</label>
                </p>

                <p>I am:<br />
                <input type="radio" name="status" value="current" id="current" />
for="current">A current customer</label>

                <input type="radio" name="plan" value="future" id="future" /><lab
future customer</label>
                </p>

                <p><label for="contact">Please contact me via:</label>
                <select name="contact" id="contact">
                    <option>Email</option>
                    <option>Phone</option>
                    <option>Mail</option>
                </select>
                </p>

                <p>
                <label for="comments">Additional comments:</label><br />
                <textarea name="comments" id="comments" |
                </p>

                </form>
```

7 Type `rows="?"`, replacing *?* with a number for the height of the field.

8 Type `cols="?"`, replacing *?* with a number for the weight of the field.

9 Type `>`.

10 Type `</textarea>`.

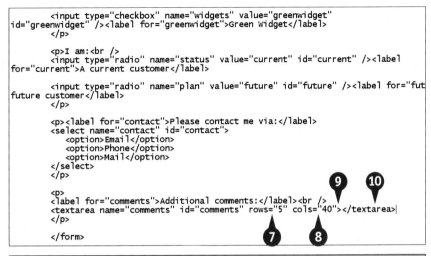

```
            <input type="checkbox" name="widgets" value="greenwidget"
id="greenwidget" /><label for="greenwidget">Green Widget</label>
        </p>

        <p>I am:<br />
            <input type="radio" name="status" value="current" id="current" /><label
for="current">A current customer</label>

            <input type="radio" name="plan" value="future" id="future" /><label for="fut
future customer</label>
        </p>

        <p><label for="contact">Please contact me via:</label>
        <select name="contact" id="contact">
            <option>Email</option>
            <option>Phone</option>
            <option>Mail</option>
        </select>
        </p>

        <p>
        <label for="comments">Additional comments:</label><br />
        <textarea name="comments" id="comments" rows="5" cols="40"></textarea>|
        </p>

    </form>
```

● When the page is viewed in a browser, the text area appears.

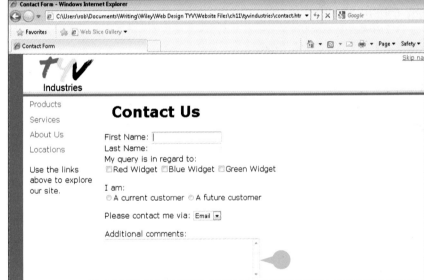

TIPS

How much text can a user enter into the field?
Some browsers limit the field to 65,536 characters, but others do not. You can set a limit yourself by using JavaScript. Several Ajax libraries, including Adobe Spry, have prebuilt controls to limit the text entered into a text area.

Can I add a toolbar to allow my user to format the text?
HTML does not provide this capability, but several implementations to do so exist. A popular, free option is the CKEditor, available for download from www.ckeditor.com.

Add a Button to Your Form

I n order to submit the data to a server, your user must click a button. HTML offers two methods by which a button can be added to the form. The first uses the `<input>` tag with a `type` attribute set to `submit`. The second uses the `<button>` tag, again with `type` set to `submit`. Both work the same, so the one you use is primarily up to you. The text that appears on the button varies between browsers, but you can add the `value` attribute to set it to text of your choosing.

Add a Button to Your Form

1 In your editor, open an HTML page that contains a form.

```
contact - Notepad    1
File  Edit  Format  View  Help
id="greenwidget" /><label for="greenwidget">Green Widget</label>
     </p>

     <p>I am:<br />
     <input type="radio" name="status" value="current" id="current" /><
for="current">A current customer</label>

     <input type="radio" name="plan" value="future" id="future" /><labe
future customer</label>
     </p>

     <p><label for="contact">Please contact me via:</label>
     <select name="contact" id="contact">
        <option>Email</option>
        <option>Phone</option>
        <option>Mail</option>
     </select>
     </p>

     <p>
     <label for="comments">Additional comments:</label><br />
     <textarea name="comments" id="comments" rows="5" cols="40"></texta
     </p>

     <p>
```

2 Type `<input`.

3 Type `type="submit"`.

```
     <p>I am:<br />
     <input type="radio" name="status" value="current" id="current" /><
for="current">A current customer</label>

     <input type="radio" name="plan" value="future" id="future" /><labe
future customer</label>
     </p>

     <p><label for="contact">Please contact me via:</label>
     <select name="contact" id="contact">
        <option>Email</option>
        <option>Phone</option>
        <option>Mail</option>
     </select>
     </p>

     <p>
     <label for="comments">Additional comments:</label><br />
     <textarea name="comments" id="comments" rows="5" cols="40"></texta
     </p>

     <p>
     <input type="submit" |    3
     </p>

     </form>
```

266

④ Type `value="?" />`,
replacing *?* with the text you
want to appear on the
button.

```
        <p>I am:<br />
        <input type="radio" name="status" value="current" id="current"
for="current">A current customer</label>

        <input type="radio" name="plan" value="future" id="future" /><l
future customer</label>
        </p>

        <p><label for="contact">Please contact me via:</label>
        <select name="contact" id="contact">
            <option>Email</option>
            <option>Phone</option>
            <option>Mail</option>
        </select>
        </p>

        <p>
        <label for="comments">Additional comments:</label><br />
        <textarea name="comments" id="comments" rows="5" cols="40"></te
        </p>

        <p>
        <input type="submit" value="Contact Us" />|
        </p>

        </form>
```

● When you view the page in a
browser, the button appears.
If you click the button, the
form's data is submitted to
the page specified in the
`<form>` tag's action.

TIP

Can I also include a button to clear the form?
Yes. HTML includes a `type="reset"` for both the `<input>` and `<button>` tags. However, you should
carefully consider before you add the button if it will actually help. Users very rarely fill out a form and
then decide to clear it; rather, most of the time the reset button is clicked by mistake, which is why most
designers do not include it.

Group Related Form Elements

The HTML `<fieldset>` tag allows you to organize your form into logical groups of elements. Grouping elements allows you to provide a better layout for your users and may cause longer forms to look less overwhelming. Within a fieldset, you can nest a `<legend>` tag to add descriptive text about the set. The fieldset will appear as a border around its fields, and the legend will display in the top-left corner of the set. Fieldsets can be nested within other sets, so you can also use it to organize subgroups, such as sets of check boxes and radio buttons.

Group Related Form Elements

1 In your editor, open an HTML page that contains a form and form fields.

2 Within the form, type `<fieldset>`.

3 Press `Enter`.

```
contact - Notepad    ◀ 1
File  Edit  Format  View  Help
  <div class="sidebar1">
    <ul class="nav">
      <li><a href="products.html">Products</a></li>
      <li><a href="services.html">Services</a></li>
      <li><a href="about.html">About Us</a></li>
      <li><a href="locations.html">Locations</a></li>
    </ul>
    <p> Use the links above to explore our site.</p>
  <!-- end .sidebar1 --></div>
  <div class="content" id="mainSection">
    <h1>Contact Us</h1>

      <form action="processform.php" method="post" >

  2 ▶ <fieldset>
          |

          <label for="firstname">First Name:</label> <input type="text" na
  id="firstname" /><br />

          <label for="lastname">Last Name:</label> <input type="text" name
  id="lastname" /><br />
```

4 Type `<legend>`.

5 Type a descriptive legend for the set of fields.

6 Type `</legend>`.

```
contact - Notepad
File  Edit  Format  View  Help
  <div class="sidebar1">
    <ul class="nav">
      <li><a href="products.html">Products</a></li>
      <li><a href="services.html">Services</a></li>
      <li><a href="about.html">About Us</a></li>
      <li><a href="locations.html">Locations</a></li>
    </ul>
    <p> Use the links above to explore our site.</p>
  <!-- end .sidebar1 --></div>
  <div class="content" id="mainSection">
    <h1>Contact Us</h1>

      <form action="pro  5 sform.php" method="post" >

      <fieldset>
  4 ▶   <legend>Contact Information</legend>| ◀ 6

          <label for="firstname">First Name:</label> <input type="text" na
  id="firstname" /><br />

          <label for="lastname">Last Name:</label> <input type="text" name
  id="lastname" /><br />
```

7 After the final form field tag in the group, type `</fieldset>`.

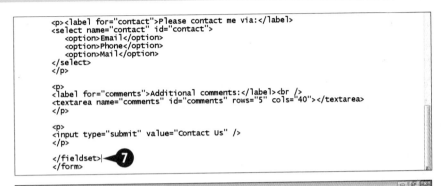

```
<p><label for="contact">Please contact me via:</label>
<select name="contact" id="contact">
    <option>Email</option>
    <option>Phone</option>
    <option>Mail</option>
</select>
</p>

<p>
<label for="comments">Additional comments:</label><br />
<textarea name="comments" id="comments" rows="5" cols="40"></textarea>
</p>

<p>
<input type="submit" value="Contact Us" />
</p>

</fieldset>
</form>
```

● When the page is viewed in a browser, the fieldset or fieldsets appear as borders around groups of fields. The legends appear in the top-left corners of the fieldsets.

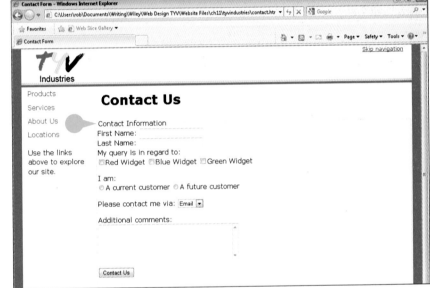

TIP

Can I control the appearance of the fieldset?
Yes. You can use the CSS `border` properties to control the width, color, or style of the fieldset border, and the `width` property to set its size. The legend can be formatted using any CSS font or text property. Background colors, unfortunately, do not work because browsers vary widely on how they choose to implement the background of a fieldset, and none of them do it well even within that variety.

Creating Dynamic Pages

Although a need for simple Web sites will always exist, many organizations today are realizing the need for and importance of having dynamic sites; that is, sites that can change and respond based on user actions.

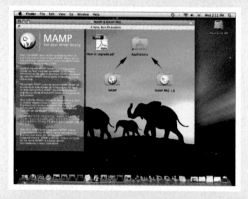

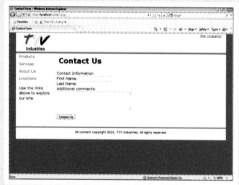

Many Web sites need to be able to respond to changes such as new members joining a site or customers adding items to shopping carts. Dynamic sites typically either retrieve information from or write data to databases, although they may also be used to send or receive e-mail, gather information from other sites, or perform any number of other tasks. HTML does not provide the capabilities to offer dynamic content. Other programming languages, however, offer the ability to generate HTML documents at the moment a user requests them.

Static versus Dynamic Sites

Static sites contain HTML pages that appear to the user exactly as the designer or developer wrote them. In order for the content on your static site to change, you must open the code in your editor, make the changes, and then upload a new copy to your server. Dynamic pages, on the other hand, contain scripts executed on the server. A dynamic page looks and behaves differently for each user who encounters it.

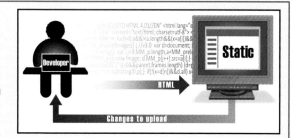

Dynamic Languages

Dynamic sites are primarily written in a server-side scripting language. Although many dozens of languages exist, some of the more popular are PHP, ColdFusion, ASP, and ASP.NET. Each language has distinct advantages and disadvantages. The examples in this chapter demonstrate how to create a simple dynamic site using PHP.

Dynamic Page Capabilities

Dynamic sites can accept and process information submitted by the user via a Web form, such as search engine forms, e-commerce site order forms, blog comment forms, and social networking status forms. Dynamic pages might also change based on the time of day the page is displayed or the region or locale of the user. They may also be updated by the Web site owner, such as the posting of a new blog entry.

Dynamic Language Editors

Scripting languages are composed of plain text, so they can be written in any editor. Most editors designed for creating Web pages offer at least some support for writing scripting languages. For example, Microsoft Expression Web has many tools designed to make creating pages in ASP. NET easier, and Dreamweaver CS5 offers a variety of features built for PHP developers.

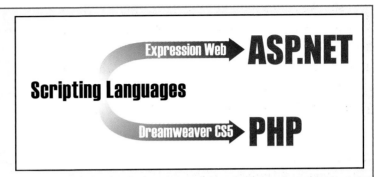

Testing Dynamic Pages

You cannot simply open a dynamic page in your browser to test it. Instead, the page must be processed by a Web server before the page displays correctly. The easiest method of testing pages is to install a Web server on your local computer, a process outlined later in this chapter.

Dynamic Pages and Static Content

Most dynamic pages contain some static content. Headings and navigation, for example, are often composed as static HTML. The presentational side of your site will likewise be mostly, if not entirely, static CSS. Mixing dynamic and static elements on the page is perfectly acceptable and, in fact, extremely common.

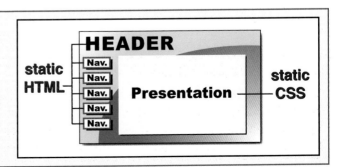

In order to develop and test PHP pages, you need a Web server and PHP installed on your computer. Most of the time, you also need a database. Although you can download and install them separately, a product known as WAMP greatly simplifies the process. WAMP, short for **W**indows, **A**pache, **M**ySQL, **P**HP, provides a single installer for Apache, a popular open-source Web server, open-source database MySQL, and PHP itself. Installing them together with WAMP, in addition to saving time, also frees you from having to worry about configuring them to work together.

Download and Install WAMP on Windows

Download and Install WAMP

① Go to http://www.wampserver.com/en/.

② Click **Downloads**.

③ Click **Download WampServer 2.0i.**

Note: The version number might be slightly different.

The File Download dialog box appears.

④ Click **Run**.

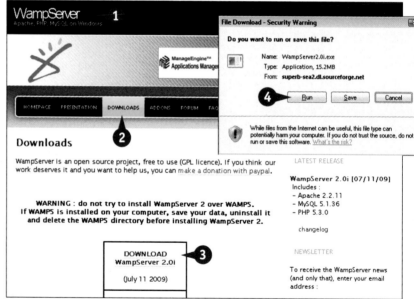

The file downloads and the installer opens.

Note: If you get any security warnings from Windows while installing, click **Yes**.

The installation wizard opens.

⑤ On the first step of the installer, click **Next**.

The license agreement appears.

⑥ Accept the license agreement and click **Next**.

The installation directory screen appears.

7 Accept the default installation directory and click **Next**.

The additional tasks screen appears.

8 Choose if you want additional icons installed and click **Next**.

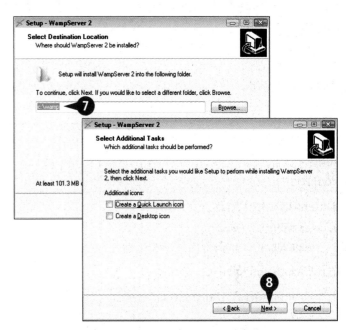

The final step of the wizard appears.

9 Click **Install**.

WAMP installs.

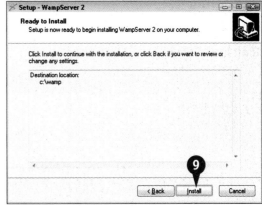

TIP

I have heard that using a single installer like WAMP has problems, and that I should manually install everything instead. Is this correct?

If you are setting up a live Web server that will be publically accessible, manually installing the Apache server, PHP, and MySQL is generally better. That way, you can control exactly what is installed and where it installs, and customize the security settings as needed. However, if you are instead setting up a local testing machine that only you will have access to, as is the case in these examples, WAMP provides a much quicker and easier installation process.

continued ▶

Once you have WAMP downloaded and installed, there are a few final steps to configure it. You need to tell WAMP which Web browser you use by default, and provide an e-mail address, although this only appears on default error messages, so for local testing computers, you do not need to enter real information. Once WAMP is installed and configured, you can test the installation by browsing to http://localhost. Localhost is the special reserved domain name that browsers use to access Web servers on the same computer as the browser.

Download and Install WAMP on Windows (continued)

The default browser prompt appears.

⑩ Click **Open**.

Note: If you are asked to allow Apache access through the firewall, click **Allow access**.

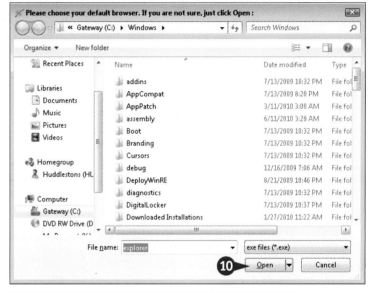

The Server Setup Wizard begins.

⑪ Type e-mail information if you have it.

Note: If this is going to be a local testing computer only, you can accept the default values.

⑫ Click **Next**.

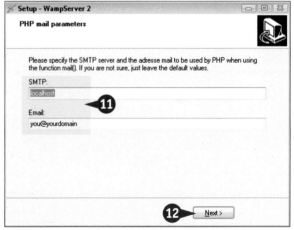

The Completing Setup Wizard screen appears.

⓭ Click **Finish**.

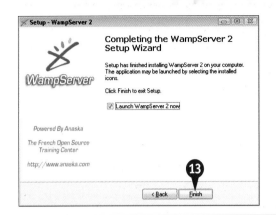

Test the Installation

① Open a Web browser.

② Type **http://localhost**.

● The WampServer page appears, indicating that the server has installed successfully.

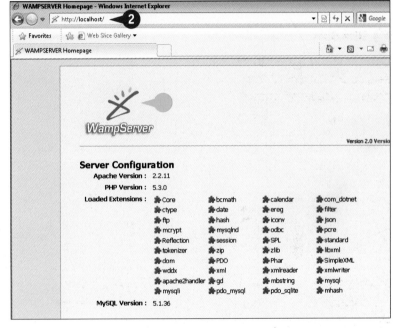

TIPS

How can I manage WAMP?
You should see a WAMP icon (🖼) in your task tray — the area on Windows that contains your system's clock. You can click this to start and stop any of the services, as well as access configuration files to modify or further control Apache, PHP, or MySQL.

Where can I get additional details on using any of the components in WAMP?
The WAMP Web site at www.wampserver.com/en has a forum where you can ask questions of other others. In addition, the Apache Web site at www.apache.org, the PHP site at www.php.net, and the MySQL site at www.mysql.com all have extensive documentation and forums.

In order to create PHP pages on a Macintosh, you must download and install a Web server, PHP, and, most likely, a database. Although all three can be downloaded independently, you can instead download and install MAMP, which provides a single installer for all three components. MAMP stands for **M**ac, **A**pache, **M**ySQL, **P**HP. Installing MAMP on your Mac simply involves dragging the downloaded folder into your Applications folder. Once complete, you can access MAMP as an application to configure and control the program.

Download and Install MAMP on a Mac

1 Browse to http://mamp. info/en.

2 Click **Download now**.

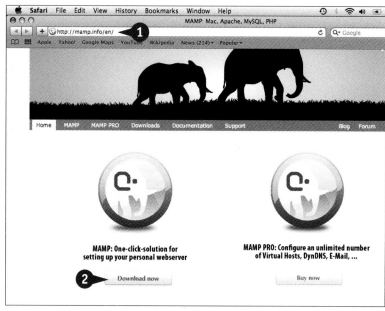

The Downloads dialog box opens and the file begins downloading. When complete, the license dialog opens.

3 Click **Agree**.

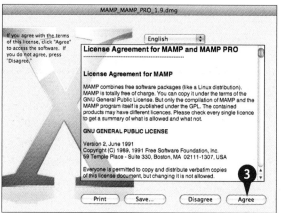

The MAMP & MAMP Pro
dialog box opens.

④ Drag the MAMP folder to
Applications.

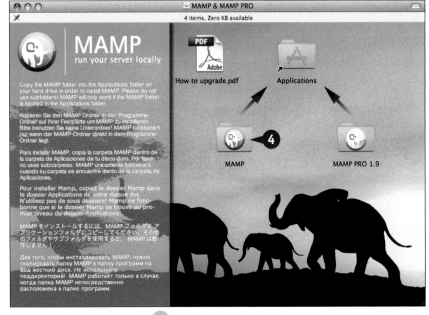

The MAMP files are copied
and the program is installed.

⑤ Open MAMP from the
Applications folder.

● The MAMP window opens,
showing that the servers
are running.

TIP

I see mention on the Web site of MAMP Pro. What is that?
MAMP exists in two versions: one free, one commercial. MAMP Pro, the commercial version, offers many additional features over the free edition. You can configure multiple servers to test different Web sites, allow external access to your server, set up e-mail, and more easily configure the components. Although the free version works well for the examples in this book, many Mac-based developers find the added features provided with MAMP Pro worth its small cost.

P HP is a relatively easy-to-learn yet extremely powerful scripting language. As a free and open-source language, it is also extremely popular and used on many thousands of Web sites, including some of the most-visited sites on the Web such as Facebook. PHP pages contain a mixture of HTML for static elements and PHP for dynamic functionality. PHP code needs to be written within a PHP delimiter, which simply surrounds the PHP block of code to separate it from the HTML on the page. You can output code to the browser using the PHP echo statement.

Create a Basic PHP Page

① Open an HTML document in your editor.

```
simplephp - Notepad     1
File  Edit  Format  View  Help
<!DOCTYPE html PUBLIC "-//W3C//DTD XHTML 1.0 Transitional//EN"
"http://www.w3.org/TR/xhtml1/DTD/xhtml1-transitional.dtd">
<html xmlns="http://www.w3.org/1999/xhtml">
<head>
<meta http-equiv="Content-Type" content="text/html; charset=utf-8" />
<title>Simple PHP</title>

</head>

<body>

|

</body>
</html>
```

② Within the body of the document, type the opening PHP delimiter <?php.

③ Press Enter.

```
simplephp - Notepad
File  Edit  Format  View  Help
<!DOCTYPE html PUBLIC "-//W3C//DTD XHTML 1.0 Transitional//EN"
"http://www.w3.org/TR/xhtml1/DTD/xhtml1-transitional.dtd">
<html xmlns="http://www.w3.org/1999/xhtml">
<head>
<meta http-equiv="Content-Type" content="text/html; charset=utf-8" />
<title>Simple PHP</title>

</head>

<body>

<?php    2
|

</body>
</html>
```

4 Type echo "Hello, world";.

5 Press Enter.

```
simplephp - Notepad
File Edit Format View Help
<!DOCTYPE html PUBLIC "-//W3C//DTD XHTML 1.0 Transitional//EN"
"http://www.w3.org/TR/xhtml1/DTD/xhtml1-transitional.dtd">
<html xmlns="http://www.w3.org/1999/xhtml">
<head>
<meta http-equiv="Content-Type" content="text/html; charset=utf-8" />
<title>Simple PHP</title>

</head>

<body>

<?php
echo "Hello, world";|

</body>
</html>    4
```

6 Type the closing PHP delimiter, ?>.

The PHP is entered onto the page.

```
simplephp - Notepad
File Edit Format View Help
<!DOCTYPE html PUBLIC "-//W3C//DTD XHTML 1.0 Transitional//EN"
"http://www.w3.org/TR/xhtml1/DTD/xhtml1-transitional.dtd">
<html xmlns="http://www.w3.org/1999/xhtml">
<head>
<meta http-equiv="Content-Type" content="text/html; charset=utf-8" />
<title>Simple PHP</title>

</head>

<body>

<?php
echo "Hello, world";
?>    6

</body>
</html>
```

TIPS

Why does the line with echo end in a semicolon?
Every PHP statement needs to end in a semicolon, which is essentially your way of letting PHP know that that statement is complete. If you do not end the statement with a semicolon, you get an error when you try to run your page.

Some pages use <? only for the opening delimiter instead of <?php. Is one more correct than the other?
PHP supports the shorter form of the opening delimiter, but not by default, so you need to modify the configuration file in order to use it. Most PHP developers prefer the longer form.

In order to run your PHP page, you must request it via your Web server and have it processed by the PHP engine. You cannot simply open the file directly in your browser as you can HTML documents. In order for your Web server to access the file, it must be saved in the Web server's root folder. In a Windows installation of WAMP, the root folder is at `c:/wamp/wwwroot`. In a Mac installation of MAMP, it is at `/Applications/MAMP/htdocs`. Your PHP files need to have a .php extension.

Save and Test a PHP Page

Save the Page

1 In your editor, open a document that contains PHP code.

2 Click **File**.

3 Click **Save As**.

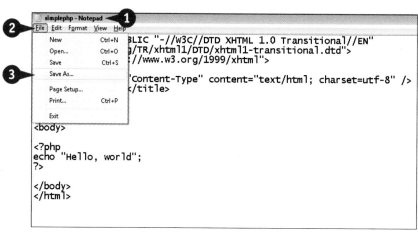

The Save As dialog box appears.

4 Navigate to your Web server's root directory.

On Windows, navigate to `c:/wamp/wwwroot`.

On a Mac, navigate to `Applications/MAMP/htdocs`.

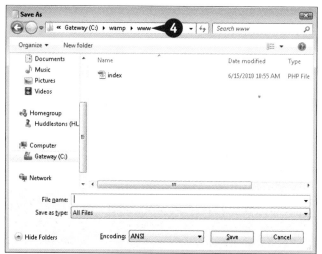

5 Type a filename.

Note: Be sure to add the .php extension.

6 Click **Save**.

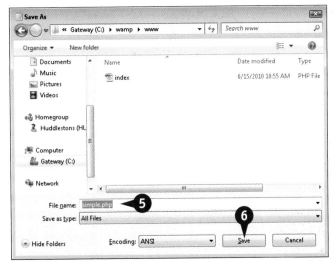

Test the Page in a Browser

1 Open your Web browser to http://localhost/?, replacing *?* with the filename you used in Step **5**.

● The browser displays the page.

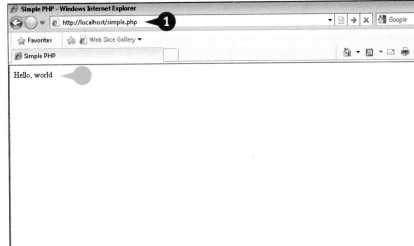

Can I organize my files in the server's root directory?

Yes. You can — and should — have subfolders for documents and images and any other assets, just as you would for a static site. You simply need to ensure that all of the site's assets are either directly in the server root or in a subfolder of the root.

Do I always need to type http://localhost in order to access my site?

Yes. PHP pages must be processed by PHP in order to work, and only your Web server can pass the pages to PHP for that processing. You thus need to request the page from the server, which is done by accessing it via http://localhost.

With PHP, you can accept data from an online form and have your site respond according to the data your use entered. Form data may be accessed in a PHP page by referencing a *super-global*, which is a special type of built-in variable in the language. The `$_POST` super-global contains a reference to any form field submitted to the page. For example, a field in HTML with a `name` attribute set to `firstName` can be accessed by writing `$_POST['firstName']`. Note that the field names are case-sensitive, so they must match your HTML exactly.

Process Form Data

1 In your editor, open an HTML document that contains an existing form.

Note: Be sure that the document is saved in the Web server's root folder.

2 Note the names of each of the fields in the form.

3 Note the filename specified in the form's `action` attribute.

4 In your editor, open a new or existing document.

5 Within the body of the document, type `<?php`.

6 Type `echo "?:";`, replacing *?* with the label from the first form field.

7 Type `echo $_POST['?'],` replacing *?* with the first form field name.

8 Type `echo "<br />";`.

9 Repeat Steps **6** to **8** for each additional form field you want to display.

---

contact - Notepad ◄ **1**

File Edit Format View Help

```
    <h1>Contact Us</h1>

    <form action="processform.php" method="post" >

    <fieldset>
        <legend>Contact Information</legend>

        <label for="firstname">First Name:</label> <input type="text" nam
id="firstname" /><br />

        <label for="last    e">Last Name:</label> <input type="text" name="
id="lastname" /><br />

        <p>My query is in regard to:<br />
        <input type="checkbox" name="widgets" value="redwidget" id="redwi
for="redwidget">Red Widget</label>

        <input type="checkbox" name="widgets" value="bluewidget" id="blue
for="bluewidget">Blue Widget</label>
```

process - Notepad ◄ **4**

File Edit Format View Help

```
<a href="#mainSection" id="skipnav">Skip navigation</a>
    <div class="header"><a href="#"><img src="images/logo.png" alt="Insert
name="Insert_logo" width="180" height="90" id="Insert_logo" style="backgr
display:block;" /></a>
        <!-- end .header --></div>
    <div class="sidebar1">
        <ul class="nav">
            <li><a href="products.html">Products</a></li>
            <li><a href="services.html">Services</a></li>
            <li><a href="about.html">About Us</a></li>
            <li><a href="locations.html">Locations</a></li>
        </ul>
        <p> Use the links above to explore our site.</p>
    <!-- end .sidebar1 --></div>
    <div class="content" id="mainSection">

    <?php   ◄ 5

        echo "First name:"       ◄ 6
        echo $_POST['firstname'];  ◄ 7
        echo "<br />";           ◄ 8
        echo "Last name:";
        echo $_POST['lastname'];
        echo "<br />";
        echo "Comments:";         ◄ 9
        echo $_POST['comments'];
        echo "<br />";
```

284

10 Save the page in the Web server's root folder, using the filename you noted in Step **3**.

11 In your Web browser, open the HTML document from Step **1**.

12 Fill in the form fields and then click the button.

● The resulting PHP page appears, showing the values from the form.

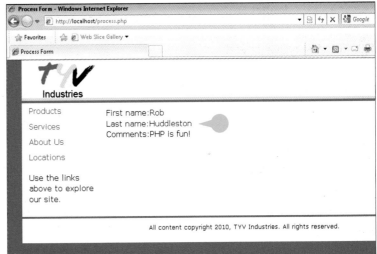

TIPS

Does it matter what method I use on the form?
Yes. The $_POST super-global reads form variables only if the method is set to post. You can use the $_GET super-global to read variables from a form that uses get. A third super-global, $_REQUEST, exists that can read form values from either method, but using it is not recommended.

What does the dollar sign represent?
PHP uses the dollar sign as the first character of any variable name. Because the super-globals are variables, they begin with the dollar sign. Variables you create yourself, as is shown in upcoming tasks, also begin with the symbol.

285

A very common request from bosses and clients alike is the ability to have the data entered into a form e-mailed to a given address. Fortunately, PHP makes this very easy through the use of its `mail()` function. The function takes three arguments: the first is the address to which the e-mail should be sent; the second, the subject of the e-mail; and the third, the message itself. Any or all of these arguments can be variables from an HTML form. Pages that send e-mail should also have additional code to display some sort of confirmation message to the user.

Send E-mail with PHP

1 In your editor, open or create an HTML form that contains fields for a user to enter a subject and message.

2 In your editor, open a new PHP document.

3 Type `<?php`.

4 Type `mail("?", $_POST['?'], $_POST['?']);`, replacing the first ? with your e-mail address, the second with the name of the subject field from the HTML form, and the third with the name of the message field from the form.

5 Type `?>`.

6 Type `<p>Your email message has been sent.</p>`.

The e-mail capability is added to the form.

---

1 emailform - Notepad

File Edit Format View Help

```
<!DOCTYPE html PUBLIC "-//W3C//DTD XHTML 1.0 Transitional//EN"
"http://www.w3.org/TR/xhtml1/DTD/xhtml1-transitional.dtd">
<html xmlns="http://www.w3.org/1999/xhtml">
<head>
<meta http-equiv="Content-Type" content="text/html; charset=utf-8" />
<title>Email Form</title>
</head>

<body>

<form method="post" action="sendemail.php">

<fieldset>
  <legend>Send Email</legend>

  <p><label for="subject">Subject:</label><input type="text" id="subject
/></p>

  <p><label for="message">Message:</label><br />
    <textarea id="message" name="message" rows="5" cols="40"></textarea

  <p><input type="submit" value="Send Message" /></p>
```

2 sendemail - Notepad

File Edit Format View Help

```
<!DOCTYPE html PUBLIC "-//W3C//DTD XHTML 1.0 Transitional//EN"
"http://www.w3.org/TR/xhtml1/DTD/xhtml1-transitional.dtd">
<html xmlns="http://www.w3.org/1999/xhtml">
<head>
<meta http-equiv="Content-Type" content="text/html; charset=utf-8" />
<title>Send Email</title>
</head>

<body>

<?php

mail("rob@filmstosee.com", $_POST['subject'], $_POST['message']);

?>

<p>Your message has been sent.</p>

</body>
</html>
```

7 In your Web browser, open the HTML document from Step **1**.

8 Fill in the form fields and then click the button.

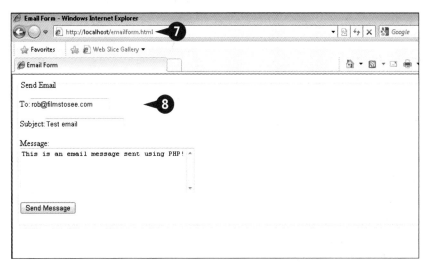

● The confirmation message appears.

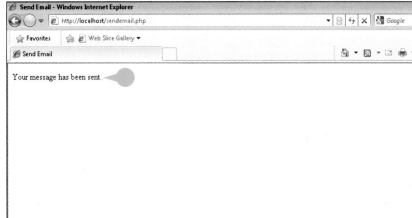

TIP

How can I test the page to be sure it really sends e-mail?
In order to test the form, you need to upload the form to a server configured with a program that can send e-mail. Any third-party Web host should have this configured already, although you may need to add additional arguments to your PHP mail function. Check your host's help files for the proper settings. You can also download and install a free SMTP program to test the page locally. If you are using a Macintosh, you can enable the built-in SMTP client. SMTP stands for **s**imple **m**ail **t**ransfer **p**rotocol, and an SMTP program is one that sends mail. Details on how to set up and configure an SMTP program for local testing on Windows can be found at www.robhuddleston.com/index.cfm/2008/7/27/Setting-up-a-local-email-testing-server. Instructions for enabling the SMTP client on a Mac can be found at www.freshblurbs.com/how-enable-local-smtp-postfix-os-x-leopard.

Managing shared assets such as common headers and navigation is a problem Web designers have faced since the medium's earliest days. Dynamic processing of pages offers a very useful solution via includes. An *include* is simply a directive for PHP to include the contents of a file into another file when it is processing the page. This way, you can have a common element such as your navigation in an independent file that is included into each of your other pages. When you need to update the navigation, you simply modify that one file.

Include External Files

1 In your editor, open a new, blank file.

2 Add the HTML you want to have in the include file.

Note: This should not be a complete file, so the basic HTML structure tags should be omitted.

3 Save the file into your Web server's root directory.

```
navigation - Notepad                    1
File  Edit  Format  View  Help
<ul class="nav">
    <li><a href="products.html">Products</a></li>
  2 <li><a href="services.html">Services</a></li>
    <li><a href="about.html">About Us</a></li>
    <li><a href="locations.html">Locations</a></li>
</ul>
```

4 In your editor, open the file into which you want to include the file created in Steps **1** to **3**.

5 In the file at the point at which you want the include to appear, type <?php.

```
contact - Notepad                       4
File  Edit  Format  View  Help
<!DOCTYPE html PUBLIC "-//W3C//DTD XHTML 1.0 Transitional//EN"
"http://www.w3.org/TR/xhtml1/DTD/xhtml1-transitional.dtd">
<html xmlns="http://www.w3.org/1999/xhtml">
<head>
<meta http-equiv="Content-Type" content="text/html; charset=utf-8" /
<title>Contact Form</title>
<link href="mainstyles.css" rel="stylesheet" type="text/css" />
</head>

<body>

<div class="container">
<a href="#mainSection" id="skipnav">Skip navigation</a>
  <div class="header"><a href="#"><img src="images/logo.png" alt="In
name="Insert_logo" width="180" height="90" id="Insert_logo" style="b
display:block;" /></a>
       <!-- end .header --></div>
  <div class="sidebar1">

  5 <?php

    <p> Use the links above to explore our site.</p>
    <!-- end .sidebar1 --></div>
```

288

6 Type `include("?");`, replacing *?* with the path to the file from Step **3**.

7 Type `?>`.

8 Save the file into the Web server's root directory.

● When you view the second file in your Web browser, the contents of the included file appear.

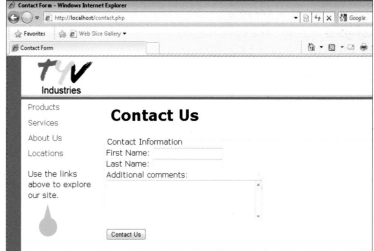

TIPS

Can my include file contain any content I want?	**How can I style my included content?**
Yes. The include file can be made up of plain HTML, PHP, or any other content you want. This file is processed as if it were part of the including document.	Most of the time, your include ends up in a document that contains a link to an external style sheet. Because the include is processed as part of that page, any CSS rules apply to it.

You can encapsulate PHP code that you need to reuse into functions. The syntax for creating PHP functions is nearly identical to that for creating functions in JavaScript: You begin by using the `function` keyword, followed by the name of the function and a pair of parentheses. The code for the function is enclosed in curly braces. You can pass arguments to the function by creating variables within the parentheses, and send a value out of the function using the `return` keyword. Functions are called in PHP by simply referencing their name.

Create Your Own PHP Function

1 In your editor, open an existing PHP document or create a new one.

2 At the top of the page, type `<?php`.

```
<?php


<!DOCTYPE html PUBLIC "-//W3C//DTD XHTML 1.0 Transitional//EN"
"http://www.w3.org/TR/xhtml11/DTD/xhtml11-transitional.dtd">
<html xmlns="http://www.w3.org/1999/xhtml">
<head>
<meta http-equiv="Content-Type" content="text/html; charset=utf-8" />
<title>PHP Function</title>

</head>

<body>

<?php
```

3 Type function `?()`, replacing `?` with a name for the function.

4 Type `{`.

5 Type the code you want to have the function execute.

6 Type `}`.

7 Type `?>`.

```
<?php

function addNums()
{
    $num1 = 10;
    $num2 = 32;
    $total = 42;
    return $total;
}

?>
<!DOCTYPE html PUBLIC "-//W3C//DTD XHTML 1.0 Transitional//EN"
"http://www.w3.org/TR/xhtml11/DTD/xhtml11-transitional.dtd">
<html xmlns="http://www.w3.org/1999/xhtml">
<head>
<meta http-equiv="Content-Type" content="text/html; charset=utf-8" />
<title>PHP Function</title>

</head>

<body>

<?php
```

290

8 At the point on the page where you want to call the function, type echo and then the function name followed by parentheses and a semi-colon.

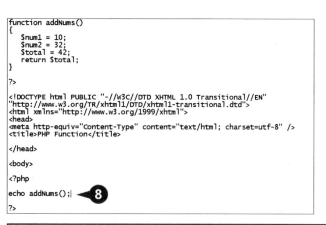

```
function addNums()
{
    $num1 = 10;
    $num2 = 32;
    $total = 42;
    return $total;
}

?>

<!DOCTYPE html PUBLIC "-//W3C//DTD XHTML 1.0 Transitional//EN"
"http://www.w3.org/TR/xhtml1/DTD/xhtml1-transitional.dtd">
<html xmlns="http://www.w3.org/1999/xhtml">
<head>
<meta http-equiv="Content-Type" content="text/html; charset=utf-8" />
<title>PHP Function</title>

</head>

<body>

<?php

echo addNums();|    **8**

?>
```

● When you view the page in the browser, the function works.

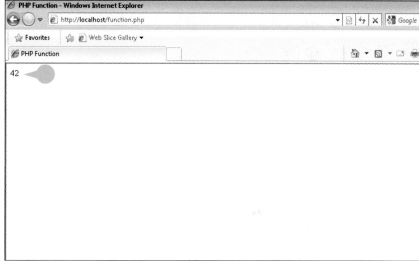

42

TIPS

What sorts of things can I use functions for?
A function can be used for any logical block of code. Most often, you use functions to designate a set of code that you need to call repeatedly, but some developers use them simply to organize the code into blocks.

Does my function have to go at the top of the page?
No, it merely needs to be written before it is called. Most developers place functions at the top of the page to keep them together and easy to find, but they can be placed anywhere.

Adding Information from a Database

Creating a dynamic site gives you the ability to allow your site to interact with a database. Databases are used to store information, which your site can then both display and manipulate.

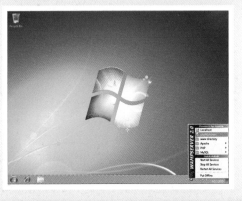

A database, in the simplest terms, is a structured collection of information, or records. Computer databases can be used to store massive amounts of information in a format that makes it easy to sort and find specific data points. Early databases were first developed in the years following World War II. In the 1970s, a new model was proposed that more efficient data storage would be possible if databases were created as a series of related tables. Today, almost every major database system on the market follows this relational database model.

Database Management Systems

A computer program that stores data is technically called a Database Management System, or DBMS. Many hundreds of DBMS systems are available today, and Web developers mostly rely on one of three systems for their work: Microsoft SQL Server, MySQL, and Oracle. Each has advantages and disadvantages. Due to its close relationship with PHP and its inclusion in the WAMP and MAMP installers, this book looks at MySQL.

Relational Databases

A relational database is one that stores its information in a collection of tables. Each table stores data about one specific topic. For example, in a database with product ordering information, the details about the products would be in a table, and the details about the customers would be kept separate in a different table. The database can then store information about the relationships between the data, so it would know which customer ordered which product.

PHP and MySQL

Although PHP can use a technology called ODBC, or Open Database Connectivity, to connect to Microsoft SQL Server, Microsoft Access, or Oracle, it includes the ability to directly connect to a MySQL database. This has the advantage of removing much of the abstraction and additional overhead required when using ODBC, but it also means that PHP applications must be written with a specific database in mind.

Structured Query Language

Also in the 1970s, a group of developers at IBM developed the Structured Query Language (SQL). SQL allows developers to write code to execute commands against a database. It allows developers to work with relational databases through a powerful language that nonetheless relies on a fairly clear syntax.

SQL Syntax

SQL is designed to be fairly easy to learn and use. It is comprised of a series of command words or phrases, all in simple English. For example, if you want to add data to a table, you use the INSERT INTO command.

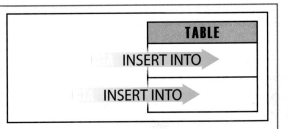

SQL Language Subsets

SQL is divided into three sublanguages: the Data Definition Language (DDL), the Data Manipulation Language (DML), and the Data Control Language (DCL). The DDL is the subset of SQL that allows you to create, alter, and delete the actual tables themselves. By far the most commonly used subset of SQL is the DML. These commands allow you to interact with your data. The DCL is the subset of SQL that allows you to create and manage user accounts.

The MAMP and WAMP installations include phpMyAdmin, a Web-based tool for administering your MySQL database. Although its overall design is not ideal, phpMyAdmin is an easy tool for those getting started using databases. MySQL is not a database, but is instead a database server: It is software that manages a set of databases. Therefore, your first step in using it will be to create a database. You can do this by simply typing the name that you want to use for your database in the phpMyAdmin databases page.

Create a Database

1 In Windows, click the WAMP task tray icon (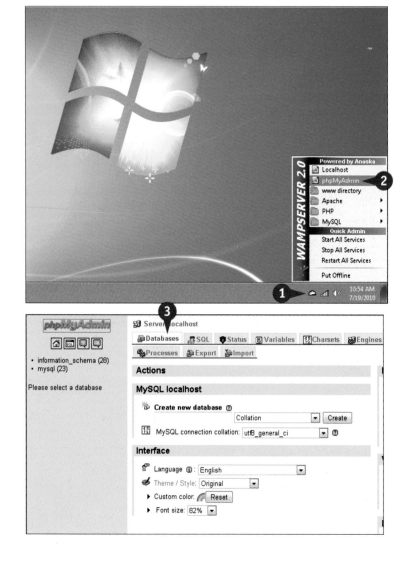).

2 Click **phpMyAdmin**.

On a Mac, you can access it by launching the MAMP application, then clicking **Open Start Page**, then clicking the **phpMyAdmin** link.

The phpMyAdmin main page opens.

3 Click **Databases**.

④ Type a name for your database.

⑤ Click **Create**.

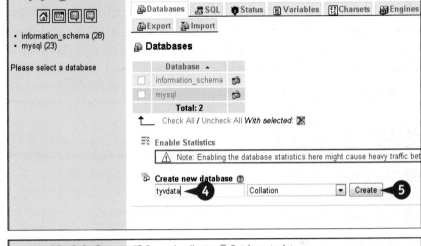

● The confirmation page opens, showing that the database has been created.

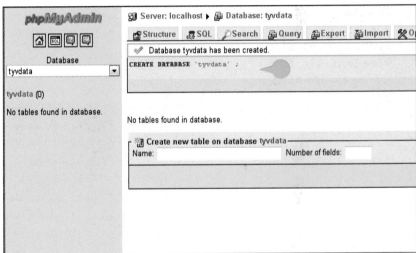

TIPS

How many databases can I create on my server?
MySQL supports an unlimited number of databases, so the limit depends on the amount of space you have on your hard drive. Third-party Web hosting companies often impose a limit of their own on databases on their system.

What are the two databases that already exist?
A default MySQL installation includes two databases: information_schema and mysql. The first, information_schema, is a database in which the server stores information about all of the other databases on the server. The other, mysql, stores information about the server itself.

Once you have created your database, you must populate it with tables. Tables make up the core of your database; they are where your data is actually stored. Tables are made up of rows of fields. Each field represents a distinct piece of your data. The data type is the kind of information that can be stored in a field. The most common are the variable-length character field, the fixed-length character field, integers, floating-point or decimal numbers, dates and times, and Boolean or true-false. You need to specify the name and data type for each field you create.

Create a Table

1 Open the phpMyAdmin page.

Note: See the previous section for instructions on opening phpMyAdmin.

2 Click the name of your database.

The database page loads.

3 Type a name for the table you want to create.

4 Type the number of fields you want to add to your table.

5 Click **Go**.

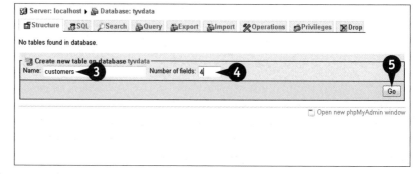

The create table page loads.

6 Type a name for the first field.

7 Select a data type.

8 Set any other desired values.

9 Repeat Steps **6** to **8** for each additional field.

10 Click **Save**.

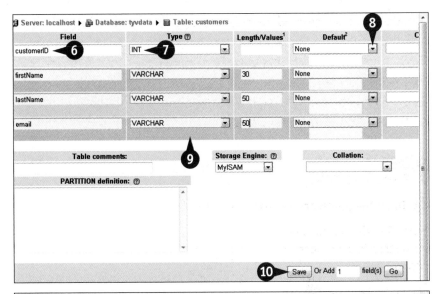

● The table page loads, showing that the table has been created successfully.

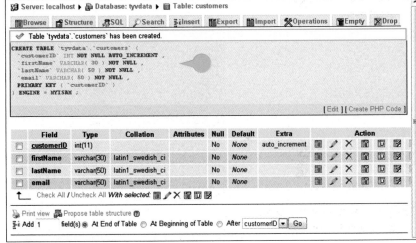

TIPS

How will I know how many fields I need?
Careful planning should always precede creating databases. Ideally, you will have already worked out how many fields you will have in each table before you begin work creating your database.

Where can I learn more about MySQL and relational databases?
The *PHP6 & MySQL Bible* (Wiley, 2009) includes much more detail on working with the database and the core concepts behind database design.

nce you have your table created, the final step before you can begin using your database with PHP is to populate your table with data. You can add data to your table with phpMyAdmin's insert tool. Accessible from the database's page, the insert tool provides a simple form that allows you to add records, or rows, to your table. You are given a list of the fields in the table and can simply type the data into a text box. Although you can add only one record at a time, you can call the form repeatedly to add more data.

Populate the Table with Data

1 Open the phpMyAdmin page.

Note: See the section "Create a Database" for instructions on opening phpMyAdmin.

2 Click the name of your database.

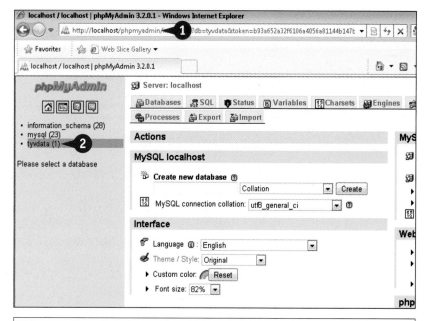

The database page loads.

3 Click the **Insert** icon (▓).

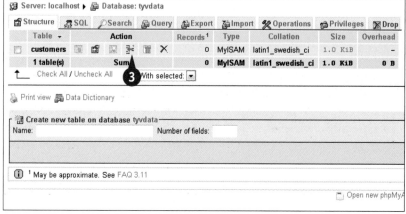

The insert page loads.

4 Type data for each field.

5 Click **Go**.

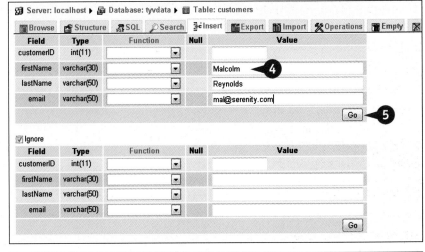

● The confirmation page loads, showing that the data has been entered.

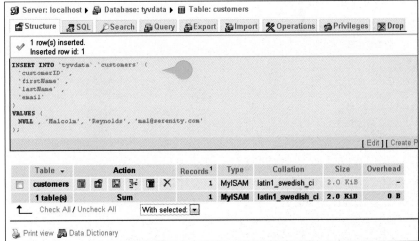

TIPS

Do I need to provide data for every field?	**Does it matter whether or not I capitalize my data?**
It depends on how the table was set up. When you create fields, you can choose to make them required, meaning that data must be provided for them every time, or optional so that they can be left blank. Which one you choose depends on the requirements of the database.	The database will not be affected either way, but you should keep in mind that the data you put into a table is exactly the data you get out. In general, you should input data in the way in which you want to eventually display it.

In order for your PHP pages to display database information, you need to connect PHP to the MySQL server. To do this, you can call the PHP `mysql_connect` function, which takes three arguments: the address to the server, the username, and the password. Once you have connected, you can call the `mysql_select_db` function, which takes a single argument: the name of the database on the server you will be using. Although these can be placed in each file, it is much easier to put these functions in their own file, which can be included into other PHP documents as needed.

Connect PHP to the Database

1 In your editor, open a new, blank document.

2 Type `<?php`.

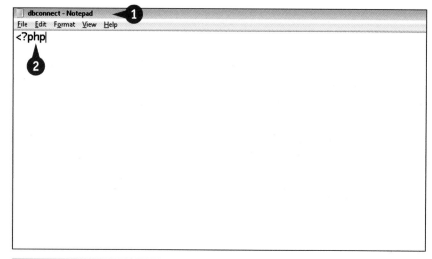

3 Type `mysql_connect ('localhost', 'root');`.

Note: A default installation of MAMP and WAMP does not set up passwords, so you do not need to provide one in this example.

4 Type `mysql_select_db('?');`, replacing *?* with the name of the database you created on your server.

5 Type `?>`.

6 Save the file in the Web server's root directory.

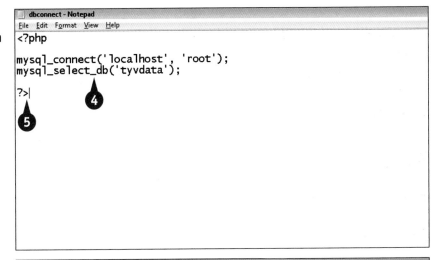

```
dbconnect - Notepad
File  Edit  Format  View  Help
<?php

mysql_connect('localhost', 'root');
mysql_select_db('tyvdata');

?>|
```

7 Open your Web browser and type `http://localhost/?`, replacing *?* with the name of the file from Step **6**.

● The page loads in the browser and is blank if no errors occur. If an error appears, recheck your code.

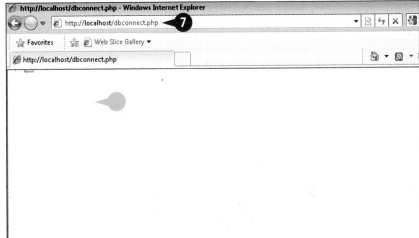

http://localhost/dbconnect.php - Windows Internet Explorer

http://localhost/dbconnect.php

TIP

Because this file contains my username and password, how can I keep it safe?
Once you have opened it in your Web browser to ensure that it works correctly, you should move it outside of your Web server's root folder. Many developers simply store it in the directory above the Web root. The Web server does not have access to files outside of its root, so a potential hacker cannot access it via a Web browser. PHP, on the other hand, can still access files outside of the root with its include function, so placing the file there limits access to it to your PHP application.

You can use PHP and a SQL statement to return the records from a table and display them on a Web page. In PHP, you can create a variable that stores the SQL statement. SQL can return the records in a table with its `SELECT` statement. Following the `SELECT` keyword, you put the names of the fields you want to return, followed by the `FROM` keyword and the name of the table. Once you have created the SQL statement, you can call the PHP `mysql_query()` function, passing the variable with the query as the function's argument.

Display the Contents of a Table on a Web Page

1 In your editor, open a new PHP page.

2 At the top of the code, type `<?php`.

3 Type `include("?");`, replacing *?* with the path to the file that contains the connection code.

Note: See the previous section for details on creating this file.

```
customers - Notepad
File  Edit  Format  View  Help
<?php

include("../dbconnect.php");

<!DOCTYPE html PUBLIC "-//W3C//DTD XHTML 1.0 Transitional//EN"
"http://www.w3.org/TR/xhtml1/DTD/xhtml1-transitional.dtd">
<html xmlns="http://www.w3.org/1999/xhtml">
<head>
<meta http-equiv="Content-Type" content="text/html; charset=utf-8" />
<title>Customer List</title>
<link href="mainstyles.css" rel="stylesheet" type="text/css" />
</head>

<body>

<div class="container">
<a href="#mainSection" id="skipnav">Skip navigation</a>
    <div class="header"><a href="#"><img src="images/logo.png" alt="Inser
name="Insert_logo" width="180" height="90" id="Insert_logo" style="back
display:block;" /></a>
        <!-- end .header --></div>
        <div class="sidebar1">
            <ul class="nav">
```

4 Type `$query = "SELECT field1, field2 FROM table";`, replacing *field1* and *field2* with the names of the fields from your database and *table* with the table name. Add additional fields, separated by commas, if necessary.

```
customers - Notepad
File  Edit  Format  View  Help
<?php

include("../dbconnect.php");

$query = "SELECT firstName, lastName, email FROM customers";

<!DOCTYPE html PUBLIC "-//W3C//DTD XHTML 1.0 Transitional//EN"
"http://www.w3.org/TR/xhtml1/DTD/xhtml1-transitional.dtd">
<html xmlns="http://www.w3.org/1999/xhtml">
<head>
<meta http-equiv="Content-Type" content="text/html; charset=utf-8" />
<title>Customer List</title>
<link href="mainstyles.css" rel="stylesheet" type="text/css" />
</head>

<body>

<div class="container">
<a href="#mainSection" id="skipnav">Skip navigation</a>
    <div class="header"><a href="#"><img src="images/logo.png" alt="Inser
name="Insert_logo" width="180" height="90" id="Insert_logo" style="back
display:block;" /></a>
        <!-- end .header --></div>
```

5 Type `$data = mysql_query($query);`.

```php
<?php

include("../dbconnect.php");

$query = "SELECT firstName, lastName, email FROM customers";

$data = mysql_query($query);    ◄── 5
```
```html
<!DOCTYPE html PUBLIC "-//W3C//DTD XHTML 1.0 Transitional//EN"
"http://www.w3.org/TR/xhtml11/DTD/xhtml11-transitional.dtd">
<html xmlns="http://www.w3.org/1999/xhtml">
<head>
<meta http-equiv="Content-Type" content="text/html; charset=utf-8" />
<title>Customer List</title>
<link href="mainstyles.css" rel="stylesheet" type="text/css" />
</head>

<body>

<div class="container">
<a href="#mainSection" id="skipnav">Skip navigation</a>
  <div class="header"><a href="#"><img src="images/logo.png" alt="Inser
name="Insert_logo" width="180" height="90" id="Insert_logo" style="back
```

6 Type `?>`.

The query is created and added to the page.

```php
<?php

include("../dbconnect.php");

$query = "SELECT firstName, lastName, email FROM customers";

$data = mysql_query($query);

?>    ◄── 6
```
```html
<!DOCTYPE html PUBLIC "-//W3C//DTD XHTML 1.0 Transitional//EN"
"http://www.w3.org/TR/xhtml11/DTD/xhtml11-transitional.dtd">
<html xmlns="http://www.w3.org/1999/xhtml">
<head>
<meta http-equiv="Content-Type" content="text/html; charset=utf-8" />
<title>Customer List</title>
<link href="mainstyles.css" rel="stylesheet" type="text/css" />
</head>

<body>

<div class="container">
<a href="#mainSection" id="skipnav">Skip navigation</a>
```

TIPS

Can I create pages that contain more than one query?

Yes. You can repeat the code to create the query as many times as you want. You only need to ensure that each query uses a different variable name. You also need to run each query separately, through repeated calls to the `mysql_query` function.

Do SQL keywords such as SELECT and FROM have to be capitalized?

No. SQL is case-insensitive. Many database developers capitalize the keywords to make them stand out and make the query easier to read, but the query functions properly if the keywords are not written in capital letters.

continued ▶

Once you have created the SQL statement and executed the query, you can display the results by using a PHP `where` loop. A loop executes a set of code repeatedly; in this case, you want the code that displays the data to repeat for each record. The data is converted into an *array*, a special type of data that holds multiple values, by calling the `mysql_fetch_array` function, and passing to it the variable you used when you called the `mysql_query` function. You can reference the values by giving the name of the array and, in square brackets, the name of the field.

Display the Contents of a Table on a Web Page (continued)

7 Within the body of the page, type `<?php`.

8 Type `while($row = mysql_fetch_ array($data, MYSQL_ASSOC))`.

9 Type `{`.

10 Type `echo "<p>";`.

```
display:block;" /></a>
    <!-- end .header --></div>
  <div class="sidebar1">
    <ul class="nav">
      <li><a href="products.html">Products</a></li>
      <li><a href="services.html">Services</a></li>
      <li><a href="about.html">About Us</a></li>
      <li><a href="locations.html">Locations</a></li>
    </ul>
    <p> Use the links above to explore our site.</p>
  <!-- end .sidebar1 --></div>
  <div class="content" id="mainSection">
    <h1>Our Customers</h1>

    <?php
        while($row = mysql_fetch_array($data, MYSQL_ASSOC))
        {
            echo "<p>";

    <!-- end .content --></div>
  <div class="footer">
    <p>All content copyright 2010, TYV Industries. All rights reserved.
    <!-- end .footer --></div>
  <!-- end .container --></div>
</body>
</html>
```

11 Type `echo $row['?'] . " ";`, replacing *?* with the name of the first field you want to display.

12 Repeat Step **11** for each additional field.

13 Type `echo '"</p>"';`.

```
  <div class="sidebar1">
    <ul class="nav">
      <li><a href="products.html">Products</a></li>
      <li><a href="services.html">Services</a></li>
      <li><a href="about.html">About Us</a></li>
      <li><a href="locations.html">Locations</a></li>
    </ul>
    <p> Use the links above to explore our site.</p>
  <!-- end .sidebar1 --></div>
  <div class="content" id="mainSection">
    <h1>Our Customers</h1>

    <?php
        while($row = mysql_fetch_array($data, MYSQL_ASSOC))
        {
            echo "<p>";
            echo $row['firstName'] ." ";
            echo $row['lastName'];
            echo $row['email'];
            echo "</p>";

    <!-- end .content --></div>
  <div class="footer">
    <p>All content copyright 2010, TYV Industries. All rights reserved.
    <!-- end .footer --></div>
  <!-- end .container --></div>
</body>
```

14 Type `}`.

15 Type `?>`.

16 Save the page in the Web server's root directory.

```
      <li><a href="locations.html">Locations</a></li>
   </ul>
      <p> Use the links above to explore our site.</p>
<!-- end .sidebar1 --></div>
<div class="content" id="mainSection">
   <h1>Our Customers</h1>

   <?php
      while($row = mysql_fetch_array($data, MYSQL_ASSOC))
      {
         echo "<p>";
         echo $row['firstName'] ." ";
         echo $row['lastName'] . " ";
         echo $row['email'];
         echo "</p>";
      }
   ?>

   <!-- end .content --></div>
<div class="footer">
   <p>All content copyright 2010, TYV Industries. All rights reserved.
   <!-- end .footer --></div>
   <!-- end .container --></div>
</body>
</html>
```

● When viewed in a Web browser, the page displays the information from the database.

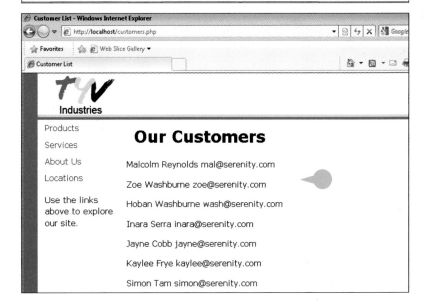

307

TIPS

What does the MYSQL_ASSOC command do?

When you call the `mysql_fetch_array` function, it can create the array of the data using either the field names or arbitrary numbers. The MYSQL_ASSOC command tells the function to create the array using the field names, which are obviously easier to remember.

Why do I need to type the period and the space in the quotes when I output the data?

PHP uses a period for concatenating, or combining, text strings. A space in quotes adds a literal space. Without this code after the `$row[]` calls, each piece of data would run into each prior piece.

Providing a search form is an effective way of allowing users to find the information they want on your site. With your information stored in a database, enabling search on your page simply involves creating a form for the user to type their search parameters, then using that data in a query that displays the results of the search. Thus, searching involves simply combining the information you have already gained in this chapter: creating and processing forms, running queries against the database, and displaying the results. You need to add a filter, using the WHERE clause, to your SQL statement to return only the records that match the search.

Search the Database

1 In your editor, create a new HTML document.

2 In the body, type `<form method="post" action="?">`, replacing `?` with the path to a PHP document.

3 Type `<label for="search"> Search:</label>`.

4 Type `<input type="text" name="search" id="search" />`.

5 Type `<input type="submit" value="Search" />`.

6 Type `</form>`.

7 Save the page in the server's Web root.

8 In your editor, open a new PHP document.

9 Within the body of the document, type `<?php`.

10 Type `include("?");`, replacing *?* with the path to the database connection page.

```
searchaction - Notepad                          8
File  Edit  Format  View  Help
<head>
<meta http-equiv="Content-Type" content="text/html; charset=utf-8" />
<title>Search Results</title>
<link href="mainstyles.css" rel="stylesheet" type="text/css" />
</head>

<body>

<div class="container">
<a href="#mainSection" id="skipnav">Skip navigation</a>
    <div class="header"><a href="#"><img src="images/logo.png" alt="Insert Logo Here"
name="Insert_logo" width="180" height="90" id="Insert_logo" style="background: #C6D5
display:block;" /></a>
        <!-- end .header --></div>
    <div class="sidebar1">
        <ul class="nav">
            <li><a href="products.html">Products</a></li>
            <li><a href="services.html">Services</a></li>
            <li><a href="about.html">About Us</a></li>
            <li><a href="locations.html">Locations</a></li>
        </ul>
        <p> Use the links above to explore our site.</p>
    <!-- end .sidebar1 --></div>
    <div class="content" id="mainSection">
        <h1>Search Results</h1>

        <?php          9

            include("../dbconnect.php");|    10
```

11 Type `$search = $_POST['search'];`.

12 Type `$query = "SELECT field1, field2 FROM table WHERE field1 = '$search'";`, replacing *field1* and *field2* with the database fields you want to return and *table* with the table name.

The query is created.

```
display:block;" /></a>
    <!-- end .header --></div>
    <div class="sidebar1">
        <ul class="nav">
            <li><a href="products.html">Products</a></li>
            <li><a href="services.html">Services</a></li>
            <li><a href="about.html">About Us</a></li>
            <li><a href="locations.html">Locations</a></li>
        </ul>
        <p> Use the links above to explore our site.</p>
    <!-- end .sidebar1 --></div>
    <div class="content" id="mainSection">
        <h1>Search Results</h1>

        <?php

            include("../dbconnect.php");

            $search = $_POST['search'];     11

            $query = "SELECT firstName, lastName, email FROM customers WHERE lastName =
'$search'";|

    <!-- end .content --></div>                   12
    <div class="footer">
        <p>All content copyright 2010, TYV Industries. All rights reserved.</p>
        <!-- end .footer --></div>
    <!-- end .container --></div>
</body>
</html>
```

TIPS

Why is the search variable in single quotation marks in the query?
SQL requires that references to data in nonnumeric fields be placed in single quotation marks in queries. If the field on which you are searching contains numeric data, you would omit the quotes.

Can I allow my user to search on more than one field?
Yes, although doing so significantly complicates your query. If you have two fields, you must account for four possibilities: that your user enters information into both fields, neither field, only the first, or only the second. Although doing so is possible, it can be difficult.

continued ▶

Once you have queried the database, you can simply display the results as you would normally, by converting the results into an array and using the where loop to iterate over them. You can also use the mysql_num_rows() function to display the number of rows the query returns, which can be helpful to your user. If your query returns no results, you can use a PHP if statement, which takes an expression that returns true or false, to display a message. You can add an else statement to display the results when the query is successful.

Search the Database (continued)

⑬ Type $data = mysql_query ($query);.

⑭ Type $num_records = mysql_num_rows($data);.

⑮ Type if($num_records == 0).

⑯ Type {.

⑰ Type echo "No records found";.

⑱ Type }.

```
<!-- end .sidebar1 --></div>
<div class="content" id="mainSection">
  <h1>Search Results</h1>

  <?php

    include("../dbconnect.php");

    $search = $_POST['search'];

    $query = "SELECT firstName, lastName, email FROM customers WHERE lastName =
'$search'";
⑬   $data = mysql_query($query);

    $num_records = mysql_num_rows($data);  ⑭

⑯   if($num_records == 0)  ⑮
    {
              echo "No records found";  ⑰
    }  ⑱

  <!-- end .content --></div>
<div class="footer">
    <p>All content copyright 2010, TYV Industries. All rights reserved.</p>
    <!-- end .footer --></div>
  <!-- end .container --></div>
</body>
</html>
```

⑲ Type else.

⑳ Type {.

㉑ Type while($row = mysql_fetch_array ($data, MYSQL_ ASSOC)).

㉒ Type {.

㉓ Type echo statements to output the results.

㉔ Type }.

㉕ Type }.

㉖ Type ?>.

```
    $data = mysql_query($query);

    $num_records = mysql_num_rows($data);

    if($num_records == 0)
    {
            echo "No records found";
    }
⑲  else
    {  ⑳
⑫        while($row = mysql_fetch_array($data, MYSQL_ASSOC))  ㉑
         {
            echo "<p>";
            echo $row['firstName'] . " ";
            echo $row['lastName'] . " ";  ㉓
            echo $row['email'];
㉖  ㉕      echo "</p>";
         }  ㉔
    }
    ?>

  <!-- end .content --></div>
<div class="footer">
    <p>All content copyright 2010, TYV Industries. All rights reserved.</p>
    <!-- end .footer --></div>
  <!-- end .container --></div>
</body>
</html>
```

㉗ Save the page in the server's Web root.

28 Open the search page in your browser. Type a term to search for and click the form's button.

● The search page displays either the results or the no results message.

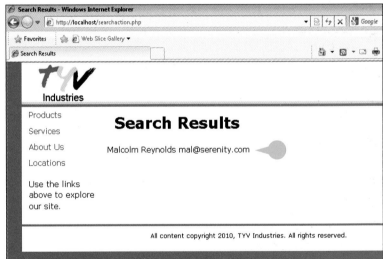

All content copyright 2010, TYV Industries. All rights reserved.

TIPS

Why does the if statement have two equal signs?
PHP uses a double equal sign to test for equality, and a single equal sign to assign a value to a variable. Thus, $x = 10$ sets the value of the variable x to 10, whereas $x == 10$ compares the value of x to 10.

Can I test on more than one condition?
Yes. PHP supports the use of `if else` statements, which are placed between an `if` and an `else`. The `if else` statement, like `if`, takes an expression as its argument.

P HP pages can perform any database operations. Although the most common uses are querying the database and displaying the resulting fields, you can also use PHP to add records to your table. Administrators need to do this to populate the table with data, but you may have situations where users will need to do so as well, such as self-registration systems. In order to insert new data, you begin by creating a HTML form. The form must contain one form control for each database field into which you want to insert data.

Insert New Data into a Table with PHP

Create the Form

1 In your editor, open a new HTML document.

2 Within the body, type `<form method="post" action=" ?">`, replacing *?* with the filename you plan to use for your PHP script.

```
<body>

<div class="container">
<a href="#mainSection" id="skipnav">Skip navigation</a>
   <div class="header"><a href="#"><img src="images/logo.png" alt="Inser
name="Insert_logo" width="180" height="90" id="Insert_logo" style="back(
display:block;" /></a>
      <!-- end .header --></div>
   <div class="sidebar1">
      <ul class="nav">
         <li><a href="products.html">Products</a></li>
         <li><a href="services.html">Services</a></li>
         <li><a href="about.html">About Us</a></li>
         <li><a href="locations.html">Locations</a></li>
      </ul>
      <p> Use the links above to explore our site.</p>
   <!-- end .sidebar1 --></div>
   <div class="content" id="mainSection">
      <h1>Insert Records</h1>

      <form method="post" action="insertaction.php">

      <!-- end .content --></div>
   <div class="footer">
      <p>All content copyright 2010, TYV Industries. All rights reserved.
      <!-- end .footer --></div>
   <!-- end .container --></div>
```

1

2

3 Type `<p><label for= " ?">`, replacing *?* with the ID you plan to use for your first field.

4 Type a label for the field.

5 Type `</label>`.

```
<body>

<div class="container">
<a href="#mainSection" id="skipnav">Skip navigation</a>
   <div class="header"><a href="#"><img src="images/logo.png" alt="Inser
name="Insert_logo" width="180" height="90" id="Insert_logo" style="back(
display:block;" /></a>
      <!-- end .header --></div>
   <div class="sidebar1">
      <ul class="nav">
         <li><a href="products.html">Products</a></li>
         <li><a href="services.html">Services</a></li>
         <li><a href="about.html">About Us</a></li>
         <li><a href="locations.html">Locations</a></li>
      </ul>
      <p> Use the links above to explore our site.</p>
   <!-- end .sidebar1 --></div>
   <div class="content" id="mainSection">
      <h1>Insert Records</h1>

      <form method="post" action="insertaction.php">

      <p><label for="firstName">First Name:</label>

      <!-- end .content --></div>
   <div class="footer">
      <p>All content copyright 2010, TYV Industries. All rights reserved.
```

3

4

5

6 Type `<input type="text" name="?" id="?" /></p>`, replacing both *?*s with appropriate name and ID values for the field.

7 Repeat Steps **3** to **6** to create any additional fields you need for the form.

```
        <li><a href="products.html">Products</a></li>
        <li><a href="services.html">Services</a></li>
        <li><a href="about.html">About Us</a></li>
        <li><a href="locations.html">Locations</a></li>
      </ul>
      <p> Use the links above to explore our site.</p>
    <!-- end .sidebar1 --></div>
    <div class="content" id="mainSection">
      <h1>Insert Records</h1>

      <form method="post" action="insertaction.php">

      <p><label for="firstName">First Name:</label>
        <input type="text" name="firstName" id="firstName" /></p>  ◀ 6
        <p><label for="lastName">Last Name:</label>
  7 ▶ <input type="text" name="lastName" id="lastName" /></p>
        <p><label for="email">Email:</label>
        <input type="text" name="email" id="email" /></p>|

      <!-- end .content --></div>
    <div class="footer">
      <p>All content copyright 2010, TYV Industries. All rights reserved.
      <!-- end .footer --></div>
    <!-- end .container --></div>
</body>
</html>
```

8 Type `<p><input type="submit" value="Add Record" /></p>`.

The form is created.

```
        <li><a href="products.html">Products</a></li>
        <li><a href="services.html">Services</a></li>
        <li><a href="about.html">About Us</a></li>
        <li><a href="locations.html">Locations</a></li>
      </ul>
      <p> Use the links above to explore our site.</p>
    <!-- end .sidebar1 --></div>
    <div class="content" id="mainSection">
      <h1>Insert Records</h1>

      <form method="post" action="insertaction.php">

      <p><label for="firstName">First Name:</label>
        <input type="text" name="firstName" id="firstName" /></p>
        <p><label for="lastName">Last Name:</label>
        <input type="text" name="lastName" id="lastName" /></p>
        <p><label for="email">Email:</label>
        <input type="text" name="email" id="email" /></p>
        <p> <input type="submit" value="Add Record" /></p>  ◀ 8

      </form>|

      <!-- end .content --></div>
    <div class="footer">
      <p>All content copyright 2010, TYV Industries. All rights reserved.
      <!-- end .footer --></div>
    <!-- end .container --></div>
```

TIP

Can I use other form field types besides text fields?
Yes. If you have a database field that can only contain certain acceptable values, such as company department names, you can and in fact should use radio buttons or select lists in the form. Fields that will contain longer pieces of information, such as a biography of an employee, should use textareas. You should use the form field type that makes the most sense for the data you need entered.

continued ▶

Insert New

Once you have created your form, you must create the PHP page to process the form. In this case, the page must contain a SQL `INSERT INTO` statement to add the record to the database. The `INSERT INTO` statement takes the name of the table, followed by a list of the fields into which you will be adding data. You then use the `VALUES` keyword followed by a list of the form fields that contain the new data. Once complete, you can use the PHP `header()` function to redirect your user to a page that displays the records in the table.

Insert New Data into a Table with PHP (continued)

Create the PHP Script

1 In your editor, open a new PHP page.

2 Delete any existing code your editor might add so that the page is completely blank.

3 Type `<?php`.

4 Type `include("?");`, replacing *?* with the path to your database connection script.

5 Type `$formfield1 = $_POST['formfield1'];`, replacing *formfield1* with the name of the first field from the form.

6 Repeat Step **5** to create shorter variable names for the remaining form fields.

7 Type `$query = "INSERT INTO table (field1, field2) VALUES ('$formfield1', '$formfield2')";`, replacing *table* with the name of the table, *field1* and *field2* with the names of the database fields, and *$formfield1*, *$formfield2* with the variables created in Steps **5** and **6**.

8 Type `$data = mysql_query($query);`.

9 Type `header("location: ?");`, replacing *?* with the path to a page that displays the table's data.

Note: See the section "Display the Contents of a Table on a Web Page" earlier in this chapter for details on creating this page.

```php
<?php
include("../dbconnect.php");

$firstName = $_POST['firstName'];
$lastName = $_POST['lastName'];
$email = $_POST['email'];

$query = "INSERT INTO customers (firstName, lastName, email) VALUES ('$firstName', '$lastName', '$email')";
```

```php
<?php
include("../dbconnect.php");

$firstName = $_POST['firstName'];
$lastName = $_POST['lastName'];
$email = $_POST['email'];

$query = "INSERT INTO customers (firstName, lastName, email) VALUES ('$firstName', '$lastName', '$email')";

$data = mysql_query($query);

header("location: customers.php");
?>
```

⑩ Open the form in a Web browser.

⑪ Fill in the form and click the button.

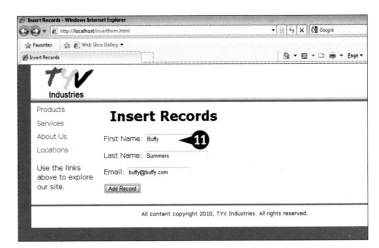

● The record is inserted into the table and the page to which the script redirects appears.

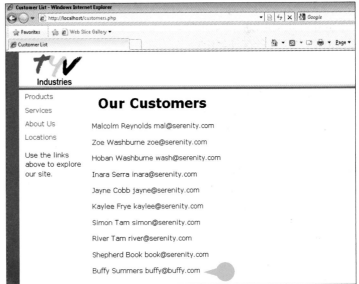

TIP

How do I troubleshoot my script if it does not work?

Debugging any complicated script can be difficult. You should first carefully review your code to ensure that you do not have any typographic errors. Pay particular attention to your use of capital and lowercase letters, single and double quotation marks, and semicolons. You can add `echo` statements at key locations in your script to get PHP to output variables and values so that you can see those values as the script executes. You can also turn on more robust error messages; for details on doing this, consult the PHP documentation at http://php.net/manual/en/.

Publishing Your Site and Getting Noticed

Once you have completed designing and coding your site, you must

get it online so that others can see your work.

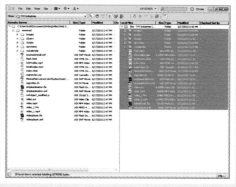

Find a Web Host

For most individuals and even small businesses, the cost of setting up, securing, and maintaining their own Web server is both technically and cost prohibitive. You can easily avoid these issues by using a third-party Web host. Web hosts provide the server space, security, and maintenance expertise to allow you to focus on the design and content of your site. You must find a host, sign up for their service, and transfer your site's files to their servers in order to get online.

Shopping for a Host

There are literally millions of Web hosts available — a Google search for "Web hosting" in June 2010 returned 89 million results. Therefore, you should spend some time comparison shopping. Hosts have widely varying fees for their services, from free to thousands of dollars per month. They also offer a wide range of services for these fees, so you must investigate which ones offer the services you want for the price you can afford.

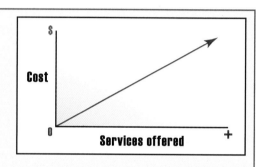

Shared versus Dedicated Hosting

Many Web hosts offer two basic services: shared hosting and dedicated hosting. With shared hosts, your site is on a server with many other sites. If one or more of those sites begins to use too much bandwidth or server resources, the performance of your site might suffer. Dedicated hosting allows you to rent an entire server for your site, so yours is the only one running on the machine. This is, for obvious reasons, a much more expensive alternative, but generally offers better performance.

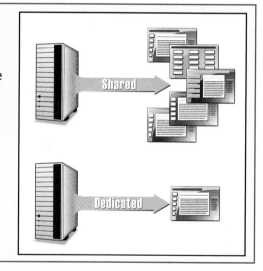

Domain Hosting

Free Web hosts generally require that you use their domain name, but most other hosts offer domain hosting, where you can purchase a domain name and use it for your site. Some hosts even offer multiple domain hosting, allowing you to purchase several domains and host them all, either as a single site that has many domains pointing to it, or as separate sites.

Hard Drive Space and Bandwidth

All hosts should offer a certain amount of disk space, a maximum allowed amount of monthly bandwidth, and some sort of control panel interface to allow you to administer your site. The hard drive space and bandwidth is more than usually sufficient for most sites, although hosts generally offer a la carte options for additional space and bandwidth should you need them.

Extra Services

Hosts generally offer e-mail services as well, allowing you to use e-mail accounts attached to your domain name. They may also offer server-side scripting features, such as support for PHP, ASP, ASP.NET, and ColdFusion, as well as space on database servers. All hosts should offer some sort of backup system to protect against data loss on their side, and many make the Web server logs for your site available, either as a raw data file that you need to analyze yourself or through a graphical interface on the control panel.

Signing Up with a Host

When you have found the host you want to use, you can sign up through their Web site. Most ask for basic contact and billing information. Many offer monthly or yearly billing, with a discount for longer terms. Once they receive your information, you should receive an e-mail from them with details as to how to log into the control panel and set up other details of your site, as well as the login information you need to upload your files to them.

Buy a Domain Name

A domain name is the recognizable identifier for your site, and becomes an important part of your overall brand. You can purchase a domain name by searching for one that is still available and then purchasing it for a small yearly fee from a company called a domain registrar. Thousands of domain registrars are in existence, and so you need to do some comparison shopping in order to find the best price. Unfortunately, you may find it very difficult to find a domain name still available that ends in .com.

Buy a Domain Name

1 Open your Web browser.

2 Browse to www. networksolutions.com.

Note: Network Solutions is merely one of the more popular registrars. It may pay to shop around before you purchase.

3 Type a domain name you would like to purchase.

4 Click **Find**.

The next page opens, either informing you that the name is available or prompting you to search again.

5 When you have found an available name, click **Add Selected to Cart**.

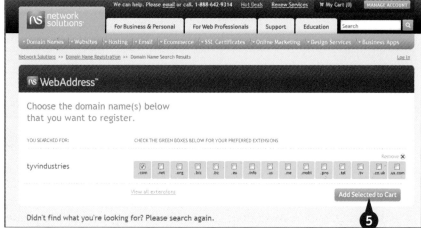

The next page opens, offering additional domains.

6 Click **No, Thanks**.

7 Complete the remainder of the steps for the checkout process.

Your domain name is now purchased.

TIP

I see a lot of other domains that end in .edu, .gov, and .mil. I also see a lot with two-letter endings such as .us or .uk. What are these?

When the domain name system was developed, six of these so-called top-level domains were created. Three were designed to be open to anyone: .com, .net, and .org. The other three were reserved, and so only nonprofit educational institutions can use .edu, only governmental entities within the United States can use .gov, and only branches of the United States military can use .mil. The two-letter top-level domains designate countries; .us is for the United States and .uk is Britain. The popular .tv domain actually belongs to the island nation of Tuvalu. Today, many other top-level domains exist as well, such as .aero and .name, but .com remains the most popular.

Publish Your Web Site Using FTP

I n order for your Web site to be visible to other people, you must transfer the files from your local machine to your Web host's servers. Although several different technologies are available to transfer files, by far the most common is FTP (**f**ile **t**ransfer **p**rotocol). FTP has been used for many years to allow for the transfer of files between computers and, in fact, predates the Web. You will also need an FTP client — software on your computer that you can use to create and maintain the FTP connection. Both Windows and Macintosh include a built-in command-line FTP.

Publish Your Web Site Using FTP

1 From the Start menu, select **Run**.

On a Mac, open the terminal from Applications ➪ Utilities ➪ Terminal.

2 In the Run dialog box, type **ftp**.

On a Mac, type **ftp** followed by the address of the server, and skip to Step **6**.

3 Click **OK**.

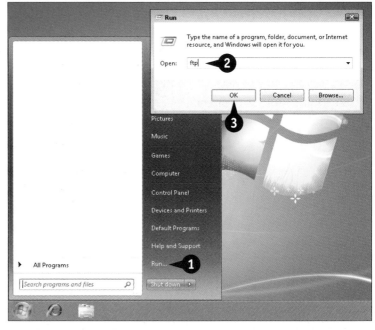

The Windows FTP window opens.

4 Type open ?, replacing ? with the address of your host's FTP server.

5 Press Enter.

6 Type your username.

7 Press Enter.

8 Type your password.

9 Press Enter.

The FTP server logs you in.

10 Type `hash`.

11 Press `Enter`.

12 Type `lcd` and then the path to the folder on your hard drive that contains your Web page files.

13 Type `mput *.html`.

Note: This transfers all files with an .html extension. If you are using another extension such as .htm or .php for your files, use it instead.

14 Press `Enter`.

All HTML files in the current directory are uploaded.

15 Type `Quit`.

16 Press `Enter`.

The command window closes.

```
C:\Windows\system32\ftp.exe
ftp> open robhuddleston.com
Connected to robhuddleston.com.
220 Microsoft FTP Service
User (robhuddleston.com:(none)): robhuddles
331 Password required for robhuddles.
Password:
230 User robhuddles logged in.
ftp> hash          10
Hash mark printing On   ftp: (2048 bytes/hash mark) .
ftp> lcd c:\wamp\www
Local directory now C:\wamp\www.          12
ftp> mput *.html
```

```
C:\Windows\system32\ftp.exe
ftp> open robhuddleston.com
Connected to robhuddleston.com.
220 Microsoft FTP Service
User (robhuddleston.com:(none)): robhuddles
331 Password required for robhuddles.
Password:
230 User robhuddles logged in.
ftp> hash
Hash mark printing On   ftp: (2048 bytes/hash mark) .
ftp> lcd c:\wamp\www
Local directory now   \wamp\www.
ftp> mput *.html          13
```

TIP

Many of the commands in FTP seem odd. Where can I find a reference for them?

FTP relies on rather arcane commands. Some common commands are included in the table below.

Command	Function
`dir`	Displays a list of the files in the current directory on the server
`cd <path>`	Changes to a specified directory on the server
`lcd <path>`	Changes to a specified directory on the client (local cd)
`mkdir <directoryname>`	Creates a directory on the server
`hash`	Displays hash symbols (#) to show the progress of a file upload or download
`get <filename>`	Downloads a file from the server
`put <filename>`	Uploads a file to the server
`mget <*.extension>`	Downloads all files with the specified extension
`mput <*.extension>`	Uploads all files with the specified extension
`?`	Displays a list of accepted commands

Set Up Remote Server Information in Dreamweaver

If you use Dreamweaver to create your site, you can also use it to upload your files to your server. The Files panel can be expanded to make file transfer easier. The first time you expand the panel, you are prompted to define a remote server. This process allows you to store the necessary remote server information so that Dreamweaver can connect to your host's Web servers and upload your files. Your hosting company will have provided you the information you must enter, most likely in the initial e-mail they sent after you signed up for their service.

Set Up Remote Server Information in Dreamweaver

1 In the Files panel, click the **Expand to show local and remote sites** button (⊡).

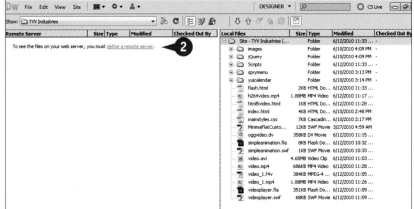

The panel expands full screen.

2 Click **define a remote server**.

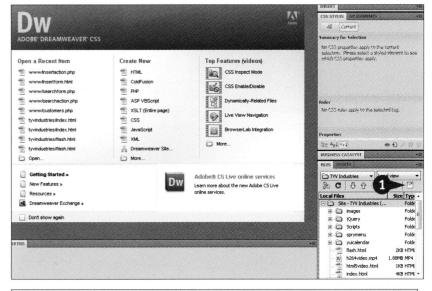

The Site Setup dialog box opens.

3 Click the plus symbol.

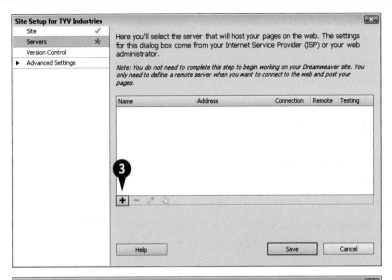

4 Type the necessary FTP information, as provided by your host.

5 Click **Save**.

6 Click **Save**.

The remote information is saved.

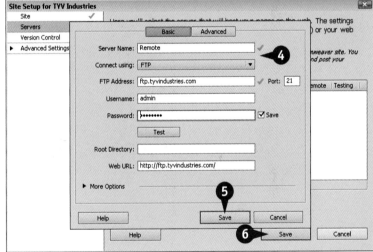

TIP

Can I define more than one server per site?
Yes. In Dreamweaver CS5, you can define as many servers per site as you want. If you are using server-side technologies such as PHP, you should define both a local testing server and a remote host server. Some companies provide their in-house designers with a testing server, a staging server for approval of pages, and a live or production server. You could define each of these and then instruct Dreamweaver as to which you want to upload the files.

Upload Your Files Using Dreamweaver

Once you have defined your remote hosting information in Dreamweaver, you can use the expanded Files panel to upload your files. When you connect to your host's server, you will see your local files on the right half of the screen and your remote files — the files on the server — on the left. You can simply drag files from your local drive to the server to upload them, or from the server to your local drive to download. You can also perform normal file system operations such as creating folders, renaming files, and moving files.

Upload Your Files Using Dreamweaver

① In the Files panel, click the **Expand to show local and remote sites** button (🗗).

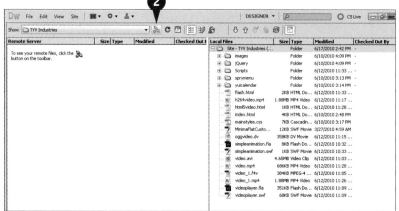

The panel expands full screen.

② Click the **Connects to Remote Host** button (🔌).

Dreamweaver connects to the remote host and displays the host's files.

3 Drag a file from the local files to the remote files.

4 Repeat Step **3** for any additional files.

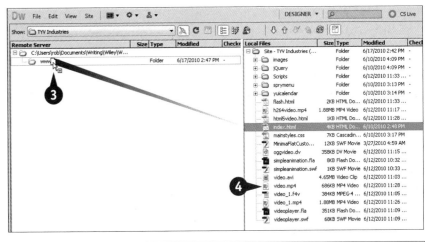

● The files are uploaded to the server.

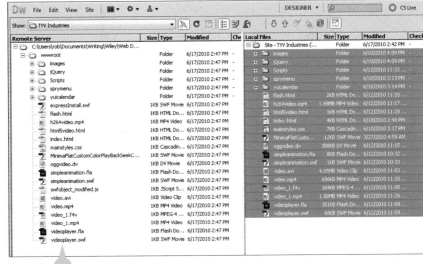

TIPS

When I upload a file, I get a dialog box asking if I want to upload dependent files. What is this?

Dependent files are primarily images and CSS files that you need to have uploaded in order for your site to work correctly. Dreamweaver is offering to automatically upload these whenever you upload an HTML document. In general, clicking **Yes** is a good idea.

How can I create a new folder on my server?

Right-click (Control+click) in the server view, click **New Folder**, and then type a name for the folder. Keep in mind that your folder structure on the server needs to exactly match that on your local computer in order for your links to work correctly.

Understanding Search Engine Optimization

Search engines are a primary way that many users will find your site, so ensuring that you your pages appear as high as possible in the results is a key factor in increasing the number of site visitors. In the early days of the Web, the first search engines were created to help users find information in the exponentially increasing number of sites. These early search engines relied on Webmasters to self-describe their pages in HTML by adding keywords and descriptions of the page content. Today, search engines use a much more complex system to index sites.

PageRank and Google

While Larry Page and Sergey Brin were graduate students at Stanford University, they developed a new algorithm that relied primarily on incoming links to a page. Their basic theory was that although a Webmaster might use misleading keywords on a page, other Webmasters would fail to perpetrate the false connection because the other Webmaster would not provide links to it. This system, dubbed PageRank, became the basis for the company Google, a company Page and Brin founded in 1998.

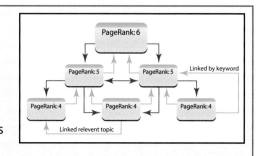

Content Is King

By far the most important key to getting good search engine rankings is to have good, meaningful content and to be sure to use the proper HTML elements to code that content. Search engines read the code in your page, and give more weight to text enclosed in heading tags than those in, say, paragraphs, the logic being that the text in headings is what the page is "about."

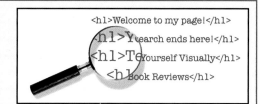

Consider Accessibility for Search Optimization

Because search engines read the code of the page, they approach your page in many of the same ways as screen readers for blind users do. So, in general, pages accessible to disabled users will get higher search engine rankings than those that are not.

Avoid All-Image Image Pages

Pages made up of nothing but images rank much lower due to their lack of meaningful text for the search engines to read. A mock-up created in a program

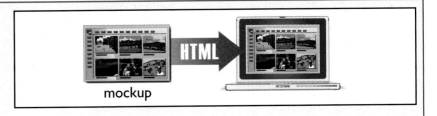

mockup

such as Fireworks can be a useful starting point in design, but converting this mockup directly into a Web page as a large image will rate very low on search engine results. It will also load very slowly and be difficult to edit later. Instead, take the mock-up as a guide for the layout, and re-create it in HTML.

Do Not Rely on Search Engine Optimization Alone

Not every site is necessarily going to benefit from high search engine rankings. Sites that are part of a larger marketing strategy may not rely heavily on search engine results at all. Placing the site's address on billboards or television advertisements may be as, if not more, effective than worrying about one's Google PageRank. Word of mouth can be an effective strategy, as can the use of social networking sites such as MySpace or Facebook, particularly for blogs or small, more local sites. Search engine optimization should fit within the site's overall marketing strategy.

Follow Search Engine Guidelines

Every one of the major search engines makes a set of guidelines available to assist Webmasters in building pages that get higher rankings. These rules are not set in stone, and, in fact, search engines change them frequently, but they should be observed as much as possible.

Guidelines
for higher rankings

☐ Create Webmaster Tools account/verify site

☐ Update settings

☐ Monitor & manage site

☐ Add sitemap for sites in Webmaster Tools account

☐ Keep up to date

Use Meta Tags

The HTML <meta> tag in the head of the document allows you to describe your page to search engines. The word *meta* is from the Greek meaning "with," and is used to refer to something that refers to itself. Thus, the tag allows you to add information about the page. The <meta> tag should be given a `name` attribute, set to either `keywords` or `description`. Either is paired with a `content` attribute. Keywords contain a comma-separated list of the words you think users are likely to type to search for your site. The description is a brief paragraph describing the site.

Use Meta Tags

1 Open a Web page in your editor.

2 In the head of the page, type <meta.

3 Type name="keywords".

```
index - Notepad
File Edit Format View Help
<!DOCTYPE html PUBLIC "-//W3C//DTD XHTML 1.0 Transitional//EN"
"http://www.w3.org/TR/xhtml1/DTD/xhtml1-transitional.dtd">
<html xmlns="http://www.w3.org/1999/xhtml">
<head>
<meta http-equiv="Content-Type" content="text/html; charset=utf-8" />

<meta name="keywords" |

<title>TYV Industries Home</title>
<link href="mainstyles.css" rel="stylesheet" type="text/css" />
<script type="text/javascript">

function hideDiv()
{
    document.getElementById("specials").style.visibility = "hidden";
}

function showDiv()
{
    document.getElementById("specials").style.visibility = "visible";
}
```

4 Type content=" ?", replacing *?* with a comma-separated list of words.

5 Type />.

```
index - Notepad
File Edit Format View Help
<!DOCTYPE html PUBLIC "-//W3C//DTD XHTML 1.0 Transitional//EN"
"http://www.w3.org/TR/xhtml1/DTD/xhtml1-transitional.dtd">
<html xmlns="http://www.w3.org/1999/xhtml">
<head>
<meta http-equiv="Content-Type" content="text/html; charset=utf-8" />

<meta name="keywords" content="tyv industries, widgets" />|

<title>TYV Industries Home</title>
<link href="mainstyles.css" rel="stylesheet" type="text/css" />
<script type="text/javascript">

function hideDiv()
{
    document.getElementById("specials").style.visibility = "hidden";
}

function showDiv()
{
    document.getElementById("specials").style.visibility = "visible";
}
```

6 Type `<meta`.

7 Type `name= "description"`.

```
index - Notepad
File  Edit  Format  View  Help
<!DOCTYPE html PUBLIC "-//W3C//DTD XHTML 1.0 Transitional//EN"
"http://www.w3.org/TR/xhtml1/DTD/xhtml1-transitional.dtd">
<html xmlns="http://www.w3.org/1999/xhtml">
<head>
<meta http-equiv="Content-Type" content="text/html; charset=utf-8" />

<meta name="keywords" content="tyv industries, widgets" />

<meta name="description" |

<title>TYV Industries Home</title>
<link href="mainstyles.css" rel="stylesheet" type="text/css" />
<script type="text/javascript">

function hideDiv()
{
    document.getElementById("specials").style.visibility = "hidden";
}

function showDiv()
{
    document.getElementById("specials").style.visibility = "visible";
}
```

8 Type `content=" ?",` replacing *?* with a brief paragraph describing the site.

9 Type `/>`.

The `<meta>` tags have been added to the page.

```
index - Notepad
File  Edit  Format  View  Help
<!DOCTYPE html PUBLIC "-//W3C//DTD XHTML 1.0 Transitional//EN"
"http://www.w3.org/TR/xhtml1/DTD/xhtml1-transitional.dtd">
<html xmlns="http://www.w3.org/1999/xhtml">
<head>
<meta http-equiv="Content-Type" content="text/html; charset=utf-8" />

<meta name="keywords" content="tyv industries, widgets" />

<meta name="description" content="TYV Industries is the world leader in widget sales" />|

<title>TYV Industries Home</title>
<link href="mainstyles.css" rel="styles    " type="text/css" />
<script type="text/javascript">

function hideDiv()
{
    document.getElementById("specials").style.visibility = "hidden";
}

function showDiv()
{
    document.getElementById("specials").style.visibility = "visible";
}
```

TIPS

Do search engines still use <meta> tags?
Google has stated publically that they do not, but other search engines might. Even though `<meta>` tags might be ignored, it does not hurt your site to add them for those engines that read them.

What else can the <meta> tag be used for?
The `<meta>` tag can be used for a variety of other purposes, such as embedding your name as the author or adding the revision date. In fact, you can set the `name` and `content` attributes to any value you want.

Use Google Webmaster Tools

G oogle is far and away the most popular search engine, so any discussion on search engine optimization must by necessity begin with pages being listed on Google. Although the company guards their specific search algorithms to attempt to impede the efforts of those who would abuse the service, they do provide a series of tools for Webmasters to help them ensure that their pages follow the company's guidelines, as well as tools to track statistics as to what keywords result in the page appearing and how the page ranks.

Use Google Webmaster Tools

1 In your browser, go to www. google.com/webmasters/ tools.

2 Either log in with an existing Google account, or create one.

Note: If you do not have an account, click **Create an account now** and follow the instructions to create the account.

3 Click **Add a site**.

4 Type the address of the site you want to track under Sites in the text box.

5 Follow the instructions to verify the site.

● The verified sites appear here.

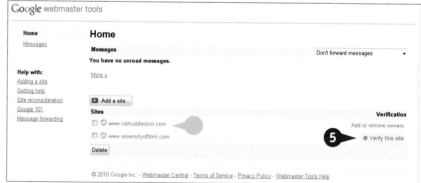

⑥ Click **Diagnostics**.

⑦ Click **Crawl stats**.

⑧ View the information provided.

⑨ Click **Your site on the web**.

⑩ Click **Links to your site**.

⑪ View the information provided.

● The number of pages linking to yours appears.

TIP

What other options are available in the tools?

On the main Dashboard page in the Webmaster tools, which can be accessed from any other page by clicking the Dashboard link, are four useful links on the far right. The first link allows you to download all of the data from the site on all of the sites you manage. The second link allows you to report spam or sites using deceptive practices to increase their PageRank. The third link serves a similar purpose, but allows you to report sites selling links. The final link allows you to appeal a prior decision by Google to remove your site from their index if they believe you violated their policies.

Create a Sitemap

One of the easiest ways to get Google and other search engines to catalog the pages in your site is to create a sitemap. This special file allows you to tell the engine what pages on your site should be added to their index. Sitemaps for search engines should follow the structure developed at the Sitemap.org Web site. The document is written in XML, a tag-based language very similar to HTML. You must always use absolute paths for your pages. Other options allow you to define how often your page is updated to try to get engines to see the latest revisions.

Create a Sitemap

1 Create a new blank document in your editor.

2 Type `<?xml version= "1.0" encoding= "utf-8" ?>`.

3 Type `<urlset`.

4 Type `xmlns="www. sitemap.org/schemas/ sitemap/0.9">`.

5 Type `<url>`.

6 Type `<loc>`.

7 Type the path to your homepage.

8 Type `</loc>`.

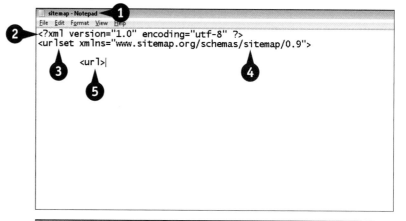

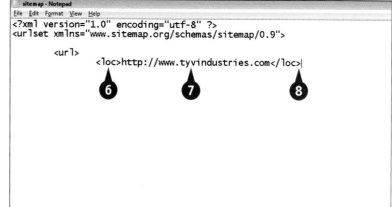

9 Type `</url>`.

10 Repeat Steps **5** to **9** to add additional pages to the sitemap.

11 Type `</urlset>`.

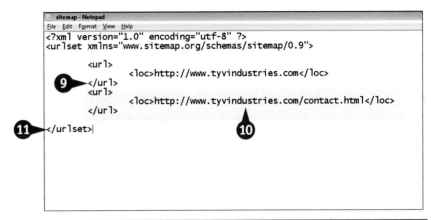

● When viewed in a Web browser, the XML should appear, showing that the document is written correctly.

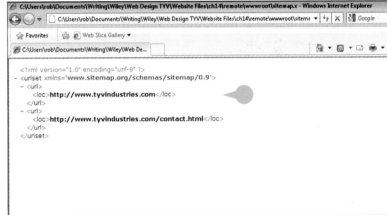

TIP

Do I need a sitemap for every site?
Sitemaps are most useful on sites with frequent changes, such as blogs. Most blog software includes a tool to generate a sitemap and keep it up to date as you add content to the blog. Many blog packages do this automatically, so you never even have to think about it. Check the documentation for your blog to see if it includes sitemap-generation features.

Prevent Pages from Being Listed on Search Engines

Occasionally, you may have pages within your site that you do not want to be indexed on search engines. For example, you may have test pages on your site that show developmental stages of upcoming features, or possibly pages you have set up for your own personal use to which you do not want to grant others easy access. A robots.txt file can prevent engines from indexing certain pages by including one or more `Disallow` statements. An asterisk disallows indexing of the entire site; a specific folder disallows indexing that folder, and a particular page blocks indexing of the page.

Prevent Pages from Being Listed on Search Engines

① Create a new blank document in your editor.

② Type `User-agent: *`.

③ Type `Disallow:`.

④ Enter either an asterisk, a path to a directory in the site, or a specific filename.

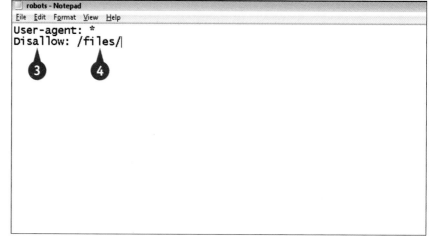

5 Repeat Step **4** to add additional `Disallow` statements as needed.

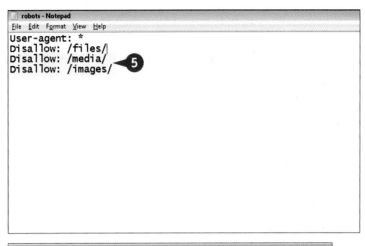

6 Save the file in your root folder with a name of robots.txt.

The page or pages specified in the text file should now be ignored by search engines.

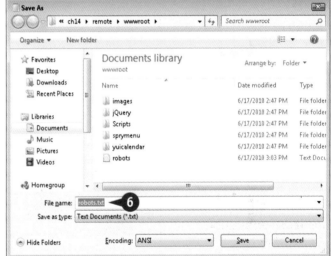

TIP

Will this absolutely guarantee that those pages will not show up in search?
Unfortunately, there is no way to guarantee that search engines will pay attention to instructions in robots. txt files. Some search engines will still display a page not indexed in the results, but not provide details such as descriptions, whereas others may not display it at all. If you have content that you want to be absolutely certain is not going to appear in search results, you should not place it on the Web.

HTML Colors

You can specify colors in HTML using six-digit hexadecimal values preceded by a number sign (#). The first two digits specify the amount of red in the color, the middle two digits the amount of green, and the last two digits the amount of blue. The colors listed below are known as *Web-safe colors* because they display accurately on older computer monitors that support a maximum of 256 colors.

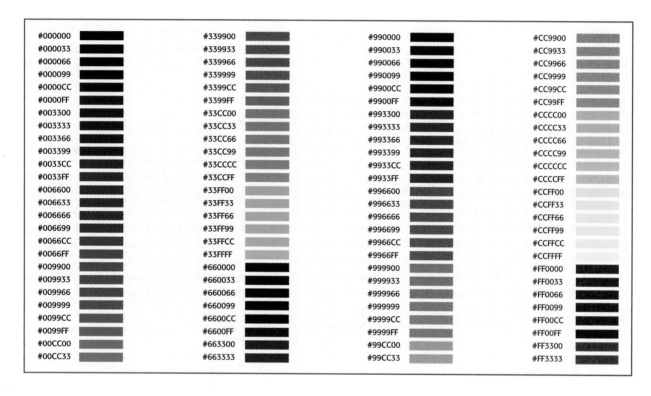

#000000	#339900	#990000	#CC9900
#000033	#339933	#990033	#CC9933
#000066	#339966	#990066	#CC9966
#000099	#339999	#990099	#CC9999
#0000CC	#3399CC	#9900CC	#CC99CC
#0000FF	#3399FF	#9900FF	#CC99FF
#003300	#33CC00	#993300	#CCCC00
#003333	#33CC33	#993333	#CCCC33
#003366	#33CC66	#993366	#CCCC66
#003399	#33CC99	#993399	#CCCC99
#0033CC	#33CCCC	#9933CC	#CCCCCC
#0033FF	#33CCFF	#9933FF	#CCCCFF
#006600	#33FF00	#996600	#CCFF00
#006633	#33FF33	#996633	#CCFF33
#006666	#33FF66	#996666	#CCFF66
#006699	#33FF99	#996699	#CCFF99
#0066CC	#33FFCC	#9966CC	#CCFFCC
#0066FF	#33FFFF	#9966FF	#CCFFFF
#009900	#660000	#999900	#FF0000
#009933	#660033	#999933	#FF0033
#009966	#660066	#999966	#FF0066
#009999	#660099	#999999	#FF0099
#0099CC	#6600CC	#9999CC	#FF00CC
#0099FF	#6600FF	#9999FF	#FF00FF
#00CC00	#663300	#99CC00	#FF3300
#00CC33	#663333	#99CC33	#FF3333

#00CC66	#663366	#99CC66	#FF3366
#00CC99	#663399	#99CC99	#FF3399
#00CCCC	#6633CC	#99CCCC	#FF33CC
#00CCFF	#6633FF	#99CCFF	#FF33FF
#00FF00	#666600	#99FF00	#FF6600
#00FF33	#666633	#99FF33	#FF6633
#00FF66	#666666	#99FF66	#FF6666
#00FF99	#666699	#99FF99	#FF6699
#00FFCC	#6666CC	#99FFCC	#FF66CC
#00FFFF	#6666FF	#99FFFF	#FF66FF
#330000	#669900	#CC0000	#FF9900
#330033	#669933	#CC0033	#FF9933
#330066	#669966	#CC0066	#FF9966
#330099	#669999	#CC0099	#FF9999
#3300CC	#6699CC	#CC00CC	#FF99CC
#3300FF	#6699FF	#CC00FF	#FF99FF
#333300	#66CC00	#CC3300	#FFCC00
#333333	#66CC33	#CC3333	#FFCC33
#333366	#66CC66	#CC3366	#FFCC66
#333399	#66CC99	#CC3399	#FFCC99
#3333CC	#66CCCC	#CC33CC	#FFCCCC
#3333FF	#66CCFF	#CC33FF	#FFCCFF
#336600	#66FF00	#CC6600	#FFFF00
#336633	#66FF33	#CC6633	#FFFF33
#336666	#66FF66	#CC6666	#FFFF66
#336699	#66FF99	#CC6699	#FFFF99
#3366CC	#66FFCC	#CC66CC	#FFFFCC
#3366FF	#66FFFF	#CC66FF	#FFFFFF

Index

Numbers

2-Up option
    using in BrowserLab, 205
    using in Fireworks, 81
    using in Photoshop, 65
4-Up option
    using in Fireworks, 81
    using in Photoshop, 65

Symbols

(pound sign), using with `href` attribute, 40
/ (slash), using with folders, 34

A

`<a>` tag, applying, 36–37
absolute paths, 34–35
accessibility
    benefits of, 243
    closed captions, 243
    cognitive disabilities, 242
    color blindness, 242
    and colors, 105
    hearing impairment, 242
    legal considerations, 243
    mobility impairment, 242
    navigation, 248–249
    and search engines, 243
    for SEO (search engine optimization), 328
    table headings, creating, 246–247
    visual impairment, 242
Acrobat.com, 203
address, getting for Web pages, 39
`<address>` tag, applying, 33
Adobe Dreamweaver
    adding Flash movies to pages in, 231
    adding images in, 188–189
    adding navigation in, 187
    adding new styles in, 198–199
    connecting to remote host, 326–327
    creating documents in, 182
    defining Web sites in, 181
    described, 8–9
    editing Photoshop images in, 194–195
    inserting copyright symbol, 186
    inserting Photoshop images in, 190–193

interface, 180
    modifying CSS, 196–197
    previewing pages in browsers, 201
    previewing pages with Live view, 200
    replacing `<img>` tag in, 184
    replacing logo placeholder, 184
    replacing main content in, 185
    resizing images in, 189
    setting up remote server, 324–325
    starter page layouts, 182–183
    uploading dependent files, 327
    using upload files, 326–327
    using with Spry framework, 218–219
Adobe Fireworks
    choosing colors in, 77
    comparing optimization settings, 81
    creating buttons in, 76–79
    creating images in, 77
    drawing in, 78
    export options, 81
    interface, 74
    modifying images in, 77
    PNG format, 80
    saving images for Web in, 80–81
    trimming room on canvas, 79
Adobe Illustrator
    adding colors to Fill Color, 83
    AI image format, 86
    changing font properties, 83
    creating logos in, 82–85
    described, 10
    Extrude & Bevel command, 84–85
    interface, 75
    removing excess canvas, 87
Adobe Kuler, using with color schemes, 106–107
Adobe Media Encoder, using with video, 232–233
Adobe Photoshop. *See also* Photoshop images
    cropping images in, 62–63
    described, 10
    interface, 58
    resizing images in, 62–63
    saving images for Web in, 64–65
    using to fix colors, 60–61
Adobe Photoshop Elements
    cropping images in, 69
    described, 10

Read Less–Learn More®

Visual®

There's a Visual book
for every learning level...

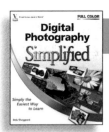

Simplified®

The place to start if you're new to computers. Full color.

- Computers
- Creating Web Pages
- Digital Photography
- Internet
- Mac OS
- Office
- Windows

Teach Yourself VISUALLY™

Get beginning to intermediate-level training in a variety of topics. Full color.

- Access
- Bridge
- Chess
- Computers
- Crocheting
- Digital Photography
- Dog training
- Dreamweaver
- Excel
- Flash
- Golf
- Guitar
- Handspinning
- HTML
- iLife
- iPhoto
- Jewelry Making & Beading
- Knitting
- Mac OS
- Office
- Photoshop
- Photoshop Elements
- Piano
- Poker
- PowerPoint
- Quilting
- Scrapbooking
- Sewing
- Windows
- Wireless Networking
- Word

Top 100 Simplified® Tips & Tricks

Tips and techniques to take your skills beyond the basics. Full color.

- Digital Photography
- eBay
- Excel
- Google
- Internet
- Mac OS
- Office
- Photoshop
- Photoshop Elements
- PowerPoint
- Windows

Wiley, the Wiley logo, the Visual logo, Master Visually, Read Less-Learn More, Simplified, Teach Yourself Visually, Visual Blueprint, and Visual Encyclopedia are trademarks or registered trademarks of John Wiley & Sons, Inc. and or its affiliates. All other trademarks are the property of their respective owners.

...all designed for visual learners—just like you!

Master VISUALLY®

Your complete visual reference. Two-color interior.

- 3ds Max
- Creating Web Pages
- Dreamweaver and Flash
- Excel
- Excel VBA Programming
- iPod and iTunes
- Mac OS
- Office
- Optimizing PC Performance
- Photoshop Elements
- QuickBooks
- Quicken
- Windows
- Windows Mobile
- Windows Server

Visual Blueprint™

Where to go for professional-level programming instruction. Two-color interior.

- Ajax
- ASP.NET 2.0
- Excel Data Analysis
- Excel Pivot Tables
- Excel Programming
- HTML
- JavaScript
- Mambo
- PHP & MySQL
- SEO
- Ubuntu Linux
- Vista Sidebar
- Visual Basic
- XML

Visual Encyclopedia™

Your A to Z reference of tools and techniques. Full color.

- Dreamweaver
- Excel
- Mac OS
- Photoshop
- Windows

Visual Quick Tips

Shortcuts, tricks, and techniques for getting more done in less time. Full color.

- Crochet
- Digital Photography
- Excel
- Internet
- iPod & iTunes
- Knitting
- Mac OS
- MySpace
- Office
- PowerPoint
- Windows
- Wireless Networking

For a complete listing of Visual books, go to wiley.com/go/visual

Visual
An Imprint of ⊕WILEY
Now you know.

Read Less-Learn More®

Want instruction in other topics?

Check out these
All designed for visual learners—just like you!

978-0-470-43638-7   978-0-470-50386-7   978-0-470-10150-6

**For a complete listing of *Teach Yourself VISUALLY*™ titles
and other Visual books, go to wiley.com/go/visual**

Visual®
An Imprint of WILEY

Wiley, the Wiley logo, the VISUAL logo, Read Less-Learn More, Teach Yourself VISUALLY, and VISUAL Quick Tips are trademarks or
registered trademarks of John Wiley & Sons, Inc. and/or its affiliates. All other trademarks are the property of their respective owners.